THE CHILD STARS

THE
CHILD STARS

Norman J. Zierold

MACDONALD: LONDON

First published in Great Britain in 1965 by
Macdonald & Co. (Publishers) Ltd.
Gulf House, 2 Portman Street, London, W.1
Reproduced and printed in Great Britain by
Latimer Trend & Co. Ltd., Whitstable

CONTENTS

LIST OF PLATES

1.

THE TRIALS OF JACKIE COOGAN

"If my father were alive, this suit would not be necessary."

With this quiet tribute to his late father, twenty-three-year-old Jackie Coogan, once America's most popular child star, instituted, on April 11, 1938, in Los Angeles Superior Court, the most spectacular lawsuit of a colorful decade in Hollywood. He accused his mother and stepfather, Mr. and Mrs. Arthur L. Bernstein, of unlawfully withholding $4 million of his past earnings and requested the court to order an accounting of these assets and to provide for a return of the money he said was originally held for him in trust.

Jackie stated that during the years when he had been one of the highest-salaried players in Hollywood, he had received an allowance of $6.25 a week. In addition, he had been given food, clothing, a place to live, an automobile, railroad transportation, a college education, and about $1,500 in gifts, $50 at a time, on his birthdays and at Christmas. He had also received $1,000 on the day before he was twenty-one. At twenty-one, even his allowance of $6.25 was cut off, and since that time he had received nothing and been forced to live on his now modest earnings as an actor.

The complaint leveled a battery of charges against the step-father. Bernstein, referred to in the action as "the trusted associate, agent, and employee of Coogan and his mother and father" before the elder Coogan was killed in May 1935 in an automobile accident, was alleged to have influenced Jackie's mother to resist his legitimate claims. Jackie further accused his stepfather of spending money on horse races, frequently betting $100 at a time, and deducting the losses from the estate. According to the complaint, Bernstein also appropriated gifts Jackie had received from admirers, including a $2,500 platinum watch received by Jackie, and still worn by Bernstein.

To add insult to injury, Bernstein had written to the Brown Derby restaurant on the stationery of Jackie Coogan Productions, Inc., stating that he would no longer be responsible for Jackie's bills. To Jackie, the move seemed pointless and rude. While he signed checks only for "convenience sake," he was at the time about to marry film starlet Betty Grable, he said, "and when a man is about to marry, he needs all the credit he can get."

That the Bernsteins had four servants in their household and owned two Rolls-Royces, while Jackie and his wife now lived modestly without servants and drove a Ford, must also have rankled.

Unable to obtain an accounting of his assets, he had tried to look over the books of Jackie Coogan Productions, Inc., and was ordered out of the office. He declared that he was also ordered out of his home at the time by Bernstein. His suit followed.

"I have shrunk from this action which I now must take," Jackie stated. "I am ready to reveal the whole story of my boyhood in order to protect the interests which my father, while he was alive, safeguarded for me.

"I have waited patiently for some time for my mother and Bernstein to make an accounting to me of my property. I owe a duty to my wife and to myself not to wait any longer.

"It is my intention at all times to see that my mother and my little brother are amply provided for. If my father had lived, no controversy of this sort would have arisen."

Judge Emmet H. Wilson appointed John E. Biby receiver of all assets in possession of Jackie's mother and stepfather, and enjoined them from disposing of any of their property. The court set April 20th to hear proceedings for a preliminary injunction.

If Jackie's suit had caused a sensation, a second bombshell was about to hit the film capital and the news outlets of the land. With awesome frankness, the defendants stated their case Jackie's money had indeed been withheld from him and, furthermore, would continue to be withheld. And the law, they stated, was completely on their side. Under the old principle of common law in England—and in many American states, including California—any money a minor earns while he is under twenty-one belongs to the parents. So stated the Bernsteins.

"I am deeply shocked," Jackie's mother, Mrs. Bernstein, told reporters. "He says he has nothing and that I refused to give him any part of the estate. No promises ever were made to give him anything.

"I'm not really bitter at Jackie," she said. "I'm just filled with regret that I should have put in so much time and spent so much money trying to make the right sort of man out of him only to discover that he is really very stupid. I say stupid advisedly, because that's what it amounts to. He is stupidly following the advice of someone who has a personal ax to grind." She was swift to add that she was not blaming Jackie's wife, Betty Grable. "You can't trap me into starting any four-cornered dogfight out of this affair," she declared. She and her son had "always been so close and there never was any trouble between us. He never came to me for an accounting of his money. He just made this legal move."

Mrs. Bernstein derided her son's account of the monies he had received at home: "I hear he says he only got about $2,500 in cash besides his keep in all the years he was working. I have to laugh at that. I'm not going to give an estimate of how much he got. I'm going to tell the court that."

Of the common-law principle being invoked, she stated, "He's going to find out a great deal more about the law before he has finished his suit, and I know he is going to feel very, very sorry for what he has done."

As to the allegations of undue influence from Bernstein, her comment was brisk: "Nobody dominates me, not even Jackie."

Not to be outdone, stepfather Bernstein was voluble with reporters. "Jackie has had all that he is entitled to, and more. He isn't entitled to that money. It belongs to us. The law is on our side. Jackie Coogan will get not a cent of income from his past earnings. Lawyers tell his mother and me that every dollar a kid earns before he is twenty-one years old belongs to his parents."

Reporting these outbursts, the New York *Herald Tribune* commented: "Mr. and Mrs. Bernstein will never be serious contenders for the title of Mr. and Mrs. America."

And *Life* related a story, which may or may not have been apocryphal: "Don't teach Jackie arithmetic," a visitor is said to have warned Mrs. Coogan, "because when he grows up he'll want to know where all his money is."

Charge was now followed by countercharge as the contenders for Jackie's earnings sparred off. Headlines told the story of the "poor little rich boy" who had earned $4 million as a child actor and had nothing to show for it. Wire services carried to Europe and the far corners of the world the tale of the once idolized young star whose mother and stepfather called his money their own.

As batteries of lawyers prepared their briefs for court, newspaper and magazine reporters went into their dusty archives to dig up the fact and fancy surrounding the career of John Leslie

Coogan, better known as Jackie. The fact, they discovered, was more extraordinary than the fancy.

In its piquant style, *Time*, on May 2, 1938, chronicled the beginnings of the Coogan career with a customary flourish: "Nearly 19 years ago in a motion picture called *The Kid*, a saucy, bright-eyed little ragamuffin, taffy hair rumpled untidily under a tattered caricature of a cap, scampered into the hearts of the world cinemaudience clinging to the threadbare coattails of Charlie Chaplin. The kid was Jackie Coogan."

Actually, Jackie Coogan's spectacular career had begun even earlier, not long after he was born, October 24, 1914, in Los Angeles, to a pair of vaudevillians who had met and married while touring the western circuit. As a young man in his teens, his father had left a job with the family drugstore in Syracuse, New York, to head for the musical comedy stage; his mother, plump, smiling Lillian Dolliver, a native of San Francisco, had gone on the stage as a child singer and dancer with the California Stock Company, which had billed her as "Baby Lillian."

Initially the Coogans intended to keep their firstborn well removed from the stage, especially from the exhausting hazards of the road. While they toured, he was shipped out to Mrs. Coogan's mother in the Oakland Hills. However, when he was only eighteen months old, his parents brought him to the old Essanay studios in Chicago and made him gurgle—then weep—for a film called *Skinner's Baby*. And again, when Jackie was two, the Coogans took him on a trip, this time for a New York engagement at the old Riverside Theatre on upper Broadway, where he watched them do their turn and nonchalantly scampered on stage, much to the delight of the audience.

At the age of three, Jackie was taken back permanently by his parents. From that time on until a memorable theatre debut a year later, he lived the life of a stage child, sitting on the knees of stage doormen and lingering in the wings, talking to the performers and picking up the patois and viewpoint of

vaudeville. An excellent mimic, he amused the touring vaudevillians with clever imitations of their acts.

His father, meanwhile, was advancing in his profession as an
"eccentric," or specialty, dancer, performing in the act of the
popular Annette Kellerman. One night in San Francisco, his
performance reached its climax with a spirited number that
transported the packed house. He came back for bow after
bow, and finally, in a burst of exuberance, the elder Coogan
grabbed his son, who had been standing in the wings, and
brought him onto the stage. Jackie, wide-eyed, listened to the
applause. He made a little bow. Then his legs began to move,
dancing the dance everyone of the period knew, the shimmy.
Something crept from the tiny, appealing figure to the vast
audience, which roared its approval. To please them, just as he
had pleased stagehands and acrobats, Jackie did one of his imitations. And in response to continuing billows of applause, he
finished up his first act with a scene his father had taught him,
David Warfield's great speech from *The Music Master*.

Pleased by the success of the boy, Annette Kellerman offered
Jack Sr. an additional $25 a week to keep the bit in the show
on a regular basis, and a few days later, the troupe opened at
the Orpheum Theatre in Los Angeles. As Jackie toddled his
four-year-old way across the stage, two eyes followed him intently, watching every movement, every gesture, every nuance
of a smile. One of Hollywood's authentic geniuses was making
one of his greatest discoveries.

"What first attracted me to the boy was a whimsical, wistful
quality, a genuineness of feeling," declared Charlie Chaplin a
short time later, after he had met Jackie and engaged him to
perform with him in *The Kid*. "He is the lovable child, carried
to the *nth* power, yet endowed with not a little of the self-con-
sciousness of an artist, and with a hundred resources as an actor. What a marvelous understanding, what delicacy of feeling.
Jackie is inspiring and inspired. Just to be in his presence is to
feel inspiration. . . ."

At the time, 1919, Chaplin was well established as the greatest comedian of what were then called the "silver sheets." *The Kid* was his first screen appearance in many months. It was his first six-reeler for First National. It was also one of the most widely heralded, expensive, and mysterious of all productions up to that time, with an original story by Chaplin himself. In a magazine interview, he told of his scenario for the film:

> I have for some time wanted to do what is for me at least, a serious picture, a picture with irony behind the incongruous and comic incidents, inspiring pity under its ludicrous aspects, with a sense of satire underlying the broadest buffoonery. The story, briefly, is this: a woman of poorest London tries to have her illegitimate child brought up in luxury and leaves it in a limousine outside of an opulent house. The car is stolen, the child deposited in an ash barrel, whence he is rescued and adopted by a tramp mender of window panes. A great part of the film is taken up with their ludicrous and sometimes pathetic adventures in the London streets. The boy—Jackie Coogan— works on the sly, breaking windows. As the tramp, I follow him, and mend the panes. Finally the boy is lost and is not to be found—indeed, he and the tramp are only united in heaven, probably the most extraordinary ever staged, a heaven satirizing the sloppiness of much contemporary altruism, with policemen enforcing brotherly love and secondhand dealers exchanging wings for the kisses of the newly arrived angels.

Released in 1920, *The Kid* achieved astounding popularity, and by his beguiling characterization of the homeless street gamin, Jackie Coogan, five-year-old unknown, leaped to fame. People flocked into motion picture theatres to watch the forlorn little figure with luminous brown eyes and a winsome smile emerging from under a battered cap.

First National, and, later, Metro Pictures rushed him into a long series of films, the earliest of which, based on solid story material, met with both popular and critical acclaim. *Peck's Bad Boy* (1921), Jackie's second film, was an appealing account of childhood scenes by George W. Peck. His third picture, the Charles Dickens classic, *Oliver Twist* (1922), was touted as "the Great Film Triumph of the Decade—with a Matchless Cast of Screen Celebrities Supporting Jackie in This His Finest Achievement." He was billed quite simply as "the greatest boy actor in the world." There would have been few to dispute the title. Columnist E. V. Durling wrote: "Insofar as Jackie Coogan is concerned, *Oliver Twist* is a better picture than *The Kid*. Teamed up with Chaplin, we all thought him cute, but there was a suspicion that perhaps without Charlie, he wouldn't be half so good. In the present instance young Coogan proves himself to be worthy of classification with those heretofore unapproachables—Pickford, Fairbanks, and Chaplin. He is an actor in every sense of the word."

In his next two films, *My Boy* and *Trouble* (1922), he again played what was becoming his customary role, the orphan waif. Both of these Sol Lesser productions for First National had sentimental scenarios by Jackie's father, Jack Coogan Sr. In *Trouble* his co-star was Wallace Beery, who was later to play a sympathetic role at the time of the lawsuit.

Story trouble became clearly apparent with *Daddy*, in 1923. Jackie's appearance was the only redeeming feature in this shopworn tale of a lost waif, son of a famous violinist, and how he comes to find his father. Charlie Chaplin, who saw the film, commented: "I didn't like some of the things they had him do. I don't like to see a child in scenes of mature emotion— weeping over a deathbed and such. A child should be joyous and free—not sentimental or emotional—joyous and sunny and natural." Critics were even more harsh with *Circus Days* later in the year.

It was after this film that Jackie made a celebrated switch from First National to Metro Pictures. To launch the four-picture, million-dollar deal, Metro commissioned the well-known author, Mary Roberts Rinehart, to write a screenplay based on the novel, *Long Live the King*. Victor Schertzinger was engaged to direct a lavish production costing more than half a million dollars. Sol Lesser had been unwilling, at First National, to put Jackie's productions under the guiding hand of Jack Sr. Joseph Schenck, of Metro, had no such scruples. *Long Live the King* was the first of Jackie's films to carry the credit line, "Produced under the personal supervision of Jack Coogan Sr." Jackie played a "lovable little prince," Otto of Lavonia, to Ruth Renick's Princess Hedwig. If the production was spectacular, the sugary soap opera plot line was decidedly less so.

A Boy of Flanders, his second picture for Metro, also dripped saccharine. The story was adapted from the well-known book, *A Dog of Flanders*, by Louise de la Ramée, who wrote under the pen name Ouida. Prominent in the cast was Teddy, a Great Dane, hero of many comedies, and child actress Toby Wing, later to be linked romantically with Jackie.

"It's different, tremendous," read the advertising posters. The world-famous story of a Belgian boy and his dog, and his fight against poverty and enemies, until, with the roof taken from him, and the coveted painting prize won by his rival, he wanders friendless and alone out on the Flemish fields in a blinding snowstorm. . . . You'll laugh and cry and be thrilled with Jackie Coogan at his triumphs and headaches." Warned *The New York Times*: the film revealed in Jackie "a steady Coogan inclination toward imitating adults."

In an attempt to counter recurrent criticism of weak plots in his son's films, Jack Sr. announced that henceforth Jackie would stick to roles like the one that had brought him such acclaim in *The Kid*. And in *The Rag Man*, his last picture for Metro under the current contract, he once again played the Kid, in a rather touching narrative about a waif who joins an old dealer in rags and junk, and helps him make a great success of his faltering enterprise.

In a single year, Jackie had made four commercial blockbusters (including *Little Robinson Crusoe*) for Metro. He appeared on the cover of *Photoplay* in November; and late in the year, *The Exhibitor*, the industry's trade journal, reported:

"There is not an exhibitor anywhere who does not know that Jackie Coogan is the surest drawing card possible to offer his patrons."

Metro signed him to a new contract, and in 1925 he appeared in *Johnny Get Your Gun*, and in *Old Clothes*, with newcomer Joan Crawford, succinctly described by one reviewer as "interesting." *Old Clothes* accentuated the problems besetting child star Jackie. *World* critic Quinn Martin attributed his previous success and popularity to "the extraordinary natural ease of the boy's bearing before the camera." Needed, said Martin, was "an entirely different kind of scenario, bringing this growing lad upon the scene in a distinctly new light. It is time to leave off exhibiting him merely as the child wonder and cast him in roles of youth written for him with a certain amount of foresight and plausibility in them."

Another reviewer found the boy actor "frankly homely, with a homeliness that lacks charm. Still without a haircut, he appears to be in a state of arrested development. When the thin story gives him a chance to act, he overacts."

By now, it was generally agreed that Jackie had arrived at the awkward age, that uncomfortable period when the winsome child turns into an ungainly adolescent. As he had grown older and taller, his parents had tried to keep him looking like a boy. His hair was worn so long that he was subjected to ridicule, and finally, he refused to work unless changes were made. "Facing the prospect of starvation or else continuing to receive about half a million a year, Dad Coogan took him to the barber," reported the New York *Telegraph*.

Jackie's first short haircut made national news. The shearing took place two weeks before his twelfth birthday, in the presence of his agitated mother and father, his gurgling younger brother, a disturbed press agent, and eleven news photographers. "You'll take a Prince of Wales haircut?" asked the barber. "I don't want a Prince of Wales haircut," Jackie replied. "I want an American haircut, Calvin Coolidge style." A week later, four-foot-six John Leslie Coogan enrolled at Hollywood Urban Military Academy. The kid with the rumpled cap, the baggy pants, the tattered shoes, and the big brown eyes was turning into a young man.

MGM, capitalizing on publicity, put him into *Johnny Get Your Hair Cut* (1926), a film written around the long-hair dilemma. In the early scenes, he was shown for the last time with his familiar long Dutch bob.

By now, the all-important exhibitors were no longer clamoring for his pictures, which appeared at ever greater intervals. In 1927 he made *The Bugle Call*, under a new contract with MGM, and, for the same studio, a film called *Buttons*. Once more, but for the last time, he was cast in the role of a forlorn waif. On a big ocean liner, he helps to frustrate the plans of the villain, who tries to come between the captain and the girl he loves. At the end, the ship hits an iceberg and Jackie stands bravely on the deck with the captain, until the last, when both are miraculously saved.

In seven short years, Jackie Coogan had turned into an adolescent boy. With that change, the meteoric career of America's most brilliant young performer came to an abrupt halt—which should not have surprised his more perceptive admirers. Inevitably, there is an evanescent quality in the child star. His days of innocence, of simplicity, of natural, spontaneous expression are all too few. At a certain point, each centimeter's growth diminishes the wistful, fleeting charm of childhood. Jackie's studios and his parents had known this well. They had scoured the libraries for stories suitable for the child star, and set the cameras to turning. Whereas *The Kid*, a carefully conceived and wrought film masterpiece, had taken a year and a day to film, the new efforts were churned out in an average of less than ten weeks each; compressed into a halcyon career were almost a score of full-length features. However, with the last *Buttons* footage in the can, and with no further call for his services, Jackie's mentors recognized the inevitable. The boy actor went off to London and played the Palladium with his dad. "Senility," said an old Hollywood veteran, "finally got him at thirteen."

If, over the years, the critics had become increasingly divided in their appraisals of Jackie—dismayed to find him growing older, regretful that, with experience, technique was becoming a part of his art—the American public, only slightly weighted in favor of women and children, loved him during his brief but glittering heyday with a fervor that bordered on idolatry.

Again and again, their adulation put him on the covers of the leading movie magazines, whose circulations at that period ran into the millions, and whose importance then was far greater than it is today. Interviews and bylined articles told every facet of Jackie's life—his breakfast menu, the hour of his bedtime, the names of his favorite actor, Fredric March, and closest friends, Charlie Chaplin and Douglas Fairbanks, Senior. In the rotogravure sections of the newspapers, he was shown clowning with Fairbanks and Rudolph Valentino. John McCormack, the beloved Irish tenor, posed with Jackie as did Conan Doyle, celebrated creator of Sherlock Holmes.

David Belasco, one of the greatest producers of his time, was seen with the popular child star, and said that one day he would coach him to play Hamlet. John Barrymore, himself a renowned interpretor of the role, gave out an unsolicited interview in which he said that he placed great faith in the boy actor's ability to master the part.

Reflecting his interest in sports, Jackie was seen with heroes of the era such as Babe Ruth. He was shown sparring with heavyweight boxer Georges Carpentier; at the wheel of a sleek motor car with Bordoni, the noted Italian racer; with Gene Sarazen, golf champion.

He was photographed with cellist-composer Victor Herbert; with John Philip Sousa, the March King, who was teaching him to lead a band. A lovely photograph showed him seated on the lap of the great pianist, Paderewski. The dignified Pole, all in white, declared that his young guest had a truly musical ear.

In the fashionable and handsome publication *Vanity Fair,* the celebrated artist Covarrubias drew a winsome and forlorn Jackie standing alone; but in a rival publication, artist Wynn placed him in a drawing called "The Immortals Greet a New Arrival," and here he was in the rather extraordinary company of George Bernard Shaw, David Belasco, Constantin Stanislavsky, Morris Gest, Walt Whitman, Edgar Allan Poe, Shakespeare, Alexander Dumas, Richard Wagner, Henrik Ibsen, and Edwin Booth.

Among the mortals of his time, his place was unquestioned. A popularity contest conducted in 1924 by *Photoplay* ranked him with the major stars: Rudolph Valentino, Norma Talmadge, Harold Lloyd, Thomas Meighan, Pola Negri, Tom Mix, Douglas Fairbanks, and a still-beloved former child actress, "America's Sweetheart," Mary Pickford.

In addition to Chaplin, numerous other figures poured out their hearts in praise of the greatest boy actor in the world:

"I can remember no piece of acting which hit me harder than that of the small boy who played with Charlie Chaplin," wrote columnist and author Heywood Broun.

"Jackie doesn't belong to any one person," rhapsodized director Frank Lloyd. "He belongs to the world. He is not a child prodigy. He is not precocious in the way that word is usually meant. Jackie is utterly natural, absolutely spontaneous and wholly unconscious and unforced. He is wholly feeling. Jackie's greatness is in his intuitive understanding—and in his eyes. He has the most extraordinary eyes I have ever seen. Every grief, every joy, every emotion and shade of emotion are mirrored in those great eyes."

Irvin S. Cobb, the humorist-author, told the world: "Perhaps the kindly angels are responsible for Jackie Coogan. If so, they did a good job. If the world doesn't spoil him, and if God lets him live with us, he will be in his maturity the blithest spirit that ever gave unending joy to countless millions—indeed, he is that now."

"Dear child," invoked a magazine writer, "we have only one prayer to offer. . . . Don't grow up!"

It is perhaps a testimonial to the extraordinary magic of his personality that when speaking of the diminutive child star, writers of stature and integrity would drool out sentimental phrases altogether reminiscent of the paid hackwork of press and publicity agents.

In 1924, between the shooting of *Little Robinson Crusoe* and *The Rag Man*, Jackie Coogan undertook a tour of America and Europe in support of Near East Relief, a campaign to aid some 70,000 orphans in Palestine, Syria, Greece, and Armenia. It was believed that the presence of the famous boy actor in this so-called Children's Crusade would draw the attention of American fathers and mothers to the tragic situation of the impoverished youngsters, the "starving Armenians," as popular usage labeled them. His whirlwind American food- and fund-raising tour on their behalf took him across the country: to Boston, where the mayor gave him the key to the city; to Albuquerque, where the Navajo Indians dubbed him "Benay Yulthid," or "Talking Eyes," and inducted him as a medicine man; to Brooklyn, where August 16th was officially declared Jackie Coogan Day, and more than 100,000 boys and girls crowded Prospect Park to help raise a million-dollar cargo of corn syrup, milk, and clothing. At every stop, the crowds were urged to buy "Children's Crusade Mercy Bonds," which carried an appeal signed by Jackie, the orphan hero of the films.

The American campaign was an overwhelming success. *Photoplay* commissioned Jackie's European diary, to be written "in his very own style, and subject to no editorial blue pencil." In it, he wrote that $1,000,037 in food and clothing had been raised and was already aboard three specially chartered ships which were heading for the Near East, where he would meet them to make the official presentation.

Wearing a sailor suit, nine-year-old Jackie Coogan sailed for Europe on September 6th on the *Leviathan*, the largest ship afloat, under the guidance of Captain Hartley. Traveling with him were his father, Jack Sr., his business adviser, Arthur L. Bernstein, and his tutor, Mrs. Kora Newell. Mrs. Coogan remained at home awaiting a baby, which was born during the course of the trip—Jackie's younger brother, Robert.

For the European pilgrimage, the young crusader was insured by Lloyd's of London for $250,000 under a policy that extended over five weeks, cost $5,000, and covered protection against favus and trachoma, described by the press as "two Eastern diseases."

It was, however, against the tumultuous crowds of people, rather than the "Eastern diseases," that Jackie Coogan had to be protected on his tour. His reception in Europe—reported in daily communiqués by the American newspapers—easily matched that of visiting royalty, perhaps exceeding it in spontaneity and exuberance, and again and again police reinforcements were brought in to hold back the crowds straining for a glimpse of the child star.

Arriving on the boat train in London, he received a hysterical welcome from thousands of women and children who flocked to Waterloo Station. In an open car, he waved and blew kisses at admirers lining his route to the Savoy Hotel, where his reception rivaled that accorded several years earlier to Mary Pickford and Douglas Fairbanks on their first visit to London.

In New York, the *World* told of the visit next day to St. James's to view the changing of the guard. "Women fought with one another for positions of vantage," reported the paper, "and Jackie was extricated from the melee with difficulty by his father, who carried him on his shoulders to the palace. It is a Coogan for a Wales, hearts touched and everybody happy." "Why?" asked the *World* rhetorically, and answered: "Dream children, these two, in a world that never loses interest in the boyish smile, the curly head, the round blue eyes that look on life with innocence."

Continuing his tour, Jackie arrived in France on the same day as Henry M. Robinson, a prominent banker who had been sent by the American Government to help carry out the Dawes Plan for French recovery from the still-recent war. France forgot Robinson in its enthusiasm for the young film idol, and at the Gare du Nord in Paris, more than 16,000 French fans thundered their welcome to "le Gosse," the French equivalent of the Kid.

Only former Premier Georges Clemenceau, who had been invited to meet Jackie, refused to share in the enthusiasm. In a telegram of regret to the elder Coogan, he said, "I do not screen well enough nor am I celebrity enough to meet your illustrious son." Thus, the flashing sarcasm of the old Tiger.

In Geneva, at the League of Nations, all activity stopped as Sir Eric Drummond, the Secretary General, received Jackie and thanked him for his help with Near East Relief.

In Berlin, police again had difficulty holding back the crowds, and from the touring staff came demands for extra police protection.

POPE RECEIVES JACKIE COOGAN, read the dispatches from Rome. Received in private audience, kneeling, Jackie kissed the Pope's ring. The pontiff, Pius XI, presented him with a silver medal bearing the papal coat of arms engraved in gold, and made a request of his chivalric young guest to help the orphanage in Athens, which he declared was very much in need. In his diary, Jackie duly recorded: "I thought it a nice thing to help the orphanage, so I cabled to have some food shipped to the orphanage." Not surprisingly, this led the Supreme Pontiff to pat his visitor gratefully on the cheek.

On the initiative of a group of eminent Fascisti, arrangements were also made for Jackie to be received by Premier Mussolini, who presented Jackie with his photograph and signed it *Al Piccolo Grande*, "To the little great one."

Finally, in October 1924, the entourage arrived at its final stop, Greece. Immense crowds lined the streets of Piraeus and Athens, where the welcome was led by the provisional President of the Republic, Admiral Coundouriostos. At Zappeon Orphanage in Athens, Jackie delivered bills of lading for the $1,000,037 worth of relief cargo, and in a ceremony at the Acropolis, on October 8, the Greek Government, in recognition of humanitarian work, decorated him with the Silver Cross of the Order of George in the presence of the American minister, Greek government and civilian officials, together with 7,000 orphans under the care of Near East Relief. For the last time, troops had to be called in to contain the crowds.

Years later, Jackie Coogan was to say that public adoration was the greatest thing in the world. He had received that adoration in a dozen countries on his European tour and as he sailed for home on the *Leviathan,* he clutched in his hand the Pope's medal, the Golden Cross of the Order of Jerusalem, one of the mostly prized of all ecclesiastical decorations, and the Silver Cross of the Order of George. His legend was international.

However, one of the most extraordinary facts of Jackie's stardom, often remarked upon at the time, was his own detachment from almost every phase of it. Reporters described him as unspoiled, as an absolutely honest interview subject. For this aspect of his upbringing, his parents were often praised, and they themselves—most notably his mother—were voluble on the matter.

"Model children are so uninteresting," she told an interviewer, removing her son from that category. "Jackie is all alive —and all boy. He has a logical brain, even if it is a small one. And I can usually appeal to his common sense and his feeling of fair play, and his manliness. . . . I don't want my son to be a Little Lord Fauntleroy. I want him to be the sort of a child that he portrays on the screen—robust and appealing and muddy—and if necessary, a little bad. . . . If he's healthy, and moderately good, I'm satisfied. If he grows up to be a real person and a hundred percent American citizen, I won't ask for anything else. I'm strong for American things."

Although Jackie associated with adults while making his pictures, in between times, she declared, he lived a "perfectly normal child's life. Both his father and I made special efforts to keep Jackie from growing up too early in life, and I believe we were successful." One of the devices used to shelter their boy was to censor his film-going. "We don't want to bring him face to face with life problems and sex situations," she said.

And summing up her recipes for bringing up brilliant child stars to be normal, manly Americans, Mrs. Coogan modestly averred: "I expect that I just use good old plain mother judgment with a bit of mother intuition and more than a bit of mother love mixed into it. I fancy that I am raising my boy just as any other average American mother is raising hers. Making just as many mistakes and having just as many successes."

While his mother told often and at length of Jackie's normal upbringing, Jack Sr. tended to note the more extraordinary qualities in his son. "To tell the truth," he said to one reporter, "Jackie is as much of a puzzle to us as to anybody else. I have seen him step out of a big emotional scene with tears still wet on his cheeks, and begin to make a railway tunnel out of a newspaper and a book."

In a 1930 interview, Mary Sharon implied that calling Jackie normal was unrealistic. "As normal as a boy who is worth two million dollars can be," she wrote. "There is the rub. Jackie can never get away from the fact that he is not like other boys. His wealth is always there like a millstone around his neck."

Jackie's childhood earnings record was spectacular. He was four years old when he began earning $25 a week for appearing in his father's vaudeville act with Annette Kellerman. At the age of five, he was paid $75 a week by Charlie Chaplin to star in *The Kid*. After the impressive success of that six-reeler, the big money began to roll in as he made film after film for First National.

In January 1923, after weeks of spirited bidding among seven film companies, Metro won out and gave the eight-year-old star a bonus check for half a million dollars to leave First National and sign with them. His contract called for four pictures over two years for a total of $1 million plus a percentage of the profits.

Photographs of the famous bonus check signing session appeared in newspapers around the world. Jackie, seated cross-legged on the desk of Metro executive Joseph M. Schenck, was holding an oversized pencil, about to endorse the remarkable document with his childish signature. Mrs. Coogan, in a great fur coat, stood stolidly behind the desk, and Dad Coogan, in a bow tie, vest, and light raincoat, gazed intently down at the half-million-dollar scrap of paper, dated January 12, 1923, and made payable to the order of Jackie Coogan.

During the two-year period of 1924-25, Jackie earned $22,-500 a week. He was incorporated by his father as Jackie Coogan Productions, Inc., becoming, effectively, Hollywood's first corporation.

Real estate purchased for him thus far was said to include one Los Angeles business block valued at $300,000; a group of store buildings; a residence; a public garage; numerous improved and unimproved business lots; and two ranches. One of the ranches, in Pine Valley, near San Diego, consisted of 1,000 acres.

A Los Angeles broker told the press in late October 1927 that he had purchased an additional fourteen lots in Los Angeles, which would bring Jackie's land holdings to $1.5 million. He was further quoted as saying there was "plenty more" Coogan money looking for good investment in real estate, and that at the normal rate of increase for the present holdings, Jackie would be a multimillionaire before the age of twenty-one.

While Jackie's film earnings had reached their peak in the mid-twenties, his income thereafter was hardly negligible. At London's Palladium, in 1928, he received $5,000 a week for appearing with his father. In 1930, making his first screen comeback in *Tom Sawyer*, he reportedly received $10,000 a week from Paramount Pictures, and as late as 1933, Metro-Goldwyn-Mayer signed him to a new contract at $1,300 a week, a far cry from his salad days but still a substantial salary.

In addition to investments and screen earnings, there were royalties on a score of merchandized items—Jackie Coogan caps, shoes, toothbrushes, school writing tablets, toys, coasters and cameras. These royalties were paid into Jackie Coogan Productions, Inc.

Even to the unpracticed eye, there must have been something incongruous about the extent of the Coogan fortune and the minuscule portion of it that passed into his hands, an incongruity which already had the newspapers calling him "the poor little rich boy." They told in detail of the devices his parents used to teach him the value of money. Among these was a schedule of sums which he received for his suggestions during the production of his films. For example, if he suggested usable subtitle material, he received 30 cents. If he thought up an original "stunt" in any scene, he was given a whopping 50 cents. Small wonder that Jackie reportedly saved his money by hiding it in out-of-the-way places around the studio.

Heywood Broun told of taking his five-year-old to California in 1923 and of visiting the Coogans. Jackie had promptly asked Broun's child if he worked for a living. The answer was no. Jackie had then replied: "I do. I sweep the floor and clean the dishes, and I get $2.50 a week for spending money." "Seemingly," said Broun, "the picture game had been sold to him as some new kind of diversion."

At thirteen, enrolled at Hollywood Urban Military School, Jackie answered an interviewer's questions about his real estate by referring the matter to his father, who, he declared, gave him money whenever he wanted it.

In the matter of finances, however, Jackie was to encounter growing needs when, as a young man, he became the escort for pretty young ingenues like Ida Lupino and Toby Wing to whom he was often reported to be engaged. At the time he began his much publicized courtship of Betty Grable, he confided in his mother, who wasted no time in getting on the phone to Mrs. Conn Grable. "If Betty thinks she is marrying a rich boy," she declared, "she is very mistaken. He hasn't a cent. Jackie is a pauper!"

An account in the New York *Post* told of how Mrs. Coogan's

calls to Betty and to her mother, attempting to break off the young couple's engagement, continued. According to Betty, "she would argue about some trivial thing just to put me in a bad light. I never could understand her attitude. Whether she thought I wouldn't make a good wife or whether she didn't want Jackie to get married, I have no idea, but she certainly made me feel badly, even to the point of tears, sometimes."

A sardonic note was introduced by Bernstein in a New York interview shortly before Jackie's twenty-first birthday. He told of Jackie's being too old to play child parts and too young at the time for juvenile roles, and then delivered himself of the comment, "He's still a kid through and through. I hope he stops growing soon. He keeps us poor buying clothes for him!"

In this extraordinary narrative, Jackie appears as a male Cinderella, sweeping the floor and virtually scrounging for pennies while his elders alternated between Rolls-Royces. His passive reaction to this situation can be explained in part by the fact that he had every reason to think his vast earnings would be his on reaching maturity.

As he neared his twenty-first birthday, in October 1935, newspaper feature stories repeatedly stated that he was about to come into control of funds generally estimated at $1 million. The million was to be paid him in four quarterly installments, starting with $250,000 on his birthday. By the following July, he was to have the million in full, plus current earnings.

JACKIE COOGAN GETS MILLION ESTATE TODAY AS HE COMES OF AGE, read a typical lead in the New York *Evening Journal* of October 24. "Coogan's father years ago established a trust fund," continued the piece, "and the kid today was to take control of the entire amount."

Reporters for the New York *Post* talked about the anniversary to Mrs. Coogan and to Arthur L. Bernstein, then not yet Jackie's stepfather, but still his adviser and business manager. In this interview of October 23, 1935, the general feeling conveyed was that life would go on pretty much as usual for the young millionaire. Bernstein jocularly suggested that there should be "some sort of ceremony to dramatize the occasion—pictures of Jackie being handed the key of the Coogan Finance Corporation, or something of the sort." Both he and Mrs. Coogan were reported as reluctant to divulge the precise extent of Jackie's fortune. "I don't want to have a lot of undesirable people, not really his friends, running after him," explained his mother. "Figures always make the wealthy a target for the unscrupulous," added Bernstein in pleasant generality.

Variety printed a disquieting story. Despite reports to the contrary, no $250,000 first installment was paid to Jackie on his twenty-first birthday, October 26th. Indeed, his status, *Variety* declared, remained unchanged. He was still a senior at the University of Southern California, where his living expenses were paid by Jackie Coogan Productions, Inc. His fortune was not to pass into his hands until the time of his mother's death.

Jackie Coogan Productions, Inc., said *Variety*, dealt in commercial paper, financed farmers and small industrialists, owned oil wells, orange groves, and, occasionally, real estate. It was founded on Jackie's screen earnings, had shown a profit through the Depression, and should be worth $2 million by the time it passed into his hands. "Setup," concluded the trade paper, "with its safeguards, reflects the native Coogan thrift back in Syracuse, New York, where the late John Coogan Sr. was cradled."

If Jackie read the *Variety* story, we have no indication that it worried him, or shook his faith in either his father or his mother. It was in his father that he placed a supreme faith. In almost every photo of the childhood era, he is seen gazing fondly up at his dad, a dapper, genial Irishman, who usually sported a cane along with a well-trimmed dark mustache, and who was a well-known and well-liked figure in the Hollywood entertainment world.

"He always had my best interests at heart," Jackie wrote in a bylined magazine article at the time of the lawsuit. "I know that sounds trite as I say it, but it is what he used to tell me time and again—and after all, he would have had no motive in lying. He knew that I would always share everything I had with my dad, that I would never let him down. I had a right to expect as much of him. He wouldn't have failed me."

Just as Jackie was approaching the anniversary which his father had said would signal his coming into his fortune, stark tragedy intervened. On May 4, 1935, Jackie and his father were driving home after a successful, happy day of dove hunting in Mexico. With them were Trent "Junior" Durkin, a former child star and Jackie's closest friend, Robert J. Horner, a young actor-playwright, and Charles Jones, manager of the Coogan ranch in San Diego County.

In hilly country some fifty-five miles east of San Diego, the excursion car was rounding a curve when Jackie saw a light tan sedan, with two women as passengers, traveling on the wrong side of the road and bearing down on them at terrific speed. At the wheel, his father swerved sharply to avoid a collision, his right tires hitting the gravel at the side of the road. Skidding helplessly, the Coogan car struck a series of heavy guard posts before plunging over the embankment, throwing the occupants out against the steep, boulder-studded side of the canyon.

Whether he jumped or was thrown from the car, Jackie could not remember. What he did recall was the sight that now met his eyes, one of indescribable horror. Jones lay dead on the ground. Robert Horner was also dead. Junior Durkin and Jack Sr., both cruelly injured, were still alive, but in desperate condition. After carrying his dad and Durkin to the roadside, Jackie hailed a passing auto, which went for medical aid. Junior Durkin died before help could reach him; and when an ambulance finally arrived, Jack Sr. was unconscious. As he was lifted into the ambulance, a priest administered the last rites. Jackie Coogan's "best pal" was dead.

Several days later, tightly taped, his face betraying pain, Jackie rose from a hospital bed to attend the funeral. His mother, dressed in black and holding a handkerchief to a tearful face, was supported on alternate sides by Jackie and Arthur Bernstein. Bernstein, wearing heavy-rimmed spectacles,

with a receding forehead and prominent, hawklike nose, was to
marry the bereaved widow a year and a half later, on December 31, 1936, and become Jackie's stepfather. Meanwhile, his
mother became president of Jackie Coogan Productions, Inc.

Unfortunately for Jackie, his father apparently had not felt it
necessary to protect his interest with the legal binding of his
will. Filed for probate in Superior Court, the document revealed that the entire estate, which consisted of stock in Jackie
Coogan Productions, Inc., was to go to his widow, and to re-
vert to the son only if Mrs. Coogan predeceased or perished
with him "in the same calamity." The will was dated July 2,
1926. While Jackie declared he was sure his father had prepared another will later than that admitted to probate, and
while he at one point stated he had obtained the first tangible
information to bolster that conviction, no later document was
ever produced.

On October 24, 1935, Jackie turned twenty-one, but it was
not until more than two years later, on April 11, 1938, that he
brought suit against his mother and stepfather. Even after that
date, however, Jackie still felt that his reluctance to take action
to acquire his earnings was perhaps understandable, given the
circumstances: "I was young and maybe any youngster would
have said to himself, as I did, 'Well, Coogan, old boy, you're
pretty nicely fixed, pretty nicely fixed! You'll never have to
worry about money, so why worry about anything else?'
Maybe I shouldn't be blamed for sitting back at that time and
not making any real attempt to stand on my own two feet and
get ahead on my own abilities, such as they were."

In the intervening period, however, the new factor in his
life, which undoubtedly played a powerful role in precipitating
the suit, was his marriage to Betty Grable. "He never would
have taken the stand," Betty Grable said in a magazine article,
"if it weren't that when we were married he realized he had
responsibilities to meet and not one cent to meet them with.
With all that he had earned, with a childhood of work behind

him, with all the talk of the trust fund created for him, the 'Millionaire Kid' didn't have enough to take me out dancing, let alone get married."

It is Betty Grable who has also given the most plausible explanation of certain elements in Jackie Coogan's character which enabled him to play so passive a role for so many years: "Any other boy would have realized that something was very wrong with his estate when the trust fund he and everyone else believed was there for him was not turned over to him on his twenty-first birthday. Instead, he was given a 'present' of a thousand dollars. And even that had a string to it. He would be given this gift, he was told, on condition that he sign certain papers which, it turns out, signed away just about everything he had. He signed them. It's hard to believe, but he did, because he is, or was, entirely without suspicion."

With considerable insight, Jackie's first wife went on to search for the origins of the credulous and compliant elements in his character, finding at least one source in his training as a child actor.

"If Jack has any fault at all, it is that he isn't aggressive enough," she stated. "Perhaps he had to 'give out' so much when he was a child that a lot of it was taken out of him. I only know he hates to fight, detests arguments or friction of any kind. I can't have an argument with Jack, because he won't argue, that's all."

Swift and total obedience to a film director's orders had made Jackie Coogan a brilliant child star. That same obedience, based on trust, had made him a near-model child in his mother's eyes. Now, however, he was to have his faith and trust severely shaken by the actions and revelations which followed his institution, in early April 1938, of a lawsuit to recover his earnings.

Having appointed a receiver to hold the assets of the Bernsteins in custody, Judge Wilson asked Mr. and Mrs. Bernstein to prepare a deposition in reply to the charges, giving an accounting of the alleged $4 million earnings. A process server, W. T. Gleason, was appointed to serve a subpoena to that effect. His task, it turned out, was far from easy.

Subpoena in hand, he called at the Bernstein residence, only to have the maid declare that Mrs. Bernstein was in Palm Springs. He tried again the next day, and was again rebuffed. When, after three days of pursuit, his prey still eluded him, Gleason resorted to a device of his own.

Armed with a pair of powerful binoculars, he chose an elevated vantage point to observe the Bernstein property. He saw a plump, square-faced woman, a dead ringer for Mrs. Bernstein, sitting in the living room talking to a lean, angular man who could easily have passed for Mr. Bernstein. In the driveway was Mrs. Bernstein's Rolls-Royce.

Hurriedly, he went to a telephone, reported what he had seen to Mrs. Bernstein, and asked whether she would surrender gracefully and accept a subpoena. The receiver at the other end was jammed loudly upon its hinges. Presenting himself again at the door of the residence, he was talking to a servant when a woman's powerful voice rang out: "Tell that man to go to hell!"

Gleason retreated to headquarters and told his story. A lawyer for Jackie went to Judge Ruben Schmidt with the tale of obstruction, and obtained an order empowering the sheriff's men to crash into the Bernstein fortress, by force if necessary. The next day, officers finally charged through the electrically operated gates and served the subpoena. Mrs. Bernstein declared herself deeply hurt at the court action and distressed that she was unable to see her son.

"Jackie did not even let me know he was filing suit," she repeated, "and now I feel that in all fairness to myself I must fight the action to clear my name."

Through her attorney, she let it be known that important points of the deposition would maintain that Jackie had never been expelled from the family home but had left of his own accord; and that his stepfather, Arthur Bernstein, never had nor wanted any of the money which Jackie claimed was his property and which he charged Bernstein with using illegally.

Having done her legal turn, Mrs. Bernstein nonetheless swore: "I'd go through fire and water for that boy!"

"All I know," declared Jackie to reporters, "is that I earned millions and don't have anything now, while my stepfather is rolling in wealth. Two times last winter I went to the Santa Anita racetrack and sat in the one-dollar seats, but I could look up and see my stepfather in the clubhouse with the rich people. I made my bets at the two-dollar window and he was making his bets at the hundred-dollar window. That's how it has been with everything else."

On April 17, 1938, Mrs. Arthur L. Bernstein, plump, darkly clad, matronly-looking, made her first appearance at the deposition hearing before Judge Wilson and provided spectators with a display of emotional histrionics which left them blinking in disbelief.

First, she discounted Jackie's tales of an unhappy home atmosphere and of financial straits. "It isn't reasonable to believe," she declared, "that a boy who found home life as unpleasant as Jackie now tells would have stayed at home, particularly when he was earning between $30,000 and $40,000 during those two years."

Secondly, she stated officially that Jackie's earnings had amounted to $1.3 million, not to $4 million, as claimed. Asked whether it was her position that this money belonged to her, she snapped, "I believe that is the law."

Thirdly, and she began crying when she said this, she felt she owed her son nothing because at the age of twenty he had grossly misbehaved. "Jackie was a bad boy," she claimed, "a very bad boy, who couldn't handle money." His father, she said, had told him, "If you had money, you'd be completely haywire in two months."

At the mention of the elder Coogan, Mrs. Bernstein broke down and sobbed hysterically. The hearing was recessed. When it resumed, she said that she remembered only one discussion of finances with her son and his father. During this discussion, she said, Jackie was told he had no estate, no money, and that all he earned belonged to his parents. Coogan Sr., she stated, had never even considered establishing a trust fund for Jackie, as was now alleged.

Mrs. Bernstein again began to cry as she related how, at twenty, her boy had done something so terrible that it caused Jack Sr. to tell him off with the statement that thereafter the most he could expect was parental "cooperation." "Jackie had done something that was bad, particularly bad," she said. "I was heartbroken. I couldn't see him. His father said, 'You are breaking your mother's heart.' He told him that we had done everything to try to make a man of him. He's my son and I love him. I've tried to make a man of him, but I don't think I've been successful."

To the charges, Jackie replied candidly, "I was flunked out of Santa Clara and I came home. I am not making much pretense that I ever was much of a student. Anyway, I was feeling pretty bad about the whole thing, and I was getting razzed from all quarters, so I did something a lot of other young fellows have done in their time. Got drunk.

"I got home about midnight and mother wasn't home yet and she didn't get home until after three; but in the meantime the alcohol didn't agree with me, and I got awfully sick and I think one of mother's fine Persian rugs suffered a little. The next morning she became hysterical and Dad and I had quite a bad time. I agreed not to drink any more and I went over to Father Mullane's at St. Brendan's Parish and took the pledge and I kept it ever since."

He did not feel that this conduct warranted his being cut off from his money, Jackie declared, adding that after all, his father had also flunked out of college at the same age.

Judge Wilson declared, "I do not think a child is bound to give his services to his parents," and stated that the allegation of undue influence on Bernstein's part must be carefully studied by the court.

On April 26th, Mrs. Bernstein surrendered to the court a 17-carat diamond, set in a platinum ring, and given her by Jack Coogan Sr. It was valued at $25,000. She also turned over a $2,500 diamond-studded platinum pocket v tch given to Jackie some years earlier by an admirer, the watch which, it had been alleged, Bernstein had appropriated for his own use.

However, when receiver John E. Biby announced plans to dispossess the Bernsteins of their San Fernando Valley mansion, from which Jackie stated he had been forced to move on demanding his earnings, as well as their two Rolls-Royces, Jackie stepped in. Through his lawyers he arranged for a stipulation in the receivership proceedings which allowed his mother and stepfather to keep the home and the two automobiles.

This conciliatory move on his part led immediately to the first rumors of an out-of-court settlement. To these, Jackie's only answer was "No comment," and his attorneys appeared contemptuous of the idea, as they did of Mrs. Bernstein's offer, a few days later, to give him a share of his earnings as a "reasonable settlement" if the court upheld her right to the money. They made it clear that they were fighting not for a part of the money, but for all of it, that they believed Jackie should decide what to give his mother, not the other way around.

To the trained observer, it appeared clear that Mrs. Bernstein's statement had public-relations overtones. It was her first utterance after hiring a top publicity agent to improve her press relations.

The move swiftly backfired. It gave Jackie an opportunity to observe, "He's an expensive press agent. I hope Mom's not spending my money on him, but my money's all the money she's got to spend."

A few days later, the publicity ace, who was supposed to make Mrs. Bernstein appear less quarrelsome to the world, quarreled with her and quit, saying that she was listening to her lawyers rather than to him.

Her lawyers, meanwhile, fought to keep the case from going to trial as ordered by Judge Wilson.

Jackie Coogan learned what was left of his childhood earnings when Biby, the court receiver, filed his inventory with the County Clerk. The most important item on his agenda was Jackie Coogan Productions, Inc. Evidently, all salaries earned by all members of the Coogan household were dumped into the corporation, which the receiver called "a family budget system."

At the time of the accounting, gross assets of the corporation amounted to only $696,204. Due to obligations outstanding and depreciations, this was further reduced to $535,923 net. Somehow, over the years, the elder Coogans and Bernstein had dissipated the better part of the colossal earnings of their young charge. Even now, Jackie could not be sure that he would ever actually put his hands on a penny of what remained of his sadly deflated fortune.

If considerable evidence existed to support his contention that his father had intended establishing a trust fund for him to protect his childhood earnings, this evidence was weakened by the firm statements of both defendants that no such intent had ever existed. As a result, although press and public sentiment ran heavily in Jackie's favor, it was generally felt that his legal position was extremely weak, and that the task facing his lawyers was a formidable one. To counter the Bernsteins' allegations, at the deposition hearing, veteran screen star Wallace Beery was called in to testify. At the time Beery and Jackie had played together in pictures, the well-known actor had become a close friend of Jack Sr.

Rubbing his jaw in a familiar meditative gesture, Beery told the court: "Not on one, but many times—more than a dozen, I think—Jack told me that he had never used or intended to use a cent the boy earned. Every penny the boy was making was being put away and saved for him, Jack said on several occasions. He was careful at all times to impress everyone that Jackie's money would be all his—and rightfully—when the kid reached a man's estate."

Concluding his testimony, Beery volunteered, "I shall be

glad to help Jackie in any way possible so that his father's wishes may be fulfilled."

From the Coogan family home in Syracuse, New York, came additional support. Friends of the family volunteered testimony that the father had often talked of preserving Jackie's money for him.

And in Los Angeles, a wealthy advertising man volunteered the information that in 1932, when he had urged Bernstein to invest in a business venture, Bernstein had turned him down, saying he couldn't invest because he was handling money for Jackie Coogan; that he and Jackie's father were building up a fund for Jackie so that when he came of age he would have a large estate.

Shortly after the hearings, new evidence came to light which greatly bolstered Jackie's case. From the long-forgotten files of the Hall of Records, his attorneys produced two documents. The first was a petition signed by both parents which would have appointed Mrs. Coogan the guardian of Jackie's estate. A second document showed that subsequently she and Coogan Sr. obtained dismissal of the guardianship proceedings, the reason being that the parents "anticipate the creation of a trust fund for the investment and preservation of the estate of Jackie Coogan." The date of the dismissal was January 8, 1923, scant days before Jackie was to sign the famous half-million-dollar bonus check from Metro Pictures which made him one of the highest-salaried stars in the history of motion pictures.

Until these guardianship documents appeared, his case had looked bleak. Now the prospects brightened. He himself declared, "Everyone has been telling me that the law is against me. I guess they're wrong. I guess the law is on my side, too." On presentation of the new evidence, the Bernstein attorneys requested a delay, which was granted.

While rumors of out-of-court settlements continued to crop up, Jackie came to New York in June for a series of personal appearances which he hoped would bolster his sagging finances. Thousands of curiosity seekers met him as he stepped off the Twentieth Century at Grand Central Station. For them and for the East Coast reporters he once again aired some of the charges that had led to his action, and repeated his assertion that his stepfather was the cause of all his trouble.

Bernstein—described by *Time* as the "slick, slanty-eyed, beaky stepfather and family adviser"—was thirty-six years old in 1922 when the Coogans put him on their payroll and asked him to guide their financial dealings. From that time until the elder Coogan's death, he played a key role in the management of Jackie Coogan's earnings and was virtually a member of the Coogan household, seeing them daily and usually accompanying them on their various travels.

When Jack Coogan Sr. died in May 1935, Bernstein was appointed administrator of his estate. Less than two years later, on December 31, 1936, the last day of the year, he took the elder Coogan's place as head of the household by marrying Lillian Dolliver Coogan, Jackie's mother. Bernstein was fifty-two at the time; his new bride was forty-two. With Jackie, just turned twenty-one, and Jackie's younger brother Robert, ten years old, they lived in a palatial residence in Encino, where the Al Jolsons, the Darryl Zanucks, and other great and influential names of the film colony resided.

Shortly after the wedding ceremony, when Bernstein moved into the Coogan home, the first signs of friction between Jackie and his stepfather came out into the open. *Time*, in reporting the strained situation, said: "One day the kid hauled off, knocked Arthur's rump over a teakettle."

As Jackie's lawsuit extended into the summer of 1938, he found additional charges to levy against his stepfather. Bernstein, he now alleged, was involved in a multitude of gambling transactions. In addition to losing $100 bets at the racetrack and charging the losses to the estate, he accused him of deriving a good living from his participation in bookmaking activities. His source for this information, he declared, was Bernstein himself.

Bernstein indignantly denied this charge. He admitted that he had done bookmaking for a short time in 1937 when the state's attorney had said it was legal to place bets at the tracks. But when this was declared illegal, he had discontinued his activity and had not engaged in bookmaking at any time since, and at no time since the beginning of the suit.

Apparently irritated by the renewed attack upon her husband, Mrs. Bernstein declared, "Jackie apparently wants all the money that Robert earned, too," referring to Jackie's younger brother. "All salaries, those of Jackie, Jackie's father, mine, and little Robert's, were turned over regularly to the corporation."

The remark stung Jackie. The relationship between the two brothers was a close one, despite the fact that Robert, born in 1924, was ten years younger, only thirteen at the time of the lawsuit. Jackie called him "Ro-bair," in the French manner, and felt very protective toward his younger brother. According to Betty Grable, for Jackie the worst aspect of the suit was the effect it might have on Robert, still living with his mother and stepfather.

As a child, Robert had tended toward plumpness, in this respect taking after his mother. When he made his film debut with Jackie, audiences happily noted the family resemblance. Dressed in coveralls, his hair cut in the familiar Dutch boy bob made famous by Jackie, Robert's evocation of that memory was sufficient to give him a brief career on his own.

In 1930, he appeared with another Jackie, Jackie Cooper, playing Sooky to the young Cooper's title role in *Skippy*, the film adaptation of Percy Crosby's popular cartoons of childhood incidents. Its success led to Robert's sole star appearance in a sequel, *Sooky*, the following year. In 1932, he appeared in *Sky Bride* with Richard Arlen and Jack Oakie, but he never again played an important role in a film. At the time of his first screen appearance, his father reportedly said, "One actor in the family is enough. Robert's going to be a businessman." While no business career of note developed, Robert appeared content to leave the movies to Jackie.

In the late summer of 1938, the opposing forces in the lawsuit engaged in another verbal sally, repeating and adumbrating their previous contentions. Jackie admitted that his father had threatened to cut him off at the time of the drunk episode, though not at all in the words that the Bernstein attorneys had used in their deposition. He also repeated that in the spring of 1937 he had asked his mother and stepfather for an accounting of his money. "Mother said I didn't have a thing coming," he reported. As for Bernstein, he had used his customary blunt manner to say, "You haven't any claim to any money. You have no right to it. It's ours."

Mrs. Bernstein talked to reporters about these statements and commented: "We've always done the best we could for Jackie, but he never seemed to grow up, so far as money was concerned. If he had this money now, it would soon be all gone." She dabbed frequently at her eyes with a handkerchief as she spoke.

In his New York *World Telegram* column, Heywood Broun added his comment: "In all the long history of impulsive parents, few, if any, have been called upon to make such a sacrifice as Lillian Coogan. She had kept the money to save her boy from himself."

In August, the Coogan-Bernstein case moved into an upbeat phase. During a recess in the proceedings, his mother left the hearing room and walked into an adjoining anteroom. To the astonishment of the spectators, Jackie followed her. "Mother," he said, kissing her on the cheek. "Jackie," she replied simply, and fervently returned the kiss. They parted.

Later, Jackie explained, "It was a kiss of affection, not of peace." He would continue the suit. Asked for her interpretation, Mrs. Bernstein, her face red with weeping, could only sob, "He's my son," as she waved aside all questions.

The incident was the prelude to a further series of delays in the proceedings. More than six months later, in early February 1939, Judge Robert Scott announced another one-week postponement. Attorneys for both parties said negotiations for an out-of-court settlement were making progress.

Several weeks later, attorneys for Jackie Coogan reported that after demanding several undisclosed changes, he was now ready to sign the settlement The Bernsteins, it was reported, were also ready to sign. The estate, according to receiver's findings, now totaled less than $300,000.

On March 19, 1939, almost a year after Jackie had instituted his suit, the Supreme Court was asked to approve a signed settlement which would release the funds from receivership and distribute them among the contesting parties. Assets were now officially listed as $291,715, mostly land holdings. The settlement assigned $126,307.50 to Jackie Coogan as his share.

The total estate included real estate in Hollywood and the Wilshire districts, plus a San Diego County ranch. The value of these holdings was listed as $218,000. In addition, there were stocks and bonds valued in the neighborhood of $50,000, and miscellaneous property and cash worth approximately $32,000. Mrs. Bernstein, it was reported, in addition to her regular half of the settlement, was to receive $20,000 worth of jewels; $16,-000 representing the film earnings of Robert Coogan; insurance on Jackie valued at $4,000; plus a note for $2,600. This added up to $42,600 more than Jackie's share. However, Jackie, in addition to real estate, was to receive rights to some of the films in which he starred—negatives and prints, plus the right to exploit them. These film and story rights, it was agreed, would make up the difference.

It was not until August 16, 1939, that the Los Angeles Supreme Court actually approved this settlement. Final liquidation of the Coogan-Bernstein holdings, after the preliminary settlement earlier in the year, disclosed a further reduction in the fortune to $252,000. Jackie accepted one-half, $126,000, as his share of the remains, and his attorneys announced that it would go into a lifetime trust fund. To Mr. and Mrs. Bernstein went a similar sum. With this final settlement, the most widely publicized trial of the decade in Hollywood came to a whimpering end.

At the beginning of Jackie Coogan's lawsuit, Superior Judge Emmet H. Wilson had said that a 1927 law giving judges the authority to approve contracts for minors virtually made the court the child's guardian, without, however, making any specific provision for the care of the minor's money. Judge Wilson proposed to correct this vagueness.

On May 4, 1939, a committee of the state assembly at Sacramento recommended passage of what was officially called the Child Actor's Bill, better known as "The Coogan Act." The measure gave the court approving the guardian's contract power to set aside half the child's earnings in a trust fund or some other form of savings, and provided for an accounting to the court of other earnings. Thus, even before the final settlement of Jackie Coogan's own lawsuit in August, his name had passed to a measure protecting the earnings of child actors of the future.

As for the child actors of the present, the newspapers reported that all was in order. The yearly half-million earnings of Shirley Temple were being invested by her parents in annuities and trust funds payable to her at intervals until she was fifty. Parents of plump, brattish Jane Withers were putting $1,000 a week into annuities and trust funds. Songstress Deanna Durbin had a $50,000 home held in trust for her, and her savings were going into special ten-year annuities. Judy Garland endorsed her checks to her mother, who, the reports declared—erroneously it later turned out—was safeguarding her money. Young Bobby Breen's sister was seeing to it that he would receive half his money at twenty-one, and the other half nine years later.

For Jackie Coogan, however, the results of his suit must have seemed in many ways a Pyrrhic victory. Of his childhood earnings—whether one used his original estimate of $4 million or his mother's figure of $1.3 million—he was to receive a scant $126,000. Of his once great popularity, the suit had brought him countless reminders, but while many friends had rallied loyally to his cause, the people who had been closest to him in childhood were now separated from him by cruel and unbridgeable gulfs.

And, even more sadly—for it represented the future, while the lawsuit looked to the past—his much ballyhooed marriage to actress Betty Grable was in serious trouble. In January 1939, after little more than a year of wedlock, the couple decided to separate. Money was the cause of their difficulties, said Jackie, admitting he was broke. Money, echoed Betty, saying she felt he needed to be alone until he was able to work out his financial problems. "The Kid," said the papers, had been separated from "America's Ideal Girl" by an empty pocketbook.

The irony of Jackie's predicament was heightened by the sudden reentry on the scene of his estranged mother. "I want my boy back and to forget the past. He'll be more than welcome," she announced, almost in tears. "I feel awfully bad about the separation, but I can't believe it is caused by financial conditions, as they say. There must be more to it." For his mother, Jackie had a cool rebuff: "Under existing conditions it is impossible to contemplate a reconciliation."

Although the young Coogans shortly reconciled, their marriage took its final turn for the worse in midyear, and in October 1939 Betty obtained her divorce. In a magazine article, Jackie wrote: "I believe that money—sad as this may seem—is the root of more marital troubles than all the other causes put together."

The haunting vision of his lost millions was not to keep him from trying his hand again—and again and again—at marriage. He had already been in the United States Army several months when he married Flower Parry, variously described by the newspapers as a Hollywood nightclub flower girl and as a George White's Scandals showgirl. Less than a year later, in April 1942, they were divorced, custody of a son, John Anthony, going to the young mother. Late in 1946, while making a nightclub comeback in which he burlesqued his classic role in *The Kid,* Jackie married Ann McCormack, blues singer, who had appeared with him in vaudeville performances. Their marriage, which also produced one child, a daughter, lasted until September 1951. The following year, he was secretly married to dancer Dodie Lamphere in Mexico City. This fourth attempt at marriage within a period of fifteen years seemed to give the lie to a statement made many years earlier by Dick Winslow, a young actor who had played with him in *Tom Sawyer.* "Jackie," said Winslow, "is practically a woman hater."

Indeed, the thread of enduring love in Jackie Coogan's life was proclaimed by newspaper headlines in January 1941, shortly before he was to go into the army. THE KID AND MA MAKE UP, they read. JACKIE BACK AT MRS. COOGAN'S HOME. Mrs. Lillian Coogan Bernstein announced that she and her son were reconciled, and that he was coming to live with her and her husband, Arthur L. Bernstein, in the ranch house they had received at the time of the settlement of the lawsuit. Jackie, furthermore, said that he was teaching his stepfather to fly.

"Are we happy?" Mrs. Bernstein echoed a reporter. "Say, I've got my family again."

"New romance?" Jackie repeated the question. "Sure, I've got a new girl—my mother."

To many, the move seemed incredible, but to those who knew Jackie Coogan best, it was understandable. In his childhood screen roles, he had played the poor, but lovable orphan waif, whose innocence was elemental, whose love was boundless. His return to a household from which he had been rudely forced, his reunion with a mother and stepfather who had caused him untold anguish, these can perhaps best be explained by the fact that as a man Jackie Coogan retained the heart of a child.

Great child stars sometimes flash like dazzling meteors through the screen heavens. Almost on sight they glow with a brilliant intensity and then, with the same startling swiftness, they burn out and fall. For Jackie Coogan, the fabulous Kid of the silents, the word career meant an unending series of unfulfilling comebacks once his childhood success was over.

"Every time a guy has been out of work for three months, they say he's making a comeback. If that's true, I've had dozens," he has said. But while it is true that the familiar headline THE KID COMES BACK has appeared in newspapers and magazines over the years, Jackie Coogan has never really come back. He has remained in the shadows of the entertainment world, playing bit parts in second-rate films, telling jokes in nightclubs, appearing on quiz shows in order to gain exposure.

Ironically, about the time of his fiftieth birthday in 1964, he began a role in a television series based on the ghoulish *New Yorker* cartoons of Charles Addams. *The Addams Family* swiftly moved into the list of top-rated evening shows, but the sight of Uncle Fester on the home screen, his bald pate shining over a round, powdered face, his leering eyes in an expression of mock evil, jarred many a sentimental memory. For the one-time symbol of youth and innocence, sentiment was perhaps less important than practical considerations. The new role provided Jackie Coogan with a steady job, not always the easiest thing in the world to come by for a half-forgotten child idol. As those in the field are swift to explain, an actor likes to work.

2.

BABY LEROY

Leroy Overacker, better known as Baby Leroy, made his film debut at eight months, rose to instant stardom, and after a brief but eventful career was retired at the advanced age of three. Seldom has screen fame come and gone so swiftly.

The first infant less than a year old to attain major billing in a feature, Leroy was born at Altadena, California, on May 12, 1932. His parents had separated shortly before his birth, and his mother, only sixteen at the time, felt a financial strain at the new arrival. Undismayed, the baby swiftly developed a sunny disposition, rocked away in his crib, and carefully bided his time.

As it happened, about this time the wise men of nearby Paramount Studios were conducting a talent hunt. What they needed specifically was a baby with a projecting underlip like that of the aristocratic Hapsburgs to play a part in a film called *Bedtime Story*, starring Maurice Chevalier. After drawing up the specifications, director Norman Taurog turned the hunt over to Rachel Smith, an Englishwoman, who was the supervisor of children at Paramount, and William Kaplan, the picture's assistant director. These two were instructed to head for the nurseries of the state's charitable institutions so that the movie salary of the chosen infant might actually relieve financial distress.

At a nursery conducted by one Captain Lee, they were told of a child now returned to its mother which might fill their bill. Accordingly, they repaired to the small farm near Altadena where little Leroy was waiting for them in an affable mood. From his crib he beamed his most winning smile at the visitors and then, when he saw them melting under the spell of his charm, he decided to give them the full treatment, and gurgled. They listened intently to the soft, seductive sound, the gurgle that was shortly to sweep America. "No use looking any further," Kaplan declared, and he and Miss Smith took Leroy immediately to the Paramount lot.

A star is a star, however, and Leroy, to the manner born, had the headliner's inevitable characteristic—temperament. By the time he arrived at the studio, he had undergone one of those swift changes of mood which were later to be the bane of his directors and co-workers. He had grown tired and peevish. When director Taurog was called from a story conference to witness the miracle child, Leroy would not even deign to smile. Furthermore, noted the director, he did not have the Hapsburg lip. Things didn't look good at all.

The wily infant, however, was only saving his energies for the big gun. He was in a room with twenty squalling thespian pretenders the day Maurice Chevalier walked in. Of all the throng, he alone ceased his howling long enough to beam a broad smile at the genial Frenchman, who could not help but take note. It was an auspicious beginning for their friendship and collaboration. And again, when Leroy faced the camera for his official screen test, he showed that he knew the ropes. Like little Shirley Temple over at Fox, he saw no reason to "give" for a long shot, but once the camera closed up on him, the trouper's instinct took hold—he seized the slats of his crib, pulled himself up to his full height, and delivered the captivating gurgle. Out of more than 1,000 aspirants, he won the coveted role, starting work at $50 a week, not bad for a six-month-old breadwinner at the height of the depression.

One technicality remained to be cleared away. Because not only Leroy, but his mother as well, was under-age, and consequently unable to authorize his appearance in films, he was legally adopted by his grandfather. The official name of Paramount's new contract player thus became Leroy Winebrenner.

The Hapsburg lip, which Leroy Winebrenner did not have, was an integral part of the plot of *A Bedtime Story*. In the film, Chevalier played a debonair man-about-town just returned from a spell of big-game hunting. At the railroad station he picks up his car only to discover that someone has left a baby in it. The butler and the rest of the help think the little visitor is the result of an escapade, and Chevalier is forced to the same conclusion on discovering that the infant has the same protruding lower lip as the master of the house. The illusion persists through a series of episodes until finally it is noted that the baby is sucking on a button lodged under the lip. This has produced the characteristic feature. In the scenes where the Hapsburg lip was needed, technicians eventually decided to retouch the negative, painting an extension onto the underlip for about 200 feet of film. So it was that Baby Leroy became a pioneer in retroactive celluloid plastic surgery.

A Bedtime Story was shot in approximately six weeks. During that time, Leroy grew considerably larger, wispy blond hair started to deck his bald pate, and two tiny front teeth made their appearance. While three sets of stand-ins, more accurately known about the studio as "lie-ins," were used in the early scenes where Leroy had his mouth wide open, the duration of the shooting was of sufficient length to permit a study of the young performer's art.

One important aspect of his playing became swiftly apparent. With an uncanny ability, he could master virtually any expression if only presented with the proper stimulus. To elicit the vast gamut of emotions that ran from tears to tantrums to a touching tenderness, the skillful filmmakers of Paramount sought out a variety of Pavlovian objects and devices. Bright things such as apples and oranges, colored balloons, and mirrors were able to draw forth appreciative smiles. Rattles and spinning tops and talking dolls provoked an expression of profound thoughtfulness. A glamorous face beaming into his own could sometimes, surprisingly, elicit a leer and at other moments a robust wail of frustration.

More elaborate ruses were often executed, however, to draw forth a desired effect. Director Norman Taurog had brought another child star, Jackie Cooper, to fame in *Skippy*, and he had children of his own. He recalled that one of them hated to blow his nose; would, in fact, burst into tears when forced into the act. The device worked unfailingly with Leroy. When the script called for him to cry, nurse Smith would put a handkerchief to his nose and the cameras would grind as he bellowed away. Since the script quite often did call for tears, there was some fear that the baby's nose might exercise itself into Durantiesque proportions. These anxieties were happily unfounded.

To evoke a real belly laugh, the studio's brightest minds resorted to another bit of ingenuity. Out of view of the camera, nurse Smith would pour water over the head of Leroy's mother, who sat regularly in attendance on the sidelines. Seeing this bit of whimsy, Leroy would howl with delight, with each precious yelp captured for the screen. His mother's reactions were not recorded.

Since the volatile young comedian's moods changed with startling rapidity and could seldom be repeated, it was necessary to catch the precise moment of inspiration for the camera. In one scene, Leroy was supposed to register surprise when Edward Everett Horton appears as a nursemaid in an apron and lace cap. Horton was kept out of Leroy's sight until shooting began, so that the one brief look of wonder could be trapped on celluloid. True to expectations, Leroy, seconds later, was already bored with Horton's appearance in female attire and his attention had wandered afield.

Occasionally, Leroy would forget himself and his position as a star and ad lib a scene as only an eight-month-old properly can. At these moments, nurse Smith would hurry away for a fresh set of raiment for her charge, and the little leading man's lie-in would be dropped into his crib. The ad-libbed footage would wind up on the cutting room floor.

"He has a habit of whispering into your ear when you are holding him," wrote columnist Sidney Skolsky with reference to this trait. "What he whispers can't be printed here, but if you believe him, you'll rush him to where he should go."

Despite these occasional mishaps, at the end of the shooting for *A Bedtime Story*, it was apparent that Paramount had come up with a winner. "The child plays quite fascinatingly," wrote one critic. "He listens intelligently. He reacts in almost an adult manner. How the director ever got him to do it is something I do not know." The review wound up with a crowning accolade: "Frankly, I have never heard an infant's gurgle mean so much."

Henceforth, Baby Leroy was treated as a star. Paramount signed him to a long-term contract; he was given his own high chair with his name on it, and script girls and assistant directors were seen respectfully trundling his wicker carriage about the lot. Maurice Chevalier settled a $1,000 annuity on him and tried to adopt him. Mae West put him into the number-twelve spot on her list of the twelve most eligible bachelors in the film colony. Moreover, declared the screen's celebrated sex symbol, number twelve would be "the most eligible bachelor for the next twenty years."

While Leroy never gave in to the pressure for interviews, his nurse and tutor, the English-born Rachel Smith, actually a studio representative of the Los Angeles City Board of Education, favored the press with her impressions of the minuscule new idol. "In the first place, he is an even-tempered, adorable, jolly little chap," she declared in clipped British tones. "We keep him that way by not letting his picture work interrupt his normal baby life. . . . He arrives on the set in a happy mood, is fresh and interested in everything." Only allowed by state

law to work two hours a day, Leroy's work was so broken up
that he was never under the lights for more than seven minutes
at a time. Proper food and regular rest periods were other features of the carefully supervised star's routine. Needless to say,
entire shooting schedules revolved around this regimented way
of life, and it was said that luminaries like Garbo and Barrymore were mere puppets in the hands of their director compared to the demanding Leroy.

Although the plump, round-faced baby's services were now
in heavy demand, not all stars felt as kindly toward him as
Maurice Chevalier. Gloria Swanson reportedly turned down
the lead in *Miss Fane's Baby Is Stolen* because the scene-
stealing Leroy was to be in it. Ruth Chatterton likewise begged
off, while Carole Lombard shouted, "Not for me! Get somebody else!" Unperturbed, Leroy cast an appreciative look at his
fan mail, which *The New York Times* said was "not surpassed
by the returns of any of Hollywood's reigning stars."

Eventually, Paramount did find players who would appear
with Leroy, and in swift succession he was cast in *The Torch
Singer*, Ernst Lubitsch's *Design for Living*, *Alice in Wonderland*, the aforementioned *Miss Fane's Baby Is Stolen*, as well as
It's a Gift, Tillie and Gus, and *The Old-Fashioned Way*, films
which led to memorable encounters with the screen's master
comedian, W. C. Fields.

On screen or off, children were anathema to Fields, and
when interviewers asked how he liked them, his standard reply was "Parboiled." The great artist was not unaware of the
risks of appearing in scenes with a beguiling infant, and in the
case of Baby Leroy, a mild case of paranoia swiftly developed.
Fields took it into his head that the infant was out to wreck
his career. As a consequence, half humorously, half seriously,
he brought out his heaviest artillery to meet the threat. On set,
he would sit in a corner, eyeing the antics of his rival, mutter-
ing vague, low threats, plotting.

He saw his chance when nurse Smith appeared, during a
break, with Baby Leroy's orange juice. "I'll give the little nip-

per his juice," Fields volunteered. While the rest of the cast studied their scripts, he quietly removed the nipple from the baby's bottle and added a healthy swig of gin from a hip flask. The amiable Leroy guzzled down the man-sized screwdriver and promptly passed into a glassy-eyed, dazed silence, which neither director Norman Taurog nor nurse Smith could comprehend.

"Walk him around, walk him around," Fields mumbled from his side of the ring. Various ministrations finally partially revived the comatose infant, but his performance, to Fields' visible delight, was far below par. "He's no trouper. The kid's no trouper!" he bellowed to Taurog. "Send him home!"

In *The Old-Fashioned Way*, the script came to the aid of Fields. During a dinner scene at a boarding house, Leroy dropped Fields' watch into the molasses, upset his vermicelli soup, and landed a spoonful of cream unerringly in his face. After dinner, Fields entered a room and came across Leroy— alone and spread out on the carpet in an inviting stance. Tiptoeing up to the infant, his face took on a happy glow as he leaned into a kick that sent Leroy flying six feet across the floor.

If Fields could throw himself with vigor into the competition with Leroy, he was also capable of sudden, impulsive gestures of kindness toward his tormentor. When he heard that the studio was contemplating dropping the option on Leroy's contract, he hurriedly wrote a small part for Leroy into one of his own screenplays.

Time yields to no man, however, and even as his most successful epics reached the screen, the seeds of decay in the career of Baby Leroy became apparent. Paramount sent out a bulletin when he took his first step, another when he spoke his first word, "Mama," to lovely Dorothea Wieck, who had finally accepted the lead in *Miss Fane's Baby Is Stolen*. Thereafter Leroy swiftly learned to say "bye-bye," "hot dog," and a few unprintable expressions which he picked up at the studio, where an alarm now went out about careless use of the language in his presence. One day word spread that Leroy was up to a cute new trick: he had learned to throw a kiss and make a loud smacking noise in accompaniment. Bing Crosby told Claudette Colbert. Claudette went in search of the prodigy and found him in the studio carpentry shop, where the carpenter was on his knees. "And what does a birdie say?" he asked. "Peep, peep!" Leroy proudly replied, sticking his finger with great dexterity into a shiny object which happened to be the carpenter's eye. Moments later, when the curvaceous Mae West also came to investigate, Leroy dropped his mother's hand and walked unaided with a remarkably determined and mature gait. Clearly, he was growing up, and for his career it was a disaster.

At the end of one film, a sharp-eyed cameraman saw a spot of white in Leroy's mouth which had not shown up in earlier scenes. Investigation showed that the shiny object was not removable. A baby tooth had appeared. Rather than scrap all the earlier footage, the rattled producers made a hard decision. The tooth was yanked.

One by one, however, Baby Leroy lost roles due to his increased size. The end was perilously near when he was withdrawn from the cast of *The Baby in the Ice-Box*. Paramount had actually bought the story for Leroy, but in the time it had taken to cast and prepare the script, he had added several inches to his frame. Richard Arlen, Sally Eilers, Robert Montgomery, and Grace Bradley had all grown older, too, but they still remained in the picture. In sad desperation, Leroy's mother and producer Charles Rogers debated fitting him somehow into a larger-sized icebox, but it was apparent to all that the ruse wouldn't work. One good look made it clear that the old boy was three years old. Baby Leroy was washed up.

Like most child stars, however, he could not resist an attempt at a comeback. At seven, he was taken by his mother to test for a part in *The Biscuit Eater*. Leroy won the role, but fell in a swamp during shooting and caught cold. Once more, he was forced to retire.

As he grew into adulthood, Leroy, with little memory of his glamorous past, turned to more mundane pursuits. As Ronald Leroy Overacker, he entered City College in Los Angeles, working part-time at his stepfather's delicatessen across Sunset Boulevard from Schwab's Drugstore, slicing ham for the hams, as one wag put it. A passion for anonymity began to form, and few of the famous stars who stopped by for a salami sandwich knew that the boy behind the counter had once appeared in films, his billing as prominent as theirs.

After serving in the Korean War as a quartermaster, the returning veteran disappeared almost completely from public view. Not until 1965 did the name Baby Leroy appear once more in a newspaper. The Les Crane television show, it was announced, planned a program on former .child stars and had sent a detective out with orders to discover his whereabouts.

The trail led to a southern California beach, where Leroy, a bronzed, lanky thirty-two-year-old, served as a lifeguard, an occupation he had been following for the past fourteen years. "I like being a lifeguard because I'm free," he told Associated Press reporter Dave Smith. "I go surfing, skin diving, skiing, or hunting, and then I see all those poor people driving to work every day. They'd love, really, to be doing what I do for a living."

Apart from his work, Leroy was reluctant to enter into much discussion. Not even his mother, it is said, always knows his current address, which he changes frequently to make it more difficult for people to trace him. His attitude toward the past is not one of bitterness, but one simply of indifference, since his memories of those long-ago days are so vague as to be almost meaningless. His independence appears to be one of the most important elements in his life.

"I come and go as I please," he says. "Nobody follows me, because nobody knows where I am. That's the way I like it."

Today's Ronald Overacker might be amused to look over the clippings of the past he has largely forgotten. There he would find an article in the now defunct *Woman's Home Com-*

panion that predicted a far different future for him. "Leroy has the traits of a born mixer, a lodge brother, and a back-slapping politician," writer Alva Johnson declared. "He is a good subordinate; a yes-child, a reflector of the needs of others. He is not the kind of boy that grows up to be President; he is the kind that grows up to be Postmaster General." If the prophecy were fulfilled today, Postmaster General Overacker would probably mark his own mail, ADDRESS UNKNOWN.

3.

WHAT WAS SHIRLEY TEMPLE REALLY LIKE?

A traditional Hollywood recipe for trouble reads: "Take one talented child, one movie set, one stage mother, and mix them all together." The recipe is apparently all but sure fire, and during the Twenties and Thirties the concoction brought what can only be described as an epidemic of trouble to the already excitable nervous system of Hollywood.

Blame it all on those villains, Charles Spencer Chaplin and Hal Roach. Chaplin had introduced Jackie Coogan in *The Kid,* which made cinema history. The following year, 1921, Roach happened to overhear some youngsters arguing in an improvised playground near his studio. When they argued for five minutes, for ten, for fifteen, and largely about nothing, it gave him an idea. He pooled the talents of several child actors— Sunshine Sammy, a Negro boy, a little tough-looking guy named Mickey Daniels, and dainty Mary Kornman—dubbed them "The Little Rascals," and put them into a short called *Our Gang.*

Across the land, young filmgoers fell in love with Jackie Coogan and Our Gang. If the one moved them to tears, the other had them howling with laughter. Sometimes the two emotions followed each other with lightning rapidity in films that had their usually restless little bodies glued to their seats. The producers, directors, and screenwriters watched these reactions with professional fascination, but someone else was giving them an equally close scrutiny. The kids' parents, especially their mothers, suddenly saw their youngsters in a new light. If Jackie Coogan could come from nowhere and win a nation's heart—along with a million dollars—and if the nondescript collection of child actors who formed Our Gang could make it, why couldn't their own little darling? In this new light, the mischievous behavior which they had for years been trying to put down took on a sudden appeal. Their little Johnny's crooked and falling teeth, if one looked at them in the right light, were actually rather "cute." Little Jennie's curls and her smile were really nothing less than solidified sunshine.

The stage mother had long been a familiar phenomenon on the American entertainment scene, but the stage had never really penetrated to every nook and hamlet of the land. The screen did. And the screen mothers soon formed an impressive troupe as they pleaded and cajoled with their less imaginative husbands, and finally coaxed them to give up their jobs, sell the house, bundle the family possessions, and oh, my God, yes, the kid, into the family jalopy to head west toward California.

In Hollywood, a talented young actress named Hedda Hopper watched them arrive, "like a flock of hungry locusts driven by the gale winds of their pushing, prompting, ruthless mothers. One look into the eyes of those women told you what was on their minds: 'If I can get this kid of mine on the screen, we might just hit it big.' I used to wonder if there wasn't a special subhuman species of womankind that bred children for the sole purpose of dragging them to Hollywood. Most of the women showed no mercy. They took little creatures scarcely old enough to stand or speak, and like buck sergeants, drilled them to shuffle through a dance step or mumble a song. They robbed them of every phase of childhood to keep the waves in the hair, the pleats in the dress, the pink polish on the nails."

Every fifteen minutes, it was estimated, one hundred children arrived in Hollywood with their ambitious parents, many of whom hoped to fulfill their own frustrated desires for a stage or screen career through their progeny. One might get a much-desired interview. Another might actually get a few days' work before the screen. The chance to earn enough during the year to pay just one week's expenses was estimated at about 1 in 15,-000.

At every studio in Hollywood, the stage mothers set up camp outside the gates, their neat, scrubbed, often frightened youngsters firmly in tow, hoping for a miraculous "discovery." Perhaps there at the magic portals, a director or a producer might catch a glimpse of their prodigy, or almost as good, perhaps the mother would recognize a figure of importance, rush up and present her "new Jackie Coogan," her "new Baby Peggy." Or the guard might for a brief moment glance the other way and give the aspiring parent an opportunity to slip through the entrance and into the studio streets where again the miracle of discovery might take place.

Understandably, Metro had a particular fascination for stage mothers during the Twenties when Jackie Coogan roamed its lot. The head of the reorganized studio, Louis B. Mayer, had set about conscientiously to build up a whole stable of child actors whom he could train and turn into long-term assets for the studio. His success was phenomenal.

Similarly, the continuing series of Our Gang comedies sent an even greater avalanche to the studio of Hal Roach. Over a period of seventeen years, an astonishing 140,000 interviews were granted to children seeking admission to the celebrated gang. Of these, 176 actually appeared on the screen, and a scant 41 were put under contract, leaving the odds for this minimum security at 3,400 to 1.

Many years later, in the Fifties, when the Our Gang comedies enjoyed a spectacular new success on television, Hal Roach was asked why he didn't remake the series. His answer was that it would be an immensely costly undertaking to organize a nationwide talent search for suitable youngsters. "In the old days," he declared, "they would come to us, and we'd review six hundred kids to find one who qualified. One of those who sat outside the office and waited day after day was Shirley Temple. She never got chosen."

Shirley Temple never made Our Gang, and a good many other prominent figures passed her by. Nonetheless, by 1935, when she was a mere six years old, she was ruling as the box-office queen of the nation and of the world. By then, virtually everyone in Hollywood was claiming the honor of having "discovered" her.

For the stage mothers streaming in from all the states of the union, there was a malicious irony in the fact that the adored boy hero of the silents, Jackie Coogan, was born right in the city of Los Angeles, while Shirley Temple grew up in Santa Monica, not more than twenty minutes from the fabled studios where fame and fortune had set up seemingly permanent shop. True love, folk legend would have it, can always be found within a fifty-mile circumference. True talent, for which agents and scouts ransacked the nation's nurseries, was waiting on their doorstep at home.

"Long before she was born, I tried to influence her future life by association with music, art, and natural beauty. Perhaps this prenatal preparation helped make Shirley what she is today," Mrs. Temple stated in 1934, when Shirley, at five, was already near the top. It is one of the few documented cases we have of a stage mother operating at the prenatal stage.

Whatever the happy reason, Shirley Temple walked when a year old, and when she was two, it became apparent that she had an extraordinary grace and sense of rhythm as she glided airily along on her toes, kept time to the music that poured from the radio or the record player, and made up tunes of her own to go with her delicate baby steps. Observing these gifts, Mrs. Temple who had herself wanted to act, decided to enroll Shirley in dancing school. Mr. Temple thought otherwise.

This quiet, retiring man, born of Pennsylvania Dutch stock in Fairview, Pennsylvania, had come to Los Angeles with his parents in 1903, and though the Temples were mostly physicians, he decided to go into banking. He met his future wife, Gertrude, daughter of a Chicago jeweler, while she was attending Polytechnic High School in Los Angeles, and married her when she was only seventeen. Despite the economic strain of an early marriage, he had done quite well. He was now a branch manager of the California bank, owned a small car and a one-story white stucco house with only a small mortgage on it, and even had a few dollars in the bank. Two sons were born early in the marriage, Jack and George, fourteen and ten years old when the Temples were blessed with the baby girl they named Shirley Jane.

The matter of dancing lessons for Shirley brought up problems, however. The country was in the midst of the worst depression of its history. The banks were particularly vulnerable. At the Bank of California there had been times when the institution was closed entirely, and later there were across-the-board pay cuts. Dancing lessons, even at one dollar a throw, seemed an extravagance.

George Temple, a conservative man, also had other questions in his mind about the lessons. He knew that the burgeoning film industry was his neighbor, that at some time that flamboyant world might reach out for his daughter if he allowed her to be placed in a vulnerable position. He wasn't sure he would like that.

His wife assured him that all she wanted was to give her daughter the pleasure of dancing with other youngsters. "We might just as well be living in Chicago or Erie for all the movies mean in our lives," she stated, and then could not resist adding, "Of course, if the movies come after her with a big fat contract—well, that will be different." At this sally, George and Gertrude Temple had a good hearty laugh.

It was a well-known fact at the time that movie talent scouts regularly explored the nation's singing and dancing schools, looking for child prodigies. If Gertrude Temple was Shirley's first discoverer, her second Columbus was swift to appear. His name was Charles Lamont, a director and talent scout at Educational Studios, and he was looking for winning youngsters, no more than 36 inches high, to be featured in takeoffs on adult movies which were to be called Baby Burlesks. Mrs. Temple had evidently not been warned of his arrival. While all the other tots, backed up by their watchful mamas, were decked out in their richest baby gowns, Shirley was dressed rather casually to accommodate a rainy day. Mrs. Temple was about to take her away when one of the other mothers suggested she give Shirley at least the chance to appear before the visitor. Mrs. Temple hesitated before making a fateful decision. She stayed.

"I remember when I was three and unknown," Shirley said in describing the event a decade later, "and some character who turned out to be a talent scout came into dancing school and I hid under the piano. Obviously no poise. He stood around for a while watching and then he said, 'I'll take the one under the piano.' "

At Educational, discoverer number three, producer Jack Hays, engaged her at $10 a day, and later signed her to a contract, holding an option on her services at $50 a picture. Not many years thereafter, when Shirley had become box-office magic with Twentieth Century-Fox, Hays filed suit against her for more than a million dollars, claiming she had walked out on him while he still had legal right to her services. In court, he produced the document which he hoped would substantiate his claim. It was indeed a standard contract. The signature, however, was in the childish scrawl of a three-year-old thespian, hardly firm enough to stand up to legal scrutiny.

For Baby Burlesks, Shirley met all requirements: height, curly hair, bright teeth, an infectious smile, and a definite, distinctive personality. She starred in *The Incomparable More Legs Sweetrick*, a takeoff on Marlene Dietrich, played Lulu Parsnips in a satire on Louella Parsons, who later became one of her biggest boosters, and wore diapers held up by great, oversized safety pins in *The Pie Covered Wagon, Polly-tix in Washington,* and other one-reelers.

Gene Mann, later impresario of the Greek Theatre in Los Angeles, became discoverer number four when he tried, albeit unsuccessfully, to get Shirley into Paramount. Over a period of two years, Shirley played leads in Frolics of Youth, a second series at Educational, as well as bit parts in a number of feature-length films at different studios, none of whom latched on to her. *Red-Haired Alibi* saw her play a small part, as did a comedy with Andy Clyde, a western with Randolph Scott and Esther Ralston, and *Out All Night,* with Zasu Pitts and Slim Summerville. "She's marvelous—she's going to be really great," declared Zasu, but nothing much happened.

By now, George Temple was a little more secure in his position at the bank, but to Gertrude Temple, the financial situation had become secondary. As she trailed her daughter from studio to studio, sometimes sitting for days in a row outside the Our Gang offices of Hal Roach, she hoped for a contract and a good part for Shirley. The big day was not far off.

Discoverer number five—bypassing Zasu Pitts—was Leo Houck, assistant director at Fox Studios, where Shirley had answered a number of calls without getting a part. Houck had nonetheless kept an eye on the bright-eyed youngster, and one evening in a movie theatre lobby he spied Shirley with her mother. They were there for a showing of the first Baby Burlesk. Houck was accompanied by Jay Gorney, a songwriter, to whom he introduced the mother and daughter. Gorney is most frequently given credit for finding Shirley Temple. At that very moment, he was searching for an appealing little girl to sing a number at the end of a picture to be called *Fox Follies.* Dimples, bright blue eyes, a riot of golden curls—the moppet facing him in the lobby seemed to have them all. "Can she sing?" asked Gorney. Mrs. Temple didn't really know. Gorney told her to bring her daughter to the studio. They would try her out.

At Fox, Gorney's songwriting partner, Lew Brown, gave her an audition, and chose her out of nearly two hundred applicants for the role, keeping up the excellent record he had begun to acquire with his "discovery" of Jackie Cooper, whom he had also cast in his first important screen role.

Shirley's final Columbus was Fox's vice-president in charge of production, Winfield Sheehan. After only two weeks of rehearsal and training, Shirley recorded the number for which she had been engaged, "Baby, Take a Bow," for the film now retitled *Stand Up and Cheer.* Her unself-conscious charm and exuberance captivated the studio. By evening, everyone on the set, including Harold Lloyd, who had witnessed the debut, was raving about Shirley Temple. Sheehan tied her down to a seven-year contract at $150 a week, and the career of the most fabulously successful child actress in history began to take wing—not, however, before Mr. and Mrs. Temple spent a long day and night debating the pros and cons of a screen career for their daughter.

By morning, the pros had a clear edge. The contract was signed. It included a highly unusual proviso: if at any time the Temples should feel that screen work was changing their daughter's personality or keeping her from being absolutely normal, they could break the agreement with the studio and retire her from the screen.

All the Temples' worldly activity was not lost on one conservative Pennsylvania Dutch relative of George Temple. "It must be that queer California climate has affected George and Gertrude," was her comment.

If the climate didn't affect them, Shirley's success certainly did. *Stand Up and Cheer,* based on an idea by the studio's leading actor, cowboy-sage Will Rogers, revolved around a national Secretary of Amusements, whose job it was to improve the country's depressed morale by organizing a series of federally supervised vaudeville acts. The revue bits and pieces, which featured some well-known Broadway names along with a penguin dressed to resemble Jimmy Durante, were loosely strung together, and Shirley's number (with veteran James Dunn), played in a white dress with red polka dots—an item of merchandise soon to play a modest role in the national recovery—did not come until the very last. It was worth waiting for.

"If nothing else," wrote *Variety*, "*Stand Up and Cheer* should be very worthwhile for Fox because of that sure-fire, potential kidlet star in four-year-old Shirley Temple. She's a cinch female Jackie Cooper and Jackie Coogan in one, excepting in a more jovial being. She's the unofficial star of this Fox musical."

In 1934, her first year with Fox, which about this time joined Twentieth Century to become Twentieth Century-Fox, Shirley made seven films. In *Change of Heart*, she had a small part with Janet Gaynor, the leading actress of the studio, and Charles Farrell; and in *Now I'll Tell* she appeared with Spencer Tracy. On loan to Paramount through a previous arrangement made by her mother, Shirley scored one of her greatest triumphs in *Little Miss Marker*, playing an orphan who reforms bookie Sorrowful Jones, better known as Adolphe Menjou. "Only a dyed-in-the-wool cynic could fail to be affected by its sterling humor and pathos," said *New York Times* reviewer Mordaunt Hall. "No more engaging child has been beheld on the screen." For Paramount she also made *Now and Forever*, with Gary Cooper and Carole Lombard.

Back at her own studio, the tremendous success of *Little Miss Marker* led to her first star billing in *Baby, Take a Bow*, and then to the highly applauded *Bright Eyes*, which had Shirley singing "The Good Ship Lollypop," and which gave another child actress, Jane Withers, her big break.

"It's sobby, but there's lots of sunshine, too," wrote critic Regina Rowe of *Bright Eyes*. In the frail story line, Shirley again played an orphan, adopted by flier Jimmy Dunn. In one memorable episode, Dunn was forced to bail out of his airplane with little Shirley clutched in his arms. A grateful nation gasped with relief at the safe descent.

By this time the billing read SHIRLEY TEMPLE IN BRIGHT EYES, with the tiny star's name preceding that of the film. The Hal Roach reject had already reached the top of her profession.

The *Motion Picture Herald*'s 1934 box-office poll of exhibitors swept Shirley into eighth place, trailing only Will Rogers, Clark Gable, Janet Gaynor, Wallace Beery, Mae West, Joan Crawford, and Bing Crosby. By 1935, even these powerful names were pushed aside, and Shirley Temple became the number one box-office attraction in America, an honor she continued to hold in 1936, 1937, and 1938, a record run. Clark Gable, Hollywood's "King," dreamed of overtaking his rival, but did not accomplish the feat until 1939. By that time, neither he nor Shirley sat on the top rung of the ladder, that position having been appropriated by another child star, Mickey Rooney.

For her year's efforts, Shirley had also received a special Academy Award. "There was one great towering figure in the cinema game in 1934, one artiste among artists, one giant among troupers," read the citation. "The award is bestowed because Shirley Temple brought more happiness to millions of children and millions of grown-ups than any child of her years in the history of the world." The next morning Shirley put her statuette, her Oscar, next to her other dolls.

During 1935, Shirley performed in four films. "The Shirley Temple situation is getting out of hand," declared *The New York Times* critic after viewing *The Little Colonel*. In this version of Annie Fellow Johnston's Southern tale, Shirley reunited her mother with her estranged grandfather, played by Lionel Barrymore, imposingly done up in a white goatee and big, bushy eyebrows that a family of wrens might well have turned into a spacious home. She also skillfully followed Bill "Bojangles" Robinson as he did his famous stair dance. After *Our Little Girl*, with Joel McCrea, came *Curly Top*, written expressly for Shirley by Patterson McNutt, and then another Southern classic, *The Littlest Rebel*, in which Southern whimsy and the thick, undiluted scent of magnolia drenched every scene. When John Boles, as her father, penetrated Northern lines to visit his dying wife and was captured, Shirley realized that only a trip to Washington, D.C., to see President Lincoln could save the doomed man. The fastest way she could raise money for the trip was to do a delightful little sidewalk dance with valet Bill Robinson. The scene in Washington, where Shirley, in hoopskirts and pantalettes, sat on the Great Emancipator's desk, swiftly became a classic of the Temple genus. An invisible orchestra softly played "John Brown's Body" as she confronted Abraham Lincoln and tearfully told him her poignant tale, muting her sobs only long enough to eat alternate slices of the apple which the President was peeling. At the end of her recital, Abe signed a reprieve. If he hadn't, it is likely that the nation's history textbooks would have been rewritten to curse him for his hardheartedness.

In March of the year, Shirley Temple placed her hand and footprints in the cement of Grauman's Chinese Theatre and wrote her message to the world: LOVE TO YOU ALL.

Captain January, with Guy Kibbee, led off 1936, providing her with the songs, "Early Bird," "At the Codfish Ball," and "The Right Somebody to Love," as well as a three-handed version of the sextet from *Lucia*, sung with Kibbee and Slim Summerville. Based on the Laura E. Richards story, the sentimental tale had starred Baby Peggy in a silent version a decade earlier. Similarly, *Poor Little Rich Girl*, with Shirley, Alice Faye, and Jack Haley, had provided a silent vehicle for Mary Pickford in 1917. In it, Shirley sang "When I'm With You" and "Oh, My Goodness."

In *Captain January*, Shirley, orphaned but happy with lighthouse keeper Guy Kibbee, uttered her classic plea when a truant officer came to take her away: "Cap! Cap! Cap! I don't want to go! I don't want to!" Variations on that phrase were among the obligatory passages in most of Shirley's films, in which tears and laughter hung as closely together as Siamese twins.

Dimples, with Frank Morgan, tended toward spectacle and was another of Shirley's pictures which virtually saved the day for Fox, which faced a box-office crisis after Will Rogers' death in an airplane crash. Oriental atmosphere pervaded the year's last entry, *Stowaway,* in which Shirley spoke some extraordinary Chinese, and sang a beguiling rendition of "Goodnight, My Love."

"What's to become of Shirley Temple is one of the burning issues of the movie industry," *Life* worried in 1937, as it summed up her progress. "She has lost some of her early prettiness and all of her babyish cuteness, but has gained enough acting tricks to leave her with a full quota of charm." While Shirley had added 7 inches to the 38 with which she had started in 1934, her charm carried her neatly through Kipling's *Wee Willie Winkie,* written for a boy, but adapted for Shirley and directed by the gifted John Ford, as well as her only other picture of the year, Johanna Spyri's classic childhood tale, *Heidi.*

In *Heidi* she persuaded her grouchy grandfather, reputed to be an infidel, to go to church each Sunday, brought about the marriage of a pastor and the village belle, and taught a crippled girl to walk. "Dear God," she prayed at the end when everything inevitably came up roses, "please make every little boy and girl in the world just as happy as I am." Happy Shirley was clearly entering the critical age for a child star, but at the box office, King Clark continued to trail considerably behind.

The following year, 1938, found him still unable to overtake his young rival, although now the studio parted her riotous blond curls and tied them back with a ribbon. "The greatest trouper of them all is still in there, at the officially certified age of eight, putting over the show for American childhood," wrote *Variety* of her performance in *Rebecca of Sunnybrook Farm.* "Any actress who can dominate a Zanuck musical with Jack Haley, Gloria Stuart, Phyllis Brooks, Helen Westley, Slim Summerville, Bill Robinson, Randolph Scott, Franklin Pangborn, etc. can dominate the world."

Little Miss Broadway, again written especially for Shirley, saw her popularity undiminished, as did *Just Around the Corner,* with Charles Farrell, Joan Davis, Bert Lahr—and Bill Robinson, back dancing with Shirley by popular demand from a following that rivaled that of Ginger Rogers and Fred Astaire. At Twentieth Century-Fox, however, the top executives grew pale and trembled when they saw their multimillion-dollar moppet weigh in at 71 pounds and measure a towering 51 inches.

While Shirley's films had hitherto been budgeted modestly at figures ranging from $400,000 to $875,000—with minimum grosses of more than $1.5 million over production costs—the studio tried to offset her advancing years with a 1939 block-buster, *The Little Princess,* based on a well-known book by Frances Hodgson Burnett, who had also written the childhood classic, *Little Lord Fauntleroy.* Twentieth Century-Fox doctored up the tale—similar in its plot line and sweet sentimentality to *Heidi*—with an expensive cast headed by Richard Greene and Anita Louise. The picture was filmed in technicolor, Shirley's first venture into that process, and cost more than $1.5 million.

A second 1939 entry was *Susannah of the Mounties,* a romantic melodrama of the Northwest, with Randolph Scott, Margaret Lockwood, Victor Jory, and a pure-blooded Blackfoot Indian boy named Martin Goodrider.

At the box office, as reflected in the *Motion Picture Herald*'s poll of exhibitors, the efforts were not good enough. Mickey Rooney topped the list, followed by Tyrone Power, Spencer Tracy, and Clark Gable, who had at last come in ahead of his long-time competitor, for whom he had a secret admiration. The fallen box-office queen lagged in the number five position.

The following year, Shirley slid out of not only the top ten, but out of the top twenty-five. *The Blue Bird,* a vapid, overblown technicolor fantasy based on Maurice Maeterlinck's nineteenth-century tale, was the first Shirley Temple picture to lose money. It was followed by a somewhat livelier entry,

Young People, with Jack Oakie and Charlotte Greenwood—the last of Shirley's pictures for her home studio.

In less than six years, Shirley Temple had made twenty-four pictures, including two on loan to Paramount, from which it was estimated that Fox's total profits ran to $20 million. Shirley herself had earned close to $3 million, one million of which was take-home pay and carefully invested for her by her parents. If a good many people felt that bad story material was responsible for her retirement, Fox was more inclined to see her waning appeal symbolized by the costume she wore at her eleventh birthday party—her first long dress.

It was, however, more than the career of a brilliant child actress that ended in 1940 when the Temples bought up the few remaining months of Shirley's contract and decided to send her to a fashionable girls' school. It was also the end of an era. Shirley Temple, with her infectious, dimpled smile, her luxurious blond ringlets and dancing feet, had burst upon the American scene at a difficult period.

"When the spirit of the people is lower than at any other time, during this depression," said President Franklin Delano Roosevelt, "it is a splendid thing that for just fifteen cents an American can go to a movie and look at the smiling face of a baby and forget his troubles."

Shirley Temple's smiling face lit up the gloomy Thirties, and there were few who did not fall under her spell as she inspired one of the wildest personality hysterias of our time. To her "bungalow"—a pleasant ten-room house on the Fox lot next to that of Janet Gaynor—trouped the great and near-great of the world. Harry Lauder, the noted Scottish entertainer, listened to her sing "Auld Lang Syne" and called her a "braw, bonnie lassie." General Pershing came to pay his respects and Shirley told him that she knew he was important because she could see that he had produced gooseflesh on her mother's arms. Al Smith, in his familiar brown derby, came by with his wife, and historian H. G. Wells checked in for a visit.

On the set of *Little Miss Broadway*, Eleanor Roosevelt came to call and left, as did all visitors, wearing a Shirley Temple police badge. Noel Coward sported his badge after a visit, along with J. Edgar Hoover, who made a particular hit with amateur police captain Shirley, and Henry Morgenthau, Secretary of the Treasury, who gave her a handful of newly minted coins. On a single morning, publisher Bernarr MacFadden and Nobel Prize author Thomas Mann both arrived to pay court to "America's Greatest Unofficial Ambassador."

The American Legion commissioned her its youngest Honorary Colonel in 1935, an honor Shirley accepted with a smart salute. James Farley made her honorary Sponsor of National Airmail Week. The Texas Rangers, not to be outdone by the American Legion, enlisted her as a captain; she became an honorary G-Woman; and the Chilean navy, to whom she was known as "Rocito di Oro," or "golden curls," made her its mascot.

The following year, her eighth birthday was greeted with 135,000 gifts and greetings from around the world, including a baby kangaroo, six crates of Easter lilies, and a prize Jersey calf from the children of Tillammok, Oregon. In the 1937 edition of *Who's Who*, Shirley's nineteen-line biography was half as long as the President's, only two lines short of Mrs. Roosevelt's, and eight lines longer than the closest Hollywood runner-up, eleven-liner Greta Garbo.

Wherever she went there were mob scenes with idolatrous fans in pursuit, trying to snip off one of her curls for a souvenir, or, failing that, a piece of her dress. When, in 1938, the Temples made the mistake of trying to sneak quietly out of town for a cross-country trip, cars suddenly began to drive up alongside the Temple automobile on both sides, hoping to catch a glimpse of Shirley, and collisions and sideswipes jammed the road until state troopers came to the rescue. With a carful of bodyguards from the studio to escort them, the Temples continued their trip, which *Life* duly reported in a cover story that gave every step of the itinerary.

While in Washington, D. C., Shirley told Mrs. Roosevelt that it did indeed rain in California. To FDR himself, who was "her willing slave all afternoon," she confided that she had just lost a tooth and that she had caught a whopper of a fish in Vancouver. Asked what happened to the tooth, she said, "I put it on the dresser and I guess it got swept off. You know how things are when you're traveling!"

When she came down with an upset stomach during the Boston phase of the trip, wire services called incessantly, and Hub newspaper reporters were put on three eight-hour shifts so that every phase of the illness could be reported to a hungry public. From London, Lord Beaverbrook's newspaper, the *Daily Mirror*, called each evening at midnight to keep English readers abreast of minute changes in Shirley's temperature, as America's star crowded the heir to the British throne, eleven-year-old Princess Elizabeth, off the front pages.

The nation and the world trembled at the kidnap and extortion threats which were periodically made against Shirley Temple. To guard against any possible violence, the studio appointed John C. Griffith, complete with gun and handcuffs, as Shirley's permanent bodyguard, with power to clear the area at the first sign of danger. Strollers in the Brentwood section of Hollywood, where the Temples lived, were sometimes amused to see the child star tooting along on a tandem bicycle, with the rear seat occupied by the burly 200-pound bodyguard. Humorous aspects of the situation notwithstanding, studio officials had no hesitancy in ordering a bulletproof limousine to carry their most valuable star to and from the studio.

While Shirley's salary rose from $10 a day for Baby Burlesks to $15 a day for Frolics of Youth, it took a healthy jump to $150 a week when she signed with Fox. After her success in *Little Miss Marker*, Mr. Temple, who left his job at the bank to manage Shirley's finances, asked that this be raised to $2,500 a week. The studio met him halfway, tore up the old contract and drew up a new one at $1,250 a week, adding a bungalow on the lot, bonus provisions, a swarm of dolls, and a Shetland pony to sweeten the pie. As Shirley's phenomenal box-office success continued, the new figure was soon doubled.

In 1936, she earned $121,422; in 1937, $162,500; by 1938, her income was the seventh highest in the land, with the Treasury Department reporting that she had earned $307,014, second only to Louis B. Mayer in the movie colony, and topping William S. Knudsen, the president of General Motors. For her last eight pictures at Twentieth Century-Fox, she hit a salary peak of $300,000 per film.

Film earnings formed only one part of Shirley's income. Entire industries were springing up as a result of her popular appeal. A manufacturer copied the red and white polka dot dress Shirley had worn in *Stand Up and Cheer*, and sold carloads of the item. Shirley Temple dolls became the rage, with one firm selling more than five million. Toys, gadgets, underwear, coats, hats, shoes, books, soap, hair ribbons, tableware, merchandise of every shape and kind, bore the name of the child Gary Cooper called "Wiggle Britches," and the sale of each item dropped additional pennies and dollars and finally thousands of dollars into her bank account. Similarly, products such as Royal Crown Cola, endorsed by Shirley Temple, paid huge sums for the privilege of being associated with the magic name.

Fortunately, George Temple had his banking experience to guide him when he took on the job of managing his daughter's finances. With great skill he channeled her earnings into three areas: government bonds; annuities with old-line insurance companies, staggered to bring in income at varying periods of Shirley's adulthood; and trust funds set up to provide maximum security for the future.

The Temples also had the great good sense to sidestep a tempting early proposition to manage Shirley's career. The offer came from none other than Arthur L. Bernstein, the stepfather of Jackie Coogan and the man Jackie held responsible for the dissipation of his own $4 million in childhood screen earnings. Mrs. Temple told of Bernstein's proposal, in an interview with author J. P. McEvoy: "You know, Bernstein wanted to handle Shirley. He came over here to the house with Mrs. Coogan one day, and walked up and down the living room waving a check for half a million dollars in my face. He told me he had just got this for Jackie and we ought to let him handle Shirley, because we didn't know anything about the picture business and we would certainly be cheated if we didn't let him take care of us. Practically every agent in town had been after us, and we didn't know which way to turn. Bernstein talked and talked until we were dizzy and then, in desperation, we called up our family doctor and asked him to come over and advise us, because he was the only professional man we knew. He has been advising us ever since. Of course, we have a lawyer now who helps us, but weren't we lucky to have such a sensible doctor!"

The wily Bernstein's plan was to use Shirley in radio broadcasts and personal appearances to boost her earning capacity in films. When the Temples told him their daughter was already under contract to Fox, he told them he would "handle" the contract. Fortunately, Shirley's parents felt themselves bound by that document, and declined the Bernstein offer.

In addition to a sensible doctor, Shirley Temple had another highly skilled gentleman in her retinue. Early in her career, the studio appointed W. M. "Doc" Bishop, a former veterinarian and police reporter, as her publicist. Bishop, who had handled publicity for prominent Los Angeles political figures, was told to devote all his energies to "that kid actress," as he once called her.

Bishop and others who handled Shirley's publicity really had a pretty easy time of it. They told the world of their star's fan mail, an avalanche of up to 15,000 letters a week, with postage on incoming mail for one year alone running to $100,000. They told of how, when Shirley's penchant for playing with dolls came to light, dolls started coming in from every corner of the world, a total of more than 3,000 in all, many of them in authentic costumes of the country of origin, others valuable antiques. They told of how Shirley had scored 155 on the Pintner-Cunningham I. Q. test, which tabbed anything over 135 as genius.

Amusingly, they reported that when Lloyds of London insured the curly-headed seven-year-old, it was stipulated that Shirley could not take up arms in warfare or join the army in peacetime. Furthermore, the insurance would not be valid if the merry moppet met death or injury while intoxicated.

Absolutely free publicity of a most remarkable variety came Shirley's way when she was nine. The Dies Committee of the U. S. House of Representatives came to Hollywood to investigate "un-American" activities in the film capital. When a witness before the Congressional group labeled Shirley Temple a "Red," an unwitting dupe of the Communists, headlines carried the story to the startled American public. The howls of laughter which greeted the news put a serious damper on the investigation and dealt a near deathblow to the Martin Dies spy-hunting expeditions.

To call Shirley Temple a Red in 1938 was really worse than spitting at the American flag. Many years later, when Shirley, by then Mrs. Charles Black, met a real, bonafide Red, he admitted to being one of her most rabid fans. The occasion was the visit to the United States of Nikita Khrushchev, Premier of all the Russias; the time, 1960, at a reception for the distinguished visitor in San Francisco. When Shirley passed him in the receiving line as Mrs. Black, she made no impression at all. Then someone told the Premier she was Shirley Temple. "His eyes got teary," Shirley related. "He grabbed my two hands and pumped them against his stomach, and it was a surprise it was so hard—just like steel."

National glory had come to Little Miss Miracle, as Shirley was sometimes called, at a time when not only the depression but also the demands of the Hays office were bearing down on Hollywood's harassed producers and forcing them to look for wholesome, uplifting, happy themes. To meet the need, Twentieth Century-Fox had found vehicles for Shirley Temple that radiated sunshine and goodness. "Of all the crusaders that battle desperately on behalf of forlorn causes I should say that the child named Shirley Temple was the most triumphant," wrote critic Richard Watts Jr. On the average, it is safe to say that Shirley did more good deeds in one picture than the Boy Scouts of America brought off during an entire year. If the stories bore a remarkable resemblance one to the other, the crowds going through the turnstiles appeared not to mind. "Why they bother with titles, or with plots either for that matter, is beyond us," the *Times* critic, Frank S. Nugent, finally concluded. "The sensible thing would be to announce Shirley Temple in *Shirley Temple* and let it go at that."

"She didn't act or make pictures," said one of her directors, David Butler. "She played wonderful games. She got into fairyland, she believed it all herself, and that's why you believed it."

The gifts which she brought to the screen were the wonder of Hollywood and of her fans everywhere. In her first feature-length film, *Stand Up and Cheer*, Jimmy Dunn muffed a line, an error which Shirley was quick to notice and correct. Fortunately the cameras were rolling. Fox, delighted by her spontaneous reaction, wrote the footage into the final version, and the upraised, admonishing index finger of the triple-threat star became a symbol which reappeared in many of her films.

Shirley herself virtually never muffed lines. Each evening before putting her to bed, Mrs. Temple read her the scenes for the next day's shooting. In the morning, they went over them once more. By the time the cameras started whirring, her mousetrap memory had committed them to a faultless order, which had old, experienced veterans watching her in awe, and inspired ace director John Ford to appreciatively dub her "One-Take Temple."

In long shots, which Shirley played with skill she knew enough not to "give," instinct telling her that the cameras would move closer when the climactic moments arrived. So professional was her trouper's second sense that even her milk teeth, it was said, never fell out while a picture was in production.

As much as any child actress within memory, Shirley Temple had that essential ability to subordinate herself completely to the director's commands, to obey. "Sparkle, Shirley, sparkle," her mother, who was constantly on the set, would say, and Shirley sparkled. If the scene called for her to cry, she would cry. "It's in the script," she declared when asked if she minded weeping.

"Crying is fun when you're not really sad," she explained. "The way I do it is just to look awfully hard at something. It's easier if I'm holding a dog or a kitten. I guess it's the way they feel—so soft and furry. But if the scene doesn't permit that, then I just stare hard, maybe at a piece of furniture or at my mother. But I don't try to think of sad things, or why I'm supposed to be crying. You see, I'm really not trying to be sad inside at all."

"What are we pretending today?" One-Take Temple would ask her mother. And to explain what transpired after the question, she declared, "Mummy reads the scenes to me, then I imagine the character, and then I change myself into that character," quite as if that were the only sensible way the thing could be done properly.

"Talent drips from her fingertips," said one of her early co-stars, Lionel Barrymore, whose grandmother, the first Mrs. John Drew, was a well-known English actress at six, and whose sister, Ethel, also went on the stage as a child. "She has an extraordinary instinct for acting, a real naturalness. She is utterly unspoiled, thanks to her wonderful mother, and I don't think she ever will be spoiled. Her talent is God-given. She's one of those miracles that sometimes occur in the theatre."

Shirley's uncanny ability to learn complex dance routines and to match abilities with the incomparable Bill Robinson had that veteran virtually hanging on the ropes. Robinson called her "the sweetest little peachblow lady in the world," and at the end of the celebrated staircase dance in *The Little Colonel*, he too was forced to refer to the Almighty to explain "little missy's" talent: "God, He made her just all by herself. No series. Just one. Uncle Bill doesn't tell her feet where to go, her heart, it tells her."

Shirley's voice was one that she could control with perfect ease, turning it deep or plaintive, lisping or dreamy. Even the Metropolitan Opera's heralded star, Rosa Ponselle, sang her praises after a visit to the bungalow. "I can quite understand why she is the greatest box-office attraction in motion pictures," she said. "She is unique and incomparable. I was astonished by the clarity of her voice. It has a richness that could be possessed only by one in a million children of her years."

In Hollywood it is said that animals make the best actors, with children running a close second. Stars of repute are reluctant to play with either.

"I want to quit," Menjou was quoted as saying during the filming of *Little Miss Marker*. "That Temple kid. She scares me. . . . She knows all the tricks. She backs me out of the camera, blankets me, crabs my laughs. . . . She's making a stooge of me. . . . Well, she's an Ethel Barrymore at four." When friends tried to reassure him by saying he would do better in later scenes of the picture, the veteran actor glumly replied, "Oh, yeah? Do you know what she does later on in this picture? She kneels down by her little white bed and says the Lord's Prayer! Anything that happens after that will go on the cutting-room floor."

It is an added tribute to the personality of Shirley Temple that eventually one great name after another, from Adolphe Menjou, Lionel Barrymore and Gary Cooper, to Carole Lombard and Rosa Ponselle, succumbed to her charm. Indeed, one of the measures of Shirley's popularity is the degree to which she overcame the prejudices of people who loathe child actors on sight—although not all were won over. There were detractors who maintained that she was a thirty-year-old midget with a shaved head and a wig; who swore that for her films Twentieth Century-Fox constructed oversized furniture that would, by comparison, give her the appearance of a child. And a good many little girls, the strongest element of Shirley's following, felt resentful as their mothers hauled them off to dancing school, and dragged them into beauty parlors where they spent impatient hours having their hair done in little ringlets like Shirley's.

And despite his toothy smile, one cannot be sure that George Murphy, on the set of *Little Miss Broadway*, was really profoundly happy each time Shirley bounced up and said, "Let's skip rope," her latest divertissement. "God, where does she get all that pep?" asked Murphy. Nor can one be sure that the arrival, on the set, of Little Miss Miracle, who loved uniforms and marching bands, shouting, "Here comes the army! Boom! Bang! Bang!" really enchanted the property boys and electricians who dutifully pretended to fall down dead, or Victor McLaglen, to whom Shirley said, after a hard day's shooting, "Mr. McLaglen, let's march a little more, please." Said McLaglen, "That little girl. How could I say no? She is too sweet," and ordered his squad to attention, signaled the drummer and bagpiper to play, then marched his squad for another rollicking fifteen minutes with his inexhaustible co-star.

One of the unconverted, writer Leonard Hall maintained candidly that "America's Lollipop has become, alas, America's Pain in the Derrière" as he inveighed against the studio that could hurl "such maudlin monstrosities at us every eight weeks, with the monotonous regularity of Old Faithful." It was precisely Shirley's innocent sweetness, her appalling perfection, that drove Hall to flinging adjectives. "This welter of unchecked love has to end sometime," he declared and sang a hymn for Shirley's co-stars: "Thrice has Mr. Dunn offered up his quivering white body on the altar of Shirley Temple's art. Gary Cooper, Joel McCrea, Adolphe Menjou, John Boles, dozens of other worthy ladies and gentlemen have stood about nobly while the little girl spoke her piece. May the great Casting Director reward them according to their deserts." Only one hope consoled the wielder of this acid pen. "Soon another baby tooth must fall," he declared. "And another and another. In anguish, executives await the inevitable hour. And so, with Christian fortitude, do I!"

Hall evidently felt about child stars as Samuel Johnson had felt about dancing dogs and female preachers. The best one could expect of them, said Johnson, was a negative lack of annoying qualities.

There were, however, astonishingly few holdouts to the persuasive powers of Shirley Temple's art. One author after another testified that while he generally disliked child performers, he did like this little Curly Top, while reviewers felt a constant need to apologize for the fact that they had thoroughly enjoyed her sentimental dramas. No one summed up this phenomenon of reluctant admiration more succinctly than critic Richard Watts Jr.: "I must confess that I invariably encounter films starring child players with skepticism and a trace of discomfort." In a thousand other newspapers, a thousand other critics had expressed this penitential opening to their reviews. "As frequently as I have seen little Miss Temple, I find myself still unreconciled upon approaching her latest vehicle," Watts continued, setting the stage for his complete capitulation: "Yet so amazing is the talent and persuasiveness of the most famous of baby actresses that each time I am slowly won over by her remarkable expertness and filled with admiration. In her guileless baby fashion she is as much a technician of the drama as Elizabeth Bergner, and every trick she manages is a miracle of persuasiveness."

After viewing the ingenuous performances of child actors in postwar French and Italian films, the art of Shirley Temple, in retrospect, at times appears mechanical and mannered. For her contemporaries, however, it was the content of her characterizations—the surfeit of sweetness and light—which sometimes met with criticism, seldom her execution, which was almost universally considered masterful.

And if her accepted professional virtuosity won over many of those with deep-rooted phobias against child performers,

Shirley's off-screen personality was calculated to swing over
the rest. "She is simple and unaffected and accepts the inevitable
photographers as naturally as if this was the way every little
girl lived her life," wrote Mrs. Roosevelt in her column, *My
Day*. To interviewers who over and over again asked the same
dull questions—"Do you like being an actress?" "Is it easy for
you to cry in a scene?" "Do you like dolls?" "How do you learn
your songs?"—she gave polite answers, only occasionally turning the tables by saying that she would interview the interviewer, or by asking the inquiring reporter to pose her questions to Corky and Poochie, her two favorite rag dolls.

To one reporter who asked "Do you like to play comedy or
more serious scenes?" Shirley sensibly replied: "I like to play
games: casino, marble games, checkers. I also like hiking.
Let's go over to the bungalow." Of another, who asked all his
questions of three congregated mothers of child stars, Mrs.
Collins, mother of Cora Sue, Mrs. Winebrenner, mother of
Baby Leroy, and Mrs. Temple, Shirley pointedly inquired,
"Why didn't you ask me the questions? I'm the star."

On yet another occasion a newspaperman asked her what
her next picture would be after *Baby, Take a Bow*. "Probably
Baby, Take a Flop," replied quick-witted Shirley.

"I love interviews," she summed up her views to one unsus-
pecting representative of the press. "They're fun. But, of
course, not when you are hungry." The nation hung on such
displays of youthful humor as though they were Wildean epi-
grams.

When Shirley visited a department-store Santa Claus on a
New York visit, he declared he had seen her films and asked a
score of questions about her work. Quietly, Shirley slid off his
lap and hurried back to her mother. "He's a fake," she declared,
and added that everyone knew they didn't show films at the
North Pole.

Shirley's no-nonsense simplicity was one of her most appealing qualities. In a single year, she posed for upwards of
1,000 stills, more than Joan Crawford and Norma Shearer com-

bined, but she took very little interest in her pictures, and seldom regarded herself in the mirror. Similarly, while she liked to be neat, she displayed only the mildest interest in jewelry or clothes, being perfectly content with white shoes and socks and the plain print dresses her mother first made for her and later bought off the rack.

Shirley's expressive, affectionate nature was reflected in the hundreds and thousands of autographed photos sent out under her name bearing the inscription, *With love, from Shirley.* To her co-star in *Our Little Girl*, handsome Joel McCrea, she confided that she would be sorry when the picture was over. When McCrea asked her why, she soberly declared, "Because I love you," and reached over to squeeze his hand. One by one she won over her co-workers with such guileless tactics, by clambering up on their laps, by putting her hand in theirs, by whispering tender and sincere sweet nothings in their ears.

Individual wooings gave way to mass seduction when the nation learned of Shirley's concern over Tarzan. As *The Lone Ranger* and *Gangbusters* were her radio favorites, so Tarzan captured her imagination in the funnies. In one episode he was left falling off a cliff. "Dear God, Tarzan is falling off a cliff," the ardent Shirley prayed. "Please save him!" The next week, when her prayers were answered, she communicated again with the Almighty. "Thank you, God, for saving Tarzan," were her heartfelt words. Along with Shirley, uncounted millions breathed a bit more easily.

To her mother, the cool-headed, sensible Gertrude Temple, went much of the credit for the development of her daughter's appealing character and screen virtuosity. For once, the traditional Hollywood recipe—a talented youngster, a movie set, and a stage mother—produced not trouble, but a very smooth-working production machine.

While there was harmony between the studio and Mrs. Temple, there is hardly a case on record of a child star more completely under the thumb of her mother. During one of Shirley's first days of shooting, a scene called for Shirley to cry. To provoke the called-for tears, someone proposed that Mrs. Temple disappear from the set, ostensibly carried off by a green-eyed monster. The plan worked, but her mother's absence threw Shirley into such a state of nervous upset that she could do no more filming for the rest of the day. After the incident, the studio saw to it that Gertrude Temple was on the set every minute that her daughter was there, paying her $250 weekly for her efforts to begin with, a figure gradually revised upwards to $1,000 per week as Shirley's own earnings took giant leaps.

"Why, Mrs. Temple is much more Shirley's director than I am," said one of the studio helmsmen, Irving Cummings. "She teaches her her lines, coaches her on how to say them, suggests Shirley's expressions, shows her how to stand and sit and walk and talk and run. There's really very little left for a director to do when Shirley arrives on the scene."

It was Gertrude Temple who also pulled the strings for Shirley's off-camera life at the studio. When she noted everyone in the commissary making a great fuss over her daughter, she quickly ordered Shirley's lunches to be served in the privacy of her bungalow. With the cooperation of studio officials, she saw to it that workers on the lot should, as much as possible, treat her like an ordinary child rather than a star. She did, however, prefer professional children as playmates for her because they tended to be less in awe of her than ordinary youngsters.

At home, the "spoiling" process which can be so distasteful in child performers was held back by Shirley's two older brothers, Jack and George, as well as by the elder Temples. Neither of the brothers had stage aspirations. Both took Shirley's stardom in easy stride. The elder Temples never moved in Hollywood society where Shirley could easily have had her head turned. Personal appearances, which could have brought in huge sums of money, were tabooed because of the bad effect this public adulation might have had on Shirley.

In an outpouring of articles for national household magazines, Gertrude Temple gave away her formulas for raising a young prodigy. Shortly after Shirley's birth she had gone to a physician, who had given the baby a series of tests and prescribed a dietary regime. Mrs. Temple had followed his prescriptions to the letter and seen to it that her baby had regular exercise and the proper amount of sleep. "A normal, healthy nervous system is a good foundation for good looks and a happy life," she sagely observed in one of her many accounts. "I do not believe a spoiled child is ever a happy one," she wrote in her short book, *How I Raised Shirley Temple.* "I do not let Shirley get the idea that she is too important in our scheme of existence. At home she feels that everything revolves around her father."

Mrs. Temple was one of the old school who firmly believed, and frequently stated, that children should be seen and not heard, and she treated her famous daughter accordingly. "Spare the rod and spoil the child" was another of the maxims to which she adhered. Shirley was taught to obey her parents and given demonstrations of the consequences of disobedience.

The remarkable thing was that the simple formulas seemed to have worked so well. Her daughter was uncommonly good-humored and well-mannered, rarely evincing even the slightest display of temper. She went to bed when ordered, slept without disturbance, and never succumbed to those common childhood diseases, the measles, mumps, or whooping cough. A balanced nature and the absence of any outward disturbing elements were, in fact, key elements in America's worship of Shirley. She was the dream child, beautiful, gay, unspoiled, the child who did not continually interrupt her elders while they were holding the floor, nor wreak havoc about the house with broken toys and fits of temper.

"The mother of a famous child star has a difficult road to travel," Gertrude Temple nevertheless ended her small opus on child-star rearing. "No mother can know how difficult until she has a small celebrity in her own home. I am sincere about this however. If the day ever comes when I feel that Shirley is becoming self-conscious or too aware of her screen importance, I shall cancel her contract immediately and let her grow up to a normal girlhood, far from Hollywood and its studios."

In 1940, Mrs. Temple exercised an option in her daughter's contract, bought it up ahead of its termination date, and enrolled her in the fashionable Westlake School for Girls. There, the retired star wore the regular uniform consisting of a white sharkskin jacket with blue collar and skirt and submitted to the standard freshman hazing, a week of wearing a sunbonnet and polishing the shoes of the seniors with a toothbrush.

The New Yorker had misgivings about the turn of events. "A young woman who has grossed $20 million at the box office in five years is not going to think very highly of Napoleon, who could only get 15 for the entire Mississippi Basin," wrote the commentator in *The Talk of the Town* column. "A girl who was accused of trying to overthrow the government before she was ten may easily wonder what was keeping Joan of Arc."

These apprehensions were premature. Shirley took easily to the life of a schoolgirl, and just as the nation had been told of every minute of her daily routine as a star, from the diet for her breakfast to the daily sessions with "Klammie," her Board of Education-appointed tutor, so now it learned of her attendance at school parties and dances, which she loved, and of her classes in French, and English, and math, where her average grade hung around the "B" mark, the phenomenal childhood memory for learning lines having become a thing of the past.

"I don't want Shirley ever to say to me: 'Mother, why couldn't I have gone to school just like any other girl?'" Mrs. Temple declared at this time. Nonetheless, to take Shirley Temple off the screen was, as someone said, pretty much like closing down an important factory. Entire segments of the economy revolved around her, and there was still a large market for the product. "They'll never let her go," declared her eminent box-office competitor, Clark Gable. "The public will want to watch her grow from a little girl to a young lady. She's their own kid, and they'll want to follow every stage."

Time passed more swiftly for Shirley than she had antici-

pated. During her days at the private school, she discovered
that she was one year older than she thought. To capitalize on
her youth, the studio had given her birthdate as April 23, 1929.
Actually, she was born on April 23, but one year earlier, 1928.
With her schoolmates, she celebrated her twelfth and thir-
teenth birthdays simultaneously.

After more than a year at Westlake, Shirley visited two ac-
quaintances on the Universal lot, youthful songbirds Deanna
Durbin and Gloria Jean. There were rumors that she would
resume her trade at that studio, under the aegis of producer
Joseph Pasternak. It was, however, the astute Louis B. Mayer
who succeeded in luring her over to MGM to join his brilliant
school of young stars. On January 2, 1940, before Superior
Judge Emmet H. Wilson, who had been the court official in the
famous Coogan lawsuit, Shirley agreed to work for her new
boss at $2,500 per week, a big cut from the $9,000 she had been
getting from Fox. The contract did specify, however, that her
billing must be the same size as MGM's and the nation's top
box-office star, Mickey Rooney.

The first publicity shots from MGM showed Shirley arm in
arm with Mickey and his screen co-star, Judy Garland, with
captions indicating that the three were scheduled to be teamed
together in the forthcoming *Babes in Arms*. While other releases said Shirley might appear with the dazzling MGM team
in the Andy Hardy series, the studio evidently thought better of both plans. When Shirley returned to the screen after her
fourteen-month retirement, it was in a modest little effort
called *Kathleen*, which also starred Herbert Marshall, Gail Pat-
rick, and Laraine Day. *Life* gave the film—the story of a moth-
erless child who struggles to win the affection of an indifferent
father—ample coverage, saying that Shirley gave a "good performance in a pretty dull story." Audiences noted that her blond
locks had grown darker, that she was almost five feet tall, and a
rather shapely hundred pounds.

Her second comeback effort, *Miss Annie Rooney*, was released through United Artists in 1942 and fared no better with

the critics. "Gingerly, very gingerly, producer Edward Small is breaking the news to the public—baby Shirley doesn't live here any more," wrote *The New York Times*. "We now see a Miss Temple in the awkward age between the paper-doll and the sweater-girl period, an adolescent phenomenon who talks like a dictionary of jive and combines this somehow with quotations from Shakespeare and Shaw."

The film's big moment came when young Dickie Moore gave Shirley her first screen kiss, a tentative peck on the left cheek. "Miss Temple seemed impressed," moaned the *Times* reviewer, "the folk in the Rivoli balcony just depressed." Built on a series of clichés, *Miss Annie Rooney* was a trite variation on the Cinderella theme, and its famous star appeared self-conscious delivering the picture's corny dialogue.

Not until David Selznick took over the reins and put her into his highly successful film *Since You Went Away*, did Shirley Temple's career as an ingenue hit its stride. For her first supporting role, as Claudette Colbert's daughter in a wartime drama, she received an Academy Award citation, holding her own with a top-notch cast that included Jennifer Jones, Joseph Cotten, Monty Woolley, Robert Walker, and her old friend from another era, the quavery-voiced Lionel Barrymore.

I'll Be Seeing You, her only film in 1944, gave her another supporting role, with Ginger Rogers and Joseph Cotten. Her restrained, natural playing swept her once more into a starring effort, as Corliss, the pixie daughter of author F. Hugh Herbert's Archer family, which had delighted Broadway in play form for more than a thousand performances. Her portrayal of the coy, flirtatious Corliss won high praise. "You've got to hand it to Miss Temple," wrote one reviewer, "she's superb in the leading role, a compound of girlish innocence and female perversity. The leap from her former saccharine didoes into this mildly terrifying teen-age role is one that required uncommon talent. The lady has got it—plus looks." The film also brought Shirley her first substantial screen kiss, administered by co-star Jerome Courtland.

The following year Shirley handed the American public another jolt when she took her first real screen drink in the most successful film of her comeback, the sparkling comedy hit, *The Bachelor and the Bobby Soxer,* a Dore Schary production, which saw Cary Grant and Rudy Vallee on the prowl for love, with Myrna Loy cast as a female judge. The picture was a sound box-office hit, and seemed to presage a rosy future for Shirley.

Unfortunately, her adolescent career never again reached the peak attained by that delightful romp. *Honeymoon,* in the same year, cast her in a Vicki Baum story with Guy Madison as the love interest. "Hers is a silly characterization which will not win her many friends," wrote *The New York Times'* Bosley Crowther. *That Hagen Girl,* her only 1947 film, had her playing her first starring role in a straight drama, a not very remarkable tale of small-town bigotry, while the following year she made two films, John Ford's *Fort Apache,* and a dated comedy about a 1905 girl crusader for the rights of women called *Adventure in Baltimore.* "Whatever strides toward maturity Shirley Temple may have made in her two or three recent pictures are completely reversed by this job," complained Bosley Crowther of the latter effort. "As the supposedly strong, enlightened maiden, she seems a mildly precocious child whose moods are expressed either by pouting or by dimpling her chubby cheeks."

The following year, 1949, saw the end of Shirley Temple's film career on a painfully low note. After a decade's absence, she returned to her former home lot, Twentieth Century-Fox, for one film, *Mr. Belvedere Goes to College,* which scored a modest success. *A Kiss for Corliss,* with David Niven, attempted to recapture the charm of F. Hugh Herbert's earlier *Kiss and Tell,* but succeeded only in part, and late in the year Shirley played the niece of a jockey in a cornball effort entitled *The Story of Seabiscuit.* Her characterization of the role, which had her laboring valiantly but not well to put over an Irish accent, was termed "to put it charitably, unusual but definitely inadequate," by the *Times*.

As a winsome, cuddly baby, Shirley Temple was the idol of a vast international following. As a subdeb, a flirtatious ingenue, she continued to exercise a hold on her public with the spontaneity of her performances. As an adult actress, she was a mechanical dud and fell from her pinnacle, although never from public view, as the grown-up roles she could not deliver on the screen had their counterpart in real life.

Romance came early to the little girl her brothers called "la Temple," and at first it was aided by the studio publicity department. To the set of *Now and Forever* sped Paramount star Baby Leroy, courting Shirley in a rakish toy roadster. Both wearing smark dark tams, the two luminaries posed for stills. Their affair, however, never got far off the ground.

Shirley's next heartbeat was her co-star James Dunn, who played with her in four films. She developed a definite crush on Jimmy at five, and suffered a severe emotional jolt when he came calling one Christmas and brought along a woman he introduced as his wife. Soon John Boles came along, however, to console her, and then other good-looking leading men, as well as twinkle-toes Robinson, who declared that he ate four quarts of ice cream a day, a fact calculated to impress a sweet-toothed baby star who had just had a soda fountain installed in her bungalow.

At Westlake School for Girls, Shirley enjoyed the dances and parties where she met young men from surrounding schools, and at the studio, she went on chaperoned dates with songwriter Nacio Brown, co-star Guy Madison, and a good many other eligible bachelors.

Serious romance came at the age of sixteen—early, as it had for her mother, and, not surprisingly, it wore a uniform. Six-foot-two John Agar was an Air Force physical-training instructor at nearby March Field. He met Shirley at a party given by Ann Gallery, the daughter of Zasu Pitts, next door to the Brentwood home of the Temples. The young couple swiftly fell in love. Although they had promised to wait two or three years before marrying, the end of the war and Agar's imminent discharge from the service hastened their nuptials.

On September 19, 1945, the seventeen-year-old star married her young soldier in what turned out to be the biggest social event Hollywood had seen since the Vilma Banky-Rod La-Roque betrothment in 1927. It was an event which made a great many Americans suddenly feel a good deal older.

"I don't want a circus," Shirley had said. "Just friends of the families." By noon, however, crowds were starting to gather in front of the Wilshire Methodist Church where the ceremony was to take place. In a holiday mood, the spectators formed little knots that grew and grew until by evening more than 5,-000 filled the street, stopping traffic, climbing lampposts to get a view of the young lovers and the "friends of the families," who happened to include Darryl Zanuck, David Selznick, Zasu Pitts, Governor and Mrs. Earl Warren, Elsa Maxwell, the Dore Scharys, as well as many of the film technicians with whom Shirley had worked over the years.

The late arrival of the Selznicks delayed the ceremony until well past eight in the evening, when a suddenly hushed congregation watched George Temple take his daughter, in traditional white, down the aisle to the tall bridegroom. Rev. Willsie Martin, who had also married Deanna Durbin, Jeannette MacDonald, and Jackie Cooper, conducted the double-ring, Episcopal ceremony, which ended with a lengthy kiss by the newlyweds.

Afterward, when the Agars tried to leave the church, a near riot broke out, and it was not until fifteen minutes later that they were able to steal out of a side door and speed, under police escort, to the Brentwood home of Shirley's parents. Here, a gypsy orchestra played at the reception, and guests joyously downed more than twenty cases of champagne before Mr. and Mrs. Agar went off to spend their wedding night at the Los Angeles Town House.

After a brief honeymoon, Agar returned to finish his tour of duty with the Air Force. It was not long, however, before he received his discharge, and with his bride set up housekeeping in what was known as "the cottage," a pleasant ten-room house on the Temples' Brentwood estate, where Shirley spent much of her highly publicized youth.

The last piece of wedding cake had barely been sliced before the oceans of copy began gushing forth telling of Shirley Temple's happiness with her handsome husband. Somehow, America wanted its dream child to go on living the dream of unblemished happiness, and Shirley was reluctant to disappoint her public, although marital difficulties began after only five months. When a daughter, Linda Susan, was born in January 1948, the world still reveled in its illusion of a happy marriage. "Well, this much I will wager," wrote the dowager duchess of the columns, Louella O. Parsons, "Miss Susie will be a happy little girl. For the happiest little girl the world has ever known is her mother."

The shock was all the greater when late the following year the headlines blazed with the news that Shirley Temple was suing for divorce and that the unhappiness of her marriage had driven her to the brink of suicide. Charging "grievous mental cruelty, Shirley's suit," *Life* declared, "stabbed sentimental movie fans in the heart."

While hundreds of curious fans crowded the courtroom, a distraught Shirley Agar told of how her husband's attitude toward her had changed after only five months of wedlock. The son of a wealthy Chicago meat-packing family, he had abandoned plans to enter the parental concern when he married Shirley. Instead, he had turned to his wife's field, appearing with her in *Fort Apache* and *Adventure in Baltimore*, winning few laurels for either. Whereas Shirley had never really entered into the Hollywood social whirl, her young husband enjoyed the glamorous activity in the film capital, and while his modest screen earnings paid for household expenses they were hardly adequate for more expensive items, such as Shirley's Adrian-designed dresses. The former child star had wanted a husband who was boss, as her mother had been at home, her directors at the studio. Agar appeared to be more of a partner.

Before the court, Shirley described the distress she felt at her husband's erratic hours and his attentions to other women. After one particularly trying scene with him, she stated, she had contemplated the action which might have taken her life. "After dinner, I jumped in my car. I was going to drive over a cliff, or something, but instead I drove to the doctor," she related. While that family counselor dissuaded her from taking any action so drastic as suicide, matters at home went from bad to worse.

The burden of Agar's complaint, a friend of Shirley's testified, was revealed to her when he confided that he found it difficult to "have any fun" with his wife. Despite the acclaim accorded her, Shirley's home life had always been sedate and carefully ordered. For war veteran Agar, the ice cream soda fountain, which had supplied Shirley with refreshments since her earliest studio days, was perhaps dispensing too mild a brew.

In approving a property settlement giving Shirley custody of twenty-one-month-old Linda Susan, and providing that Agar's share of community property be set up in a trust fund for the child, Judge Herndon took the occasion to remark, "This plaintiff occupies a place in the hearts and affections of the country, and the failure of her marriage was a distressing disappointment to many people." As if to wipe away that disappointment, he restored the plaintiff's maiden name of Shirley Temple.

Agar, touring with a play in Buffalo, did not appear in court, nor did he contest the divorce. "There is much I might have said and might say now," he said in a prepared statement. "However, as I see it, no constructive purpose would be served by recrimination or airing our respective sides in public."

The dream marriage of the dream child was over.

Another, a more successful attempt at matrimony, was soon

to begin. To get away from the memories of her unhappiness, Shirley and her parents took a trip to Honolulu, where she was sunning herself on the beach when a good-looking, dark-haired young man stopped to talk, asking somewhat naïvely, "Are you a secretary on the island?" To Shirley, the remark signified his acceptance of her as a young woman rather than as a film star, and she was delighted.

On December 16, 1950, Shirley Temple married the young man, Charles Black, at his parents' home in Monterey and disappeared on a quiet honeymoon. The press did not learn of the event until after the fact, largely because of Black's dislike of publicity, an incongruous taste for the bridegroom of the most publicized child actress of all time, but one which appeared to suit her well.

The son of James B. Black, president of the Pacific Gas and Electric Co. of San Francisco and reputedly one of the wealthiest men in California, young Black had been a wartime naval officer, twice cited for bravery in the Pacific, and holder of the Navy's Silver Star. Of medium height, dark-haired, with the graceful, easy movements of a college athlete, he was recalled to active duty after the marriage, and served as Lieutenant Commander Black, in Washington, D. C. Here Shirley spent several happy years tending her duties as housewife, and accompanying her husband to state functions. "She was more excited to be treated as a housewife and Mrs. Black than about being Shirley Temple," a friend revealed at the time.

After returning to civilian life, Charles Black became a television time salesman, living near Atherton, California, and moving to Redwood City when he took on an assignment as an executive with a large electronics corporation. A son, Charles Black Jr., was born to Shirley at Bethesda Naval Hospital on April 28, 1952. Complications followed the Caesarean birth and came close to threatening the young mother's life. Shirley recovered, however, and a third child, Lori, also brought forth by Caesarean, was born on April 9, 1954. As an indication of the Blacks' tendency to shy away from publicity, the first photos of young Charles Jr. did not appear until he was seven months old. Black also adopted Shirley's child by her earlier marriage.

While her agent repeatedly called Shirley with prospective screen roles, including the offer of a role as a dipsomaniac that had her reeling with laughter, Shirley firmly turned them all down. "I worked for twenty years," she declared, "and I believe that is long enough." Her only contract, she stated, was her marriage contract. Stage offers also came, but these, too, were turned aside, Shirley being still convinced, as she had been over the years, that she would find it boring to repeat the same role night after night. In fact, she confessed, she hates the very term, "show business," and uses "entertainment world" in its place.

The only dent in her retirement came with a foray into television in the late Fifties. Not surprisingly, her role was that of mistress of ceremonies for a series of dramatized fairy tales called *Shirley Temple's Storybook,* in which she also played a small, prescribed number of roles herself.

"During my early days as a movie actress, I lived in a story-book world," she declared at that time, "and what a delight this was for a little girl. Nothing was impossible and it all seemed real. . . . But how can any of us, however grown up, deny the importance of make-believe in our lives. Aren't all of us living and working for things that we *hope* will come true? To me, fairy tales are not primarily intended to teach us something we do not know, or to remind us of things we should be doing. Their purpose is to entertain, to let us escape from reality."

Looking back on the past, Shirley said that she had had "the best kind of childhood anyone could have." Instead of having the world's favorite children's classics read to her, she lived the parts: "I *was* the little Colonel and Heidi, and in one picture, I actually sat on Abraham Lincoln's knee."

Nonetheless, Shirley had by now largely turned her back on the past, not only for herself, but for her children. Of the baby

Barrymore of another era she said, "I feel like I know her. I feel like she's a relative of mine. Yet, I'm sort of detached and critical." Did she sing the many songs from her pictures, which delighted children of another generation, to her own youngsters—songs like "The Good Ship Lollypop"? No. "You know, I got awfully tired of singing that even as a kid," she stated. "I simply was asked to sing it too many times."

An entertainment career would be all right for her own children, she has said, if they really wanted it. She has always hastened to add, however, that she and her husband "haven't seen many signs of such inclinations yet—except for Lori. She was quite put out that I wouldn't let her sing a song on my first TV show." Shirley finally let all three children make their entertainment world debuts with small roles in "Mother Goose" on her *Storybook* series.

The strongest indication of her attitude about a career for her children was manifested, however, when, some years earlier, her first daughter, Linda Susan, was cast as a fairy in a school version of *Cinderella,* and then given a small role in *Jack and the Beanstalk.* To the accompaniment of staccato reports in the Washington newspapers, Shirley angrily withdrew Linda Susan from the school because the second performance was to take place in a public auditorium rather than in the relative privacy of the school. "I was not going to let her appear before four hundred people," she declared. "It is a sad commentary that Linda Sue must be parted from her good little friends at Christmas time, but I had not and will not allow anyone to commercialize on my daughter's presence."

As a child, indeed, as a baby, Shirley Temple had been boxed and sold around the world to the tinkling tune of millions of dollars. Perhaps, in her heart of hearts, there was resentment, expressed by actions rather than by words. "Shirl is a real girl—no delusions of grandeur," husband Charles Black has said, and it is as Mrs. Charles Alden Black, wife, mother, community leader, that the former screen idol prefers to face the world.

"Our Gang" in *Tire Trouble* (1924)

Daniel Blum Collection

Above: Jackie Coogan and Charlie Chaplin in *The Kid* (1920). *Below:* Signing a new contract with Nicholas M. Schenck of MGM. Younger brother Robert and the elder Coogans are interested witnesses.

Jane Withers in *This Is the Life* (1935).

At thirty-seven, Mrs. Black is an attractive woman who carries herself very straight and still has the brisk, somewhat mechanical walk that delighted her childhood fans. The petal-smooth skin of yesteryear retains its vibrant glow, and the big, saucer-like eyes still burst easily into a smile. The blond curls have, however, long ago turned from honey-gold to bronzish red, and the baby voice has turned to a mellow contralto.

Active in community affairs, the Blacks are a conservative family who like to entertain informally once or twice a week, and who can be counted upon to dig in and work for the Republican Party, having paid visits to President Eisenhower and Vice-President Nixon while they were in office. They support the Peninsula Children's Theatre Association, a group of ninety housewives and mothers who stage plays for children at cost. For this group, Shirley has worked as an usher, hospitality chairman, and publicity head. No one has yet asked her to perform.

Shirley Black's greatest community interest, however, is with handicapped children. Each Monday she is a receptionist at the Children's Health Council for Mentally and Physically Retarded Children. She also works for the Allied Arts Guild, which sells art goods for the benefit of a children's convalescent home. She is active in the Women's Auxiliary of the local Society for Crippled Children and Adults, and acts as chairman of the local Multiple Sclerosis Society—members of these various organizations, and Shirley herself, were probably surprised to see Shirley Temple in the company of Theda Bara and Jean Harlow in a recent film compilation called *The Love Goddesses*. The film's Shirley, implied the producers, was in truth a sex object, a nymphet, the forerunner of Nabokov's Lolita.

Everybody always wanted things to come out just right for Shirley Temple, and apart from the circumstances of her first unhappy marriage, the wish seems to have come true. At what price, it is hard to say. As a child, it was reported that when Shirley read the novel *The Yearling*, she skipped the end where the deer is shot because she could not bear to hear about animals or human beings suffering. Many years later, when she and husband Charles Black lived in Atherton, California, they put down 3,000 square feet of green cement to form a patio around their rambling twelve-room house. "We did that," Shirley declared, "because we didn't like the idea of grass going patchy on us." Today, Shirley Temple Black is continuing her campaign against the blemishes of life with her compassionate work for children. "I'm a pushover for fairy tales," Shirley has said. As the years go on, her admirers—and their numbers are still legion—will watch with fingers crossed to see just how similar life and dreams can be.

4.

JANE WITHERS:
DIXIE'S DAINTY DEWDROP

"I want to write a story," Jane Withers told a magazine interviewer at the height of her popularity as America's favorite problem child. "This is the story. My father's a great millionaire, and my mother's a great society mother. She takes me to these bridge parties and I throw mud over everybody. I'm just terrible. I'm never good for one minute all through the picture. That is my idea of a swell story . . . it gives you a chance to yell your head off . . . Garbo and Dietrich never yell at all. That's the trouble with being a glamour girl—no yelling."

For the better part of a decade, Jane Withers yelled, and kicked, and bit, and screamed, while movie audiences bestowed their approval. She early evidenced a remarkable insight into those audiences. "Of course, at the end, just to satisfy everybody, I get a good spanking," she explained. "The minute they slapped me in *Bright Eyes*, everybody just yelled and waved, they were so happy. Well, I don't mind. I had my fun. So let them have their fun, too."

Bright Eyes, in 1935, provided the prototype for Jane's later characterizations of "the meanie everybody loves." The film was essentially a vehicle for Twentieth Century-Fox's sensational new child discovery, Shirley Temple, who already had a near monopoly on celluloid sweetness and light. As a contrast —almost an antidote—to her engaging, positive qualities, director David Butler began interviewing a series of tiny soubrettes with a bent for more traditional mischief and mayhem. Round-faced, freckled, homely Jane, shepherded by her mother, was one of those paraded before him, making little impression, however, until her mentor coaxed her to do a number of imitations developed for earlier radio appearances. Butler began to take note, and, in an intuitive moment, asked whether the child could imitate a machine gun. Jane's arms folded, her eyes took on the hard squint of a miniature Edward G. Robinson, a finger shot menacingly into firing position, and the tiny revolving body suddenly shook to the thoroughly convincing "Ra-ta-ta-ta!" of an imaginary machine gun. She was given the part with no further formalities.

When the film was released, fond mothers and daughters smiled approvingly and somewhat complacently as Shirley Temple told Santa Claus she wanted a doll for Christmas. Their smiles turned to howls of laughter when Jane bemoaned the fact that she had not received a machine gun and turned on her lively imitation. Critics gasped with delight. "Into *Bright Eyes* producers inserted an eight-year-old chunk of human ratsbane called Jane Withers," wrote Withers idolator Leonard Hall. "This appalling child kicked and yowled and bit her way through the film so magnificently that millions roared with glee. . . ."

While other studios had ransacked nurseries and dancing schools at home and abroad to find *another* Shirley Temple— Warner Brothers having gone as far as South Africa to find Sybil Jason—Twentieth Century-Fox had come up with Shirley's foil in Jane Withers. Where Shirley was the model child, incredibly bright, unbelievably pretty and gifted, ever obedient—the sum of what most parents would have liked their dream child to be—wild-eyed, mischievous, uncontrollable Jane was much closer to the real thing, the noisy, brawling youngster actually making a mess of the living room before departing, strictly against orders, for some neighborhood gangland mayhem.

The contrast continued as far as personal appearance: Shirley with her lovely golden ringlets, her bright blue eyes, her delicate, measured movements; Jane, with dark, Buster Brown bangs over the forehead, pigtails trailing behind, dark brown, mildly malicious eyes that photographed black, and a pudgy restless body that moved in sudden, impulsive lurches.

As a happy studio tailored screen vehicles to the diverse talents of its two prodigies, Shirley grew from good to better to perfect, while Jane capitalized on her tomboyish, fun-loving, fight-loving nature, seldom making a picture in which there was not at least one good tussle. After *Bright Eyes,* she was immediately given star billing in *Ginger,* playing with her male counterpart on the screen, mean, surly Jackie Searle, who seldom got through a film without suffering a good beating. Miraculously, in *Ginger,* Searle actually scored a knockout over one of the other boys in the cast.

Critic Richard Watts Jr. bemoaned the fact that "this talented and likable child actress should be forced to go in for sweetness and light when her forte is infant frightfulness." Nonetheless, he felt the film did have its virtues, allowing Jane to impersonate Garbo and Zasu Pitts, to do a balcony scene from *Romeo and Juliet,* and to be "roguish, slangy, hard-boiled, humorous, and pathetic, and to demonstrate her gifts for heckling her elders and putting them at their ease."

The plot of *Ginger* provided a fair forecast of Jane's future films. As the orphan daughter of two actors, she was reared by an alcoholic old man, once a Shakespearean trouper, who still managed to mumble speeches from the classics. When the old veteran was put in jail for engaging in a brawl, Jane was adopted by a somewhat dotty society woman who considered herself an authority on child-raising, despite the fact that she had made a thorough mess of her own family. The plot showed her trying to reform little slum-orphan Jane, who, all the while, was busily inculcating *her* with her own particular democratic virtues, including frequent use of such daring expressions as "Skip it" and "For crying out loud."

In his review, Watts concluded that the film made "little Miss Withers at least the number two child actress of the American screen." Reporters and interviewers in the Thirties tried repeatedly to stir up a feud between number one, queen Shirley, and her studio runner-up. Although Shirley and Jane never became playmates or friends, the feud never developed, and as recently as January 1965 a grown-up Jane appeared on a television program and loudly declared, "God bless Shirley Temple," when the moderator tried once again to stir up flames from the ashes of the nonexistent rivalry.

The rivalry existed perhaps less in the actual careers of the two popular child stars than in the minds of their followers. And perhaps one of the strongest sources of Jane's appeal was her confirmed position as the underdog, not only in her films, but in reality, as second fiddle to Shirley. Reportedly, many of the films which Jane made were first offered to Shirley and rejected by her governing council, a fact which would account for the great similarity in plot structure between Withers and Temple films. Like Shirley, Jane did an enormous amount of good on the screen. Like Shirley, she could reform wayward characters, like the smugglers in *Always in Trouble,* or manage to bring together troubled lovers, as in *Paddy O'Day.* Like Shirley, she was often lost or orphaned, but for those who were kind to her, she could accomplish near miracles; in *45 Fathers* she saved her wealthy benefactor from marrying a gold-digging socialite, and in *Pepper* she turned grouchy millionaire Irvin S. Cobb into a reasonably likable old codger.

Similar plots could take on a different coloring as a result of the points of emphasis. The emphasis in Withers films was usually on the difficulties she encountered, the terrible fixes she was suddenly in, and the tomboyish ferocity with which she challenged her fate—a fate, more often than not, largely of her own manufacture. Typical was *Little Miss Nobody,* in which Jane once again played the golden-hearted orphan. In her review, Regina Crewe declared that *"Little Miss Mischief* might well be Jane Withers' *nom de theâtre. . . .* With the aid of the scenarists . . . she manages to get into more jams than a subway rider."

Trouble was the byword for Jane's films, and their titles give a good indication of their spirit and contents: *Arizona Wildcat,* with Leo Carillo, a frequent Withers co-star; *The Holy Terror,* which permitted Jane to work mayhem with a toy airplane; *Always in Trouble,* in which a monkey named Gertrude became Jane's friend, but not before it had taken a good bite out of her leg; *Wild and Woolly; Rascals; Chicken Wagon Family,* which had Jane sliding down a fire rail, singeing her behind; and *Pack Up Your Troubles,* with the zany Ritz Brothers. If a film like *Gentle Julia,* based on popular Booth Tarkington characters, appeared to indicate a shift in direction, the change was more apparent than real. "The picture is Jane Withers from beginning to end, which it probably was meant to be," wrote one reviewer. "And since she lends to her portrayal of the tomboy Florence a sincerity, and at times her customary pointed malice, it is entertaining."

Over a period of six years, Jane made twenty-seven straight starring films. Moving into her teens, she passed through adolescence often playing Tarkington-type characters and beating the jinx of the difficult transition period with her easy comic ability. In the Forties, she made *Small Town Deb,* with a plot born of Jane's own fertile imagination, for which she received $3,000 and screen credit under the name "Jerrie Walters"; *Golden Hoofs,* an appealing little racetrack film with Buddy Rogers; and *Girl From Avenue A,* which had Jane wearing her first long stockings. *Boy Friend,* her nineteenth movie for Twentieth Century-Fox, brought her her first film kiss, a delicate peck on the cheek. *A Very Young Lady* gave her two leading men, John Sutton and Richard Clayton, as well as twenty-seven changes of costume, while *Her First Beau,* made while Jane was on loan to Columbia, co-starred her with Jackie Cooper.

When Shirley Temple had announced her retirement from the screen in 1940, it was felt that Jane would now inherit features of better quality. While Shirley's films had seldom been really big budget, they were all considered "A's," using the studio's top production facilities. Despite the withdrawal of the miniature queen of the lot, however, Jane continued to play in second-string pictures. Of her forty-seven films, all except one, a Samuel Goldwyn entry entitled *North Star,* were low-budget "B's." The modest entries brought Jane Withers fame, a following both fervid and faithful, and fortune.

After *Bright Eyes,* she jumped from $5 and $7.50 for one-day calls to a contract salary of $150 per week. Succeeding efforts catapulted her from obscurity to number thirty-four in box-office appeal in 1936. The high rating forced a reluctant studio to boost her weekly pay from $150 to $1,500 and to allow her to lend the Withers name to product endorsements, a right which Fox had previously withheld. Mrs. Withers was put on salary as a consultant at $150 per week.

In 1937, Jane placed sixth among the box-office champs. In 1938, she placed eighth, trailing only Shirley Temple, Clark Gable, Sonja Henie, Mickey Rooney, Spencer Tracy, Robert Taylor, and Myrna Loy, and edging out Alice Faye and Tyrone Power. The high standing jumped her salary from $1,500 to $2,-500 per week. If Shirley Temple got the prize roles, the redoubtable Jane was doing remarkably well with the rejects. Only a narrow rung below the leader, she was neatly holding her own.

If Shirley had received more than 5,000 dolls from all corners of the globe, Jane was not really unhappy with her collection of 1,500. If Mrs. Eleanor Roosevelt had stopped on the set to visit Shirley, let it not be forgotten that Pauline Longworth, daughter of Mrs. Alice Roosevelt, had stopped by to sip soda pop with Jane. If Shirley had placed her tiny hand and footprints in the celebrated cement of Grauman's Chinese Theatre, Jane, after all, had left her somewhat larger footprints in the cement at Shaefer's Center at the New York World's Fair.

Like Shirley, Jane was the object of kidnap and extortion plots, and maintained her own personal bodyguard, a rangy Texan named Jack Trent. And if Shirley was mascot of the Chilean Navy and an Honorary Colonel of the American Legion, Jane was the mascot of the Georgia Tech football team, as well as "The World's Only Honorary Chief Air Hostette of American Airlines," a title copyrighted in her name by company president C. R. Smith. When Temple addicts repeated over and over again the real-life virtues of their baby Bernhardt, Irvin S. Cobb spoke up for the Withers claque. "If Jane Withers is a sample of what a movie career does for children, a law should be passed forcing all youngsters to have such an experience," stated Cobb. "I have yet to know a sweeter, more well-bred, gently considerate and wholly natural little girl."

Although the younger of the pair, Shirley had already been married for almost two years to John Agar before Jane followed her example, on September 20, 1947. After the conclusion of her forty-seventh film, Danger Street, she became the bride of William Moss Jr.

While making her cavalcade of pictures, Jane was taught by her mother to cook, to sew, to budget her $4.25-a-week allowance, and to participate in family discussions on the expenditure of money. "I am training Jane to be a poor man's wife," declared Mrs. Withers. "I want her to know all the things a girl who marries a man making a modest salary, say, forty dollars a week, should and must know." The training as a poor man's wife was not immediately necessary. Her mother's careful investment of her earnings had made Jane independently wealthy. Bridegroom Moss was a Texas oil millionaire and part-time film producer. The affluent young couple made their home in Midland and Odessa of the Panhandle State, spending time in California only for Moss's producing activities.

Three children, Wendy, William, and Randy, were born, but the marriage went through difficult days. An estrangement was accompanied for Jane by an ailment which temporarily paralyzed her arms and legs. A reconciliation was effected in July 1953, but by the following July the couple went to the divorce courts.

A settlement gave Jane half of their community property, including oil lands valued at $500,000, $1,000 a month alimony, and a $24,000 education-insurance fund for the children. "Hollywood and the movies had nothing to do with it," Jane said of her divorce. "My life in Hollywood has always been wonderful. And so are the people."

With her children, Jane returned to California, taking courses in cinema at the University of Southern California. "I thought I'd learn something about the movies . . . the technical side . . . maybe I could get a job," she declared. One day, guest speaker George Stevens, the noted director, spotted her among his listeners and offered her the role of Vashti Snythe in his forthcoming film, *Giant*. Jane took the role in the Edna Ferber epic on condition that the harsh view of Texans be modified. To Vashti, a blowsy, scatterbrained millionairess, high on diamonds but low on polish, she brought a genial comic interpretation that won praise from the critics, but, curiously, elicited no rash of further acting offers from Hollywood producers.

Jane ventured into a second, apparently more happy marriage, when, on October 18, 1955, she became the wife of Ken Errair, an insurance broker and a former member of the singing Four Freshmen. Two new members, sons Kenneth and Kendall, joined the Errair household, set up in a thirty-three-room mansion in a lovely residential area next door to the Hollywood film studios.

Today, in addition to managing her large family, the once more bouncy and buoyant Jane paints, designs her own clothing, and does extensive charity work. She is also a regular Sunday school teacher. "In the future, I'd like to do a film with a religious background," she has stated. "Faith has played such an important role in my life." With no screen roles forthcoming, however, she has had to content herself with occasional television appearances, most notably, a much-used commercial in which she appears as a lady plumber.

The sight of the one-time child star on the home screen churns up a heady nostalgia for viewers nearing middle age, just as the sight of daughter Wendy used to remind people on the street of the girl who used to be mean to Shirley Temple on the screen. At the time, Jane, despite the fact that she still recalls with great joy her days as a child star, made it very clear that Wendy would not follow in her footsteps. "Wendy is going to stay a little girl," she declared. "I was so busy I missed the wonderful business of growing up. I don't want that for Wendy."

Jane herself was the product of a very different mother. Lavinia Ruth Elble had wanted desperately to attempt acting, but her parents considered her "strange notion" ridiculous, refusing even dancing lessons. As a consequence, when Walter Withers, an employee of a rubber-manufacturing company in Atlanta, Georgia, proposed marriage, Lavinia Ruth accepted on one condition—that if they had a daughter and she showed a genuine flair for acting, she could train her for a career. The condition was accepted. Accordingly, when a baby girl was born in 1926, the name Jane was chosen because it would fit easily onto a theatre marquee.

To her mother's delight, Jane began humming melodies at seven months. She sang before she talked, danced before she walked, providing ample grounds for Mrs. Withers to register her at Atlanta's Boston Academy to study tap, ballet, and caracter dancing. At the age of three, she sang "Little Pal" at a local theatre's amateur night, and at four, she had her own radio program, specializing in impersonations. To her title of "Atlanta's Sweetheart" was added that of "Dixie's Dainty Dewdrop." As such, she reigned over the Georgia capital until her mother took her to Hollywood in 1932. One-day calls, bit parts that often wound up on the cutting-room floor, dubbing voices for animated cartoons, and benefit and vaudeville appearances were her lot until the day director David Butler asked her to imitate a machine gun. That was the day Dixie's Dainty Dewdrop turned into America's favorite screen brat. Dixie's loss was the nation's gain.

5.

THE TRUE JUDY

One of the truly remarkable American entertainers of her generation was born in Grand Rapids, Minnesota, on June 10, 1922, to the very untheatrical name of Frances Gumm. Less than a dozen years later, she was to drop both Frances and Gumm. And even at birth, Frank and Ethel Gumm didn't really like the name Frances. Already the parents of two daughters, they wanted their third child to be a boy. Indeed, the evening edition of the Grand Rapids *Independent* announced the birth of Francis Gumm Jr., and described the event as presenting young Mr. Francis Gumm, owner and manager of the local New Grand Theatre, with his third— daughter. Only at the very last minute did the disappointed parents substitute the feminine version of the father's name for the newborn child, a red-faced, pug-nosed, rather homely baby.

It is not uncommon for parents to take as their favorite the child who initially failed to fulfill their hopes. Frances Gumm's father reached out to his third daughter in this way, calling her his "Baby" and giving her a place in his heart. Frances's mother, too, had a special feeling for her. But Ethel Gumm was that most intriguing figure of the entertainment world, a stage mother, who chose to fulfill her own dreams and fantasies through the careers she planned for her daughters. When the fantasy began to realize itself, Ethel Gumm's obsession became ever more resolute and all-embracing, and the mother love she felt expressed itself through that enactment. Did Baby Frances understand? Could any child understand that the uprooting of the family, the endless traveling, the separation from the father were all expressions of mother love? A stage mother's love?

Pretty Ethel Milne was playing the piano in a movie theatre in Superior, Wisconsin, when she met Frank Gumm. He had just graduated from Sewanee University, a handsome, gay young Irishman, and had left his Southern home to spend the vacation in Superior. At the same theatre where Ethel played, Frank found work. He was a tenor; his job, to deliver a few numbers and then lead the audience in community singing. After the two youngsters had met and married, they decided to merge their musical abilities to form a vaudeville act, billing themselves as Jack and Virginia Lee, Sweet Southern Singers. Somehow that sounded right. With a minimum of success, they went from one small town to another on the vaudeville circuit, gradually acquiring a family as they traveled; a daughter, Sue, was born in 1916, a second girl, Virginia, three years later. To raise their growing family, the Gumms settled in Grand Rapids, Minnesota, and here their third daughter, Frances, was born. A dozen years later, when she had already taken the new name by which she was to become internationally famous, she sometimes told reporters that she had been born in Murfreesboro, Tennessee. Somehow, that sounded right.

It was in Grand Rapids, however, that Baby Frances made her stage debut. It was a Saturday night, at her father's motion picture theatre, during the Christmas season in 1924. Baby Frances was two and one-half years old, seated on her grandmother's lap in the theatre. On stage were Virginia and Suzy Gumm, going through a singing routine which their mother had arranged and staged. Watching them, little Frances squirmed restlessly. Grandmother Gumm, a real stage *grand-mother*, recognized a problem and saw its solution. She took the child in her arms, carried her down the aisle, and deposited her on stage. Virginia and Suzy had the good sense to flee for the wings. Tiny Baby Frances surveyed the scene, appeared happy with the friendly round of applause which greeted her, and burst into the chorus of the only song she knew, "Jingle Bells." Since it went rather swiftly, she repeated it, and hearing more applause, she launched into a third chorus, and then a fourth. By now, her somewhat frantic father was shouting "Get off!" But Baby Frances sallied into still another chorus of glittering "Jingle Bells," and only left the stage when Frank Gumm swept her away in his arms.

Frances Gumm had had her first taste of the swelling acclaim of an audience. It was a wonderful, unforgettable sound. She was to hear it often in the years ahead, in countless cities, even in far-off lands. It was to grow in intensity until it sang like the sea at high tide, and like the balming sea, it could sometimes give her comfort, making her warm when she felt cold, making her well when she was ill and alone, always making her heart leap with love.

Ethel Gumm heard the sound, too. For her it rekindled the dream of success, of fame, of a glorious spotlight beaming down like a star, not on her, but on her children—especially, now, on little Frances. The reception accorded Jack and Virginia Lee, Sweet Southern Singers, had been tepid, if not cool. Perhaps the dream could be realized through the children. Frances was immediately pressed into service, becoming part of the act of "The Gumm Sisters," who performed every Saturday night at the theatre in Grand Rapids and from time to time fulfilled engagements in nearby towns.

For her three daughters, Ethel Gumm sewed costumes, chose numbers, worked out routines, made the musical arrangements, and played the piano at performances. Grand Rapids and Minnesota offered too limited a horizon, however. In the newspapers and fan magazines, she read about Hollywood, and the many youngsters who were flourishing in films, and bringing delight to a happy nation. Why not the Gumm sisters? Why not Virginia, and Sue, and Frances?

Soon after Frances's debut, the Gumms put up their white frame house for sale. Frank Gumm sold his theatre. Portable possessions were piled into an automobile and the family set out for California, doing their act in every town along the way that would give them a booking. When they finally arrived in Los Angeles, Frank Gumm had difficulty finding a suitable job. After a brief, unfruitful stay, the Gumms settled eighty miles to the north, in Lancaster, California, where he became the owner and operator of the local movie theatre.

For the Gumms, with the memory of a lively, green Midwestern town still fresh, Lancaster was a lonely place. Situated in a harsh, barren semidesert, it provided little in the way of culture or refinement. The townspeople were as inhospitable as the countryside. To them the Gumms were show people, a not altogether desirable breed, never really acceptable.

As a consequence of the chill that ran through the sterile air, the three sisters looked forward to out-of-town bookings of their act, which their mother arranged. For Mrs. Gumm, Lancaster was only a stepping-stone to Hollywood. During the family's brief stay in Los Angeles, she had signed up her daughters with Meglin Kiddies, a booking agency for child acts, and now each weekend she took them to Los Angeles to see what she could line up in that city or in the rest of the state.

When the entire family was booked, it went on in shifts. Jack and Virginia Lee, Sweet Southern Singers, went on first. Jack Lee always introduced his partner as "a tiny, pretty lady, with pretty, tiny hands." This introduction never failed to bring tears to the eyes of little Frances Gumm, and these continued to flow as Virginia Lee sang "I've Been Saving for a Rainy Day." While Jack Lee, in his rich, tenor voice, sang a number of songs, sometimes including melodies he had composed himself, Virginia, with her pretty, tiny hands, played the piano, rather badly. The young sisters sang as a trio, but they also divided up into specialties, Baby Frances sometimes taking a spirited turn as a belly dancer in colorful Egyptian regalia. The reception accorded the acts was not always favorable. Columnist Sidney Skolsky later recounted how, when the Gumms were playing the Alhambra just outside of Los Angeles, schoolboys brought along box lunches to the theatre and sent the contents flying toward the hapless performers—whirring tokens of disapproval.

For the family, these were also difficult days financially, with the father just getting started in a business which was gradually to flourish. The income from the acts was welcome, although pitifully small, as they performed at theatres, benefits, luncheons, wherever they could get an audience. One evening, the three sisters received the lamentable sum of 50 cents for their efforts.

Eventually, Frank Gumm's business began to thrive, enabling him to buy two additional theatres in neighboring towns. With the financial necessity removed, he hoped that his family would give up their trouping and turn his house into a home. But Ethel Gumm continued to follow the dream. When Virginia and Sue returned to school, she would get into the car with Frances and drive off to book her as a single. Now it was just Frances and her mother. Whenever possible, Frank Gumm would follow after and catch the performance, but the family bonds seemed to be growing weaker, and the laughter that had rung through the large white frame house in Grand Rapids was seldom heard in the Gumm residence in Lancaster. Too often it was empty.

And Frances Gumm, the baby of the family, became a quiet, pensive child. In solitude, she would play with modeling clay and talk to her dolls, all of which she named Peggy, in an attempt perhaps to give one thread of continuity to the shifting sands that carried her young life to so many distant towns, all of them away from the father she loved and who loved her.

Occasionally, waiting to rehearse at a theatre, she would

meet other boys and girls, young entertainers usually accompanied by their mothers. Friendships would begin to grow—bonds forged of a restless, lonely life. Donald O'Connor was one of these. Briefly they would meet and quickly separate, for one-day stands were the order of the day, and the day after the engagement they would pack up and take to the road again.

After each trip, Frances and her mother would return to the scorching, unfriendly heat of Lancaster. At the school there, she wanted to be accepted, and she felt that her talent might bring her popularity. Her teacher told her, however, that roles in class plays and musicals were based on grades. As a consequence this strange casting director relegated husky-voiced Frances Gumm to the chorus.

It was on stage, while giving a performance, that Frances felt most assured and relaxed as a child. At the age of six, she had one of her first real successes. In a solo act at Loew's State Theatre in Los Angeles, dressed as Cupid, she sang "I Can't Give You Anything but Love, Baby," and brought down the house. At that time, and even much later, however, she dreamed of being an actress rather than a singer, influenced perhaps by a newspaper critic who described her ungraciously as "the leather-lunged blues singer," and by a theatre owner who advised her to give up show business. "You may sing loud," he told her, "but you don't sing good."

In the early Thirties, Mrs. Gumm decided that she could bear Lancaster no longer. With Frances, she established a permanent beachhead in Los Angeles, to be followed by her husband, who bought a local theatre, and her two older daughters. She quickly enrolled Frances in Mrs. Lawlor's School for Professional Students. Here, at the age of ten, Frances Gumm met a brash but openhearted boy named Mickey Rooney and took an instant liking to him. The out-of-town trips continued as before, however, and shortly one of them was to provide a wedge that would open the fabled portals of Hollywood to Frances Gumm.

In 1933 Ethel Gumm packed her children once more into an automobile, heading this time for Denver, which she viewed as a gateway to the relative big time of Chicago. The Denver engagement worked out as planned, but the weeks passed and nothing came through for Chicago. Ethel Gumm refused at this time to accept any money from her husband, who disapproved of the trip, and things began to look grim. Finally, an offer came for the act to appear at the Century of Progress Exhibition of the Chicago World's Fair. For several weeks, the hungry, valiant Gumm sisters gaily sang and danced to distracted Fair visitors, only to discover, as payday came and went, that the strange-looking people in charge of the concession had quietly skipped town.

Fortunately, Ethel Gumm heard of an act which had suddenly been forced to cancel a booking at the Oriental Theatre, and instantly pushed her weak and strained offspring into the breach. It was an important victory. The Oriental was a respectable theatre in a major town, with dapper Georgie Jessel headlining the current bill. Only one thing went radically wrong. As the revivified sisters approached the theatre for the evening performance, they gazed up in horror at the glittering marquee. There for all the world to see, the Gumm Sisters were billed as the Glum Sisters, the result of an electrician's error. Loneliness, hunger, and abuse had come the way of the battered trio, who had taken them in stride, but now even their name was to be taken away. They rushed to find George Jessel to tell the master of ceremonies of this final humiliation.

Since Gumm rhymed not only with glum, but also with crumb and bum, a really drastic change was in order, said the veteran showman. Riffling through the evening newspaper, he came upon a column written by a friend, drama critic Robert Garland. Garland was the name he suggested to replace Gumm and Glum. For Frances Garland, it seemed a God-given opportunity to correct another mistake. She had never liked the name Frances, much preferring the title song of a Hoagy Car-

michael song called "Judy." And so at Chicago's Oriental
Theatre, an unknown electrician put the wrong name in lights
and gave the world Judy Garland, an entertainer who would
generate enough electricity to light up half the theatre mar-
quees in the world.

For a while, though, Judy Garland had about as much success as Frances Gumm. Methodically, she made the rounds of
the casting bureaus of the Hollywood studios, where she would
launch into a song, accompanied by the stalwart piano of her
mother, now known as Mrs. Garland. Everyone liked her voice,
but no one hired her. If she were five, they said, they could
cast her in child parts; if she were eighteen or nineteen, she
could play young romantic roles. But Judy Garland was in
between, at the awkward age, and they could think of nothing
for her to do.

Mrs. Garland was never at quite such a loss. In the summer
of 1934, she took her daughters to the Cal-Neva Lodge at Lake
Tahoe in Nevada, where they had also appeared the year before. Their second summer at the resort seemed to pass as une-
ventfully as the first. They were already back on the road
rambling home toward California, when Virginia screamed to
her mother that she had forgotten something. Mrs. Garland
whirled the car about and sped back to the lodge, where Judy
rushed inside to retrieve a hat box.

When one of a group of men seated around a table asked her
to sing for them, she hurriedly inquired if the man over at the
piano knew "Dinah." Smiling, he said he did. His name was
Harry Akst, "Dinah's" composer. Judy sang to his accompaniment, and then the man who had first spoken to her introduced
himself as a songwriter and executive at Columbia Pictures.

Several days later, back in Hollywood, he arranged for her to
audition with a number of key people at Columbia. They listened but were less impressed than the executive, who now
proceeded to steer Judy toward agent Al Rosen. Rosen once
more made the rounds of the studios with Judy. As before, she

met with a pleasant reception and no real encouragement until one day Rosen called to say an audition had been arranged at Metro-Goldwyn-Mayer. For Judy Garland, née Gumm, the great moment had arrived.

At previous auditions, carefully dressed and manicured, she had gone with her mother to the studio. On this auspicious day, her mother was out, and Judy was playing in the backyard when the call came. In the emergency, her father took over, and together they went down to Metro, where Judy sang for Jack Robbins, talent chief, and Roger Edens, rehearsal piano player. These two immediately felt the power of the personality before them. They called in Ida Koverman, influential executive secretary to the head of the studio, Louis B. Mayer. With Edens replacing her father at the piano, Judy, recently billed as "the little girl with the great big voice," once more walloped out "Zing! Went the Strings of My Heart!" Koverman picked up the phone to call her boss and a minute later announced that he was coming.

The meeting between one of the great movie moguls of his time, Louis B. Mayer—"L. B.," as he was known to studio, friends, and enemies—and the twelve-year-old child actress from Grand Rapids, Minnesota, is a part of the annals of Hollywood. Mayer, under constant pressure, highly temperamental at best, now furious at being interrupted, came flying into the room and stared at the young girl before him, his eyes expressionless. He could see that she was rather stocky, on the short side, with a plain, freckled face, brown hair, large brown eyes, a little pug nose that was not unattractive. In a navy blue middy blouse, gray slacks, and grass-stained sneakers, she had about her a natural quality that was, indeed, very appealing. Roger Edens once more struck up the introductory chords of "Zing!" Louis B. Mayer listened intently to a voice that was young and rich and full, with an emotional power that stayed in the air after the song was over. For a moment he sat in silence, then rose, still without a word, and left. By his orders,

Judy Garland was given a Metro-Goldwyn-Mayer contract without even the technicality of a screen test. And now the grim, golden years could start to unfold.

Sadly, they began with the death of Frank Gumm, only a few months after Judy, in October 1935, signed her first Hollywood contract. Frank Gumm, with his full-throated Irish laugh, had bequeathed to his daughter a wonderful, almost indestructible sense of humor. To him, laughter was a necessity, like food and breathing, and for her it became a necessity and sometimes almost a salvation. She would have liked to share more with her father, to be closer to him, as she felt he wanted to be closer to her. But they had had so little time together. And now all time had run out.

The pundits of Hollywood, who have psychoanalyzed Judy Garland to an exhaustive fare-thee-well, were later to see her marriages to men considerably older than herself as a continuing search for her father. Before the marriages began, however, there was another father substitute in the corporate person of MGM, home of Leo the Roaring Lion. For the next fifteen years, the studio played the fiddle in her life and the obedient star danced endlessly to the relentless tune.

"Oh, the early days at MGM were a lot of laughs," Judy has said. "It was all right if you were young and frightened—and we stayed frightened. Look at us—Lana Turner, Elizabeth Taylor, Mickey Rooney, and me—we all came out of there a little ticky and kooky."

Under sunny California skies, Metro-Goldwyn-Mayer, which the redoubtable L. B. ruled like a feudal kingdom, was turning out stars the way Rolls-Royce turned out automobiles, geared to last a lifetime—Norma Shearer, Clark Gable, Joan Crawford, Spencer Tracy, Robert Montgomery, Greta Garbo, Jean Harlow, James Stewart, Jeannette MacDonald, Nelson Eddy, Greer Garson, Walter Pidgeon, Robert Taylor, Eleanor Powell, Myrna Loy, William Powell and many more. These glittering names, surrounded by every brilliant production facility, made motion pictures that were fed to the rapacious American public, which passed through the turnstiles at the rate of 90 million admissions a week.

Into this highly competitive, authoritarian barony wandered little Judy Garland, "the poet of the family," according to her sister Virginia. "Her poems are serious and introspective," she wrote. "A few years ago, she had a volume of her poems printed and bound as a surprise Christmas present for our mother. Judy is devoted to her. Like many other things about her real self, her poems aren't what people might imagine them to be. But they do reflect her personality as I know it actually is. They are earnest, tender, lyrical."

At the MGM film factory, Judy, the tender poet, heard herself referred to as a "property," an "investment." She was told that she had a great responsibility to the studio which had taken her on as a nobody and was going to make a star out of her.

For a time, as in the lull before a storm, excessive concern seemed premature. Like the other film makers, MGM didn't know what to do with a thirteen-year-old girl. They enrolled her in the studio school, where she studied with her old friend Mickey Rooney, and with Jackie Cooper, Freddie Bartholomew, and another young singer, Deanna Durbin. With Mickey, her pal, she sometimes went off to the beach, while she and Deanna became wary friends, each wondering whether the other's option would be taken up at the end of the three-month periods. With Roger Edens, who had played for her audition, she studied two hours daily, going over arrangements he wrote for her. From time to time, she was asked to sing at studio birthday parties, no extraordinary effort for her $150 a week salary.

Eventually, the studio cast her in a short called *Every Sunday*, with Deanna Durbin. The mediocre effort brought glory to no one. After viewing it, MGM officials decided to drop Deanna Durbin's option. Universal snapped it up, and, under the aegis of producer Joseph Pasternak, cast her in a series of sensationally successful musicals in which her high, unfaltering

soprano saved the studio from bankruptcy and brought
Deanna international fame. MGM, betting on the contralto of
Judy Garland, loaned her out to Fox where she made her first
full-length movie, *Pigskin Parade*. The 1936 feature, which occasionally makes it to the *Late, Late Show* on television, also
featured a much publicized newcomer, Betty Grable. *Pigskin
Parade* won no laurels.

"I went to the preview of my first picture, *Pigskin Parade*,
with my mother. . . . I thought I'd look as beautiful as Garbo
or Crawford—that makeup and photography would automatically make me glamorous. Then I saw myself on the screen. It
was the most awful moment of my life. My freckles stood out. I
was *fat*. And my acting was terrible. I burst into tears. 'Mom-
mie,' I said, 'let's go.' I was ready to go back to vaudeville. 'You
shouldn't expect a miracle,' my mother comforted me. 'Be patient. Wait, and some day you'll look beautiful on the screen!'
Well, I'm still waiting."

More than twenty-five years ago, Judy Garland's candid
comments to a fan magazine showed that she could look at
herself with a humorous smile. The matters she touched on
were nonetheless of immense concern to her. Her family nick-
names had been "Baby," and "Monkey," and "Pudge," and now
as she looked at herself in the mirror she saw that she was
indeed a chubby, rather short little girl on a lot that had always worshipped beauty.

Her acting ability was another very real cause of concern.
Judy Garland had played half the tank towns in half the conti-
nental United States, but she had never had professional
training, never read a single line. She had learned by doing, by
watching her parents—no raging successes they—and other
vaudeville actors go through their paces. Now she was at one
of the great film studios of the world, wondering uneasily
about every move, every gesture, about timing, comparing herself to that unself-conscious young veteran, Mickey Rooney,
and finding herself sadly wanting. Curiously enough, the studio

scarcely concerned itself with her acting, never provided her with a coach, a lesson, even a handbook.

It was Mickey Rooney who finally taught her certain acting essentials which she was never to forget. "Honey, you've got to believe what you're doing," said the generous "Mick," putting a comforting arm around his friend. "Make like you're singing as though you meant it. Live the part." Many aspects of her art began to be comprehensible after this, but all through her film career torturing doubts about her ability dogged the steps of Judy Garland, invisible to the audiences who viewed only the end product, a joyous two hours of screen virtuosity.

With her career going nowhere in particular, with her friends mostly studio friends, whom she seldom saw away from the lot, with her two sisters both recently married to musicians, Judy found the life of a film starlet a lonely one. In her desire to capture what she viewed as a more normal life, the life of the ordinary youngster, she enrolled in Hollywood High, not even mentioning to the other girls that she had an entertainment background. As a result, she was one of the gang, an acceptance which greatly pleased her.

Unaccountably, one of the vice-principals of the school ended this idyll when he called her in and said, "People like you should not be allowed to go to school with normal children. You belong with your own kind." Judy did not return to Hollywood High. Sadly, but without explanation, she asked her mother to place her back in the school on the Metro lot, a school in name only, since there was no school building, no playgrounds, no resident faculty, no football games or proms, only four or five little actors and actresses arriving for their scheduled hours with the tutors, disappearing again into the Hollywood Hills huddled in the back seats of chauffeur-driven limousines.

Dorothy Gray, a childhood friend and classmate at MGM, has described the dilemma she and Judy faced in their search for normalcy: "We theatrical kids used to be embarrassed when our pictures were in the paper because the other—normal—kids we knew would tease us. I guess we were robbed of our childhood."

As she neared the end of her studio classes, Judy found that state law had required she register in the school of her district when she began high school work at MGM. Technically, this entitled her to get a diploma the normal way. When the time came for her class to graduate, she turned up at University High School, wearing a regulation blue organdy dress, carrying two pink sweetheart roses provided to all the girls by the school. Proudly, she marched with the rest of her class, perfect strangers all, to take her diploma from the principal's hand in the traditional graduation ceremony.

At MGM, the birthday parties went on. With the anniversary of the "King," Clark Gable, close at hand, Roger Edens wrote an introductory verse to the song, "You Made Me Love You." Ida Koverman led Judy and Edens to the set where Gable was filming *Parnell*, with Myrna Loy. During a lull in the shooting, everyone gathered around the piano, and Judy sang "Love Letter to Clark Gable" straight from the heart, as though she meant it, as Mickey had told her to do. When she had finished, a deeply moved, misty-eyed "King" came over and kissed her. Later, he sent Judy a gold charm bracelet with the inscription *To my girl friend, Judy Garland, from Clark Gable*. Judy treasured the memento, and Gable never forgot the song, which followed him through the years, or the event, which formed a bond between these two stellar figures of one of the golden eras of Hollywood.

"Love Letter to Clark Gable" and Judy Garland were swiftly put into a film called *Broadway Melody of 1938*, starring Robert Taylor and Eleanor Powell. Also in the cast were Buddy Ebsen, hoofer George Murphy, and Sophie Tucker, who predicted that young Judy Garland would one day take her place and become the new "Red Hot Mamma" of show business.

That day was still far away. Meanwhile, Judy was well received in several pictures which were a prelude to the big time. In *Everybody Sing*, she co-starred with Allan Jones in the story of a mad household of stage people whose waning fortunes she gallantly retrieves. Bosley Crowther wrote in *The New York Times* that "Judy Garland of the rhythm, writin' and 'rithmetic age is a superb vocal technician." In *Listen, Darling*, Judy played with schoolmate Freddie Bartholomew in a pleasant light comedy about two youngsters who kidnap a matrimonially eligible widow, lock her in a trailer, and start touring the countryside in search of a suitable husband. Critic Frank S. Nugent described the picture as "winsome," and reported that Judy had "a fresh young voice which she uses happily" on the film's melodies.

To season their young star, MGM sent Judy east for a personal appearance tour in 1938. *Variety* reported favorably on her turn in Detroit and Columbus, Ohio. A greater test came when she made her first appearance on the huge stage of Loew's State Theatre in New York, where six-foot letters on the marquee announced the bill, spelling Garland quite correctly. Roger Edens, who had come east to accompany her on the piano, tells the story of the tense and triumphant debut: "There was this unknown fifteen-year-old girl alone for the first time on an enormous stage, nervous, and singing much too loudly. The audience was coughing and a baby started crying. People laughed at the baby and Judy stopped her song, laughed, and started again. That one thing steadied her and she wrapped that audience up from then on. She has been able to handle an audience ever since."

During her New York stay, Judy, ever anxious about her lack of formal training, took her first and solitary music lesson from a professional coach. This mentor asked her to sing with a pencil placed between her teeth, and then complained that her diction was bad. Judy never went back after that first lesson, never took another until twenty years later. She is unable to this day to read a note of music. A remarkably retentive memory enabled her to undergo the rigorous working schedule which was soon to begin.

A scant few scenes in a film called *Thoroughbreds Don't Cry* really broke the ice. The scenes were with the volatile Mickey Rooney. In their brief encounter, MGM officials felt something happening, a contrast in personal styles perhaps, the time-honored meeting of the extrovert and the introvert, a celluloid chemistry at work. The decision was made to write a part for Judy into Mickey's next series opus, *Love Finds Andy Hardy*.

Although Los Angeles Mayor Bowron officially named the Hardys the First Family of Hollywood, they were more accurately, in the late Thirties and early Forties, the First Family of America, average in their modestly complicated lives, their aspirations, and their compromises. Judy Garland played in three installments, *Love Finds Andy Hardy*, *Andy Hardy Meets Debutante*, and *Life Begins for Andy Hardy*, and then went on to star with Mickey Rooney in a series of fabulous song-and-dance musicals.

Before this string of extravaganzas began to unwind before a dazzled and delighted America, Judy made the one picture as a child for which she will always be remembered, the unforgettable *Wizard of Oz*. Since L. Frank Baum had published the first Oz book, called *A New Wonderland*, in 1900, more than 9 million copies had been sold. Between 1904 and 1919, when he died, Baum wrote one Oz book a year. Thereafter, under the sponsorship of his widow, fourteen additional volumes appeared, and in 1939 sales ran to 100,000 annually.

In recent times, Samuel Goldwyn had acquired the film rights, holding them five years before dropping the idea and selling the rights to Mervyn LeRoy, who had long wanted to film the classic fantasy. It was generally thought that when the film was made, it would be the enormously popular Shirley Temple who would play the lead role of Dorothy, the Kansas farm girl who goes off in search of the Wizard. When Shirley, rigidly tied to a million-dollar schedule by Twentieth Century-Fox, proved unavailable, LeRoy cast about in MGM's own backyard. There he came across Judy Garland.

Judy, it appeared to LeRoy, was a natural. She had just the

spontaneous, unaffected quality required for Dorothy. Like Dorothy, she was born in the Midwest. Her age would work out satisfactorily. Above all, she had a wonderful voice, and Le-Roy was filming the fantasy as a musical, with music and lyrics by the talented Harold Arlen and E. Y. "Yip" Harburg.

Nonetheless, looking more carefully at his choice for Dorothy, his "natural," LeRoy and the studio decided that her teeth were wrong, her hair was wrong, and her clothes were wrong. MGM ordered a corset, fitted her with a blond wig, capped her teeth, and refashioned her nose. Then suddenly, the studio reversed itself, leaving Judy pretty much intact, although it was decided to henna and plait her hair, and put her on a diet.

Tensions often ran high during the filming of the expensive project, and seven directors worked on the film which Victor Fleming finally brought in. Technically, all the stops were pulled out in the $2 million technicolor effort. More than 9,000 actors were employed during two years of filming, which utilized practically all of MGM's 29 sound stages, and 65 tremendous sets. Tricks were accomplished with live actors which had hitherto been possible only for cartoonists. To the enchantment of the classic fairy tale, the film makers skillfully added a secondary level of unconscious reality, as Dorothy and Toto, her dog, were whirled away on the black wings of a rushing tornado to Munchkinland, the realm of kindly dwarfs, there to set out for the Emerald City of the Wizard of Oz, a beautiful land of happiness where every dream comes true.

When the final version of *The Wizard of Oz* was unveiled to the public in 1939, it scored a popular and critical bull's-eye. "Not since Disney's *Snow White* has anything quite so fantastic succeeded half so well," wrote Frank S. Nugent in *The New York Times*. The cast was unanimously acclaimed for stellar interpretations: Frank Morgan, as the dotty Wizard of Oz; Ray Bolger, the nimble Scarecrow; Bert Lahr, superbly touching as the Cowardly Lion; Jack Haley, an appealing Tin Woodman; Billie Burke as the Good Witch; Margaret Hamilton as the Wicked Witch; and veteran Charles Grapewin as Uncle Henry.

Highest praise was reserved for the film's star. "Judy Garland's Dorothy," declared Nugent, "is a pert and fresh-faced miss with the wonder-lit eyes of a believer in fairy tales." To her characterization, which won her a special juvenile Academy Award, Judy brought a wistfulness and charm which have always clung to her. "I think the American people put their arms around me when I was a child performer," she declared years later, "and they've kept them there—even when I was in trouble." And it is true that even today the public seems to see in Judy something of the innocent child, the little girl lost, skipping along a Yellow Brick Road, singing of bluebirds flying over the rainbow, and wondering "Why then, oh, why, can't I?"

From the double impetus of her success as Dorothy in *The Wizard of Oz* and her teaming up with Mickey Rooney, Judy's star shot into the Hollywood heavens and reached the dizziest heights. *Babes in Arms*, in 1940, sent her with Mickey to Grauman's Chinese Theatre to leave her hand and footprints in the world's most glamorous cement in the time-honored ceremony that symbolizes the ascent to stardom. Budgeted at the comparatively low figure of $800,000, the film smashed all house records when it opened in New York. Around the world, it swiftly topped any MGM release except the studio's all-time leader, the epic *Gone With the Wind*.

Competing for critical attention with Mickey Rooney could be an exhausting process. At a time when Judy's career was just beginning to catch fire, Mickey had already clambered to the top. In 1939, the Motion Picture Exhibitors' box-office poll named him the number one box-office attraction in the land. A great many critics, too, were held tightly in the palm of the youthful scene-stealer's hand, and while they paid respectful attention to Judy once she began appearing with him, they often left little doubt as to the relative position of the two stars.

"From beginning to end, *Babes in Arms* is swell, and this reviewer," announced one of the species, "is having a laurel crown made for Mickey in recognition of his excellent imitations of Lionel Barrymore, Clark Gable, and Franklin D. Roosevelt. Adult young Rooney runs away with this picture, which considering the fine cast, is another way of saying that he's terrific." The fine cast, of course, included Judy Garland, who was said to do "some nice things" with her singing.

"There is no doubt that the fact that the Rooney-Garland combine is such an attractive one has contributed to Judy's triumphs," wrote one reviewer at the time, "but that very combination may be preventing Judy from getting the individual notice she deserves, for it is no easy job to hold the center of the stage with an old hand like Rooney pulling all sorts of mugging tricks out of the bag."

Happily, the two young stars were fond of one another and enjoyed working together. When they went to New York for personal appearances to coincide with the release of *The Wizard of Oz*, newspapers called them "the two most popular young movie stars in the world today." Both their fan clubs met them as they arrived at Grand Central Station. Police reinforcements to prevent bedlam were continued throughout their stay, as they drew the largest crowds in the Capitol Theatre's nineteen-year history, 15,000 people often trying to get into a theatre that seated only 5,400.

At the opening performance, it was Mickey who was perhaps the more nervous. He had not appeared before a live audience in many years, not since he had traveled the vaudeville circuit as a kid, while Judy had done a solo act at Loew's State only the year before. In the wings, the two friends grabbed each other's hand and listened to the stomping of feet and the staccato applause. "Come on, Toots, we'll knock 'em dead," Mickey shouted. Arm in arm they ran out to face the joyous mob. "If Hollywood must come in person," wrote one reviewer, "this is the way it should do it."

To interviewers wondering if romance might draw the two even closer together, Judy candidly and somewhat wistfully declared, "I like and admire him, but we don't see each other often between pictures." It was an obvious conjecture. Both were the children of vaudevillians, and had traveled the road from town to town, knowing its hazards and loneliness. As children, they had gone to school together. Always within view of each other, each had taken his own road and climbed to the top. Here, too, they could understand one another, knowing as no one else could the perils of success, its isolation, its demands. And so they could comfort each other and form a comradely alliance that was to endure for a lifetime.

"Mickey understood me," Judy Garland wrote a generation later, in an eloquent account of her life in *McCall's*. "And he must have known I was crazy about him. People used to ask him why we never had a romance, and he told them that his life was such a mess—and he seemed to think it always would be—that he didn't want to get me involved in it."

If Mickey understood her, very few others understood Judy Garland at this time—or Mickey Rooney, for that matter. "Off screen Judy and Mickey are normal, happy young people who enjoy the sort of thing that the kid around the corner likes," reported a magazine of the period. Twenty years later, with the wreckage of half a dozen broken marriages strewn along the road, it didn't look that way.

And at the time, if Judy Garland enjoyed the things the kid around the corner likes, Metro, which certainly didn't understand her, and her mother, increasingly preoccupied with a Mr. Gilmore, did not seem to provide them for her. "Hollywood can't hurt my daughter!" Mrs. Garland wrote almost defiantly in a bylined magazine article. "As long as Judy is the girl I know she is, movies or movie life can't hurt her. She is happiest when she is busy, and you know the old saying, 'The devil finds uses for idle hands.'" Of the lonesome youngster who longed for closer friends of her own age, she wrote, "I believe her work and association with adults have helped develop her character. Judy wants to go on making pictures, minding her own business, developing and improving her mind, building a sane and normal future for herself."

Growing up as a star under the aegis of the Metro Lion could bring a heavy strain to the maturing process. Even when very young, Judy, posing in front of the mirror, had dreamed of being a demure and sophisticated young lady with a long dress. On the MGM lot, she saw the glamorous queens of the studio, Norma Shearer and Joan Crawford, Greta Garbo and Jean Harlow, wearing the beautiful creations of the studio's famous designer Adrian. She hoped that the day for her first Adrian had finally arrived when she was to go to the premiere of her great success, *Babes in Arms*. "Too young," said Louis B. Mayer. Hearing the story, a sympathetic Hedda Hopper told the startled L. B., "Not too young to make ten million dollars for your company." Judy got the dress, but the basic attitude of MGM did not change.

In a rare explosion of frustration, she declared, "That's the only legitimate bone I have to pick with Hollywood. Anywhere else in the world, once you're out of high school, have celebrated your nineteenth birthday, and drive a car, you automatically step out of the Junior Miss class. But in Hollywood, people won't forget how you looked when you were 'that age.' "

The attempt to stunt Judy's growing up and to control her life to meet the needs of MGM reached alarming proportions as she approached young womanhood. When her mother remarried, Judy took an apartment of her own, with a roommate. The roommate was a girl she had known for many years, someone she looked forward to living with. She was also, Judy soon found out, a spy actually on the studio's payroll, regularly reimbursed for telling MGM the names of the people Judy saw, what she ate, when she went out at night and at what time she came in. Sudden calls from Louis B. Mayer, lecturing her on the harm she was doing to herself and MGM, became explicable. After discovering the betrayal, a deeply wounded Judy cried bitterly and wandered about forlorn and off balance for days. By her mother, signs of rebellion were met with the simple words, "I'll tell Mr. Mayer." No threat could have been more fearful to the sensitive young girl than this appeal to the stern patriarch who ruled the lot.

Judy Garland's first real romance began at a time when the pressures of stardom at a despotic studio, troubles at home, and her own desperate search for maturity all converged to confound and harass her. The prospect of life with handsome orchestra leader David Rose, based upon a sincere love, offered a hope that an oasis of stability and comfort might be at hand in her troubled young life.

She had gone out with other young men, all from the film world, often appearing at studio gatherings and Hollywood openings, seldom two dates in a row with the same escort. She liked jam sessions, and readily invited people to her home, where there was a radio in virtually every room, at least one always on, very loud, for Judy insisted that music wasn't good unless it was loud.

Music, one of the enduring loves of her life, was an important factor in drawing her to Rose. Although twelve years her senior, he was still a young man and already a successful, established orchestra leader, specializing in symphonic arrangements of popular songs. Born in London, he had studied at the Chicago College of Music, and was now the conductor on the popular Tony Martin radio program. He met Judy at the radio studio where she also performed, appearing with Bob Hope on his perennial Tuesday night show.

On Judy's eighteenth birthday, their engagement was announced, much to the dismay of MGM, which disapproved of outside influences on its stars. For a time, the young couple contemplated a big church wedding. On July 26, 1941, while dining with Judy's mother and stepfather, Mr. and Mrs. William Gilmore, they made the decision to marry immediately, a move which was probably hastened by increasing studio opposition to the romance. With the Gilmores, they flew to Las Vegas, and were wed shortly after one A.M. in a simple ceremony that formed a sharp contrast to the more elaborate wedding, a short time before, of Deanna Durbin to young film director Vaughn Paul. Judy gave her age as nineteen; the bridegroom was thirty-one.

Like a neglected, irate parent, MGM was quick to strike back. Less than twenty-four hours elapsed before an unexpected call from the studio asked Judy to report back to the set immediately to work on *Babes on Broadway*. Her mother advised her to continue the honeymoon, but Rose, accustomed to professional demands on his personal life, spoke for a return to Hollywood. "Studio work comes first in the life of the motion picture star," ran the newspaper story. Stepping from the plane in Hollywood, Judy voiced her hopes for the marriage. "Even if we don't get any sort of honeymoon right now," she declared, "we're the happiest couple in the world. This is no ordinary Hollywood marriage. It is the result of a wonderful romance of two years and it's the real thing."

"The real thing" lasted a year and a half, until February 1943, when a long separation began that ended in divorce in June 1944. Conflicting careers, said the self-appointed experts.

The studio was, in fact, always calling. And Judy, for whom the sweet smell of success was growing intoxicatingly strong, always obeyed. Occasionally, MGM would add spice to the proceedings by showing Judy how much they disapproved of the marriage. At the Academy Award ceremonies, Judy and her new husband were carefully omitted from the star-studded tables in the limelight and shunted off to the side by themselves. Hedda Hopper, noting Judy's look of dejection and humiliation, quietly joined the isolated pair.

Apart from the matter of conflicting careers and MGM hostility, the nineteen-year-old bride was ill-prepared for marriage in other respects. Her mother, evidently a good housekeeper, had never asked her to help in the home. And the house the Roses lived in needed a good deal of attention. Judy had persuaded Rose to leave his small but comfortable home in the San Fernando Valley, where many of his friends resided and where he indulged his hobby, miniature railroads, and to move into the swank mansion which had once been the home of Jean Harlow. To his train collection, with one thousand feet of track circling the house, Judy added a splendid new depot. But in the long run, the need for a guiding hand from the woman of the house became apparent.

When a couple came to work for the Roses, it was Judy's mother who hired them. Noting their young mistress's inexperience, they treated her like a child. Judy, in search of dignity and an area of capability, felt humiliated and useless. "When I knew I was going to be married," she declared later, "all I thought about was what I would wear and how romantic it would be to live with my husband." Sadly, there was no one to teach her more, and Judy, distracted by her demanding work, forgot dinner engagements, and let the servants have their way.

With no acrimony, the couple separated, and Judy obtained a divorce. Rose did not contest the action. In a signed agreement, the two parties relinquished any property claims against each other. Judy was once more free and alone.

At the studio, a backbreaking production schedule was getting into high gear, with new songs to be memorized, dance routines to be developed, wardrobe fittings, makeup sessions, recording sessions, sittings with the still photographer, publicity meetings, and then the exhausting work before the cameras, days on end, during shooting, with almost no rest, sixteen-hour days, eighteen-hour days, often finishing at four or five in the morning, just in time to catch a glimpse of the unchanging California sun making its way over the Hollywood hills to start another day. "Nothing Ever Happens to Judy," was the title of a 1943 magazine article. Hard as the fan magazines try to drum up items of interest to their voracious readers, the author was forced to admit, "Nothing ever happens to Judy but work."

While on the vaudeville circuit she had developed the habit of staying up late and sleeping well into the morning; a totally different routine was required for making films. Shooting might begin in the early hours of the day, and whenever possible, it was important to go to bed early. For Judy, retiring at nine, or ten, or even eleven in the evening simply didn't work, no matter how severe her exhaustion. Insomnia, an unpleasant malady at best, became an almost hallucinating ailment under the pressure of a demanding schedule. Finally, near dawn, she would fall into a brief torpid sleep, only minutes before the alarm would wake her up to start a new day on the relentlessly sunny, bustling MGM lot.

When pressure and exhaustion had pursued her in the past, Judy had taken to gulping down sweets to bring back her energy. Now, sleepless, insecure, in desperate search of a remedy for her worn-out state, she reached frantically for rich foods, only to find that all the bells in her private Hollywood hell began to jangle when she so much as looked at a dish of ice cream in the studio commissary.

At wardrobe fittings, care was taken to place her before a mirror with a dress form of a fat woman beside her. "Now look at yourself," she would be admonished. "Do you want to look like that dummy, or do you want to be a star?"

Judy Garland wanted to be a star. Comparison with the pretty young things in the MGM commissary had helped induce an earlier regime of dieting. Now, severe pressure from the studio called for more drastic remedies, like black coffee, and more black coffee, and cigarettes, which gradually increased their place in the diet until as many as four packs a day were nervously puffed away.

During filming, strict orders went out from Louis B. Mayer himself as to Judy's luncheon menu, which seemed to consist almost exclusively of chicken soup. "I swear there must have been a vat full of chicken soup at the MGM commissary with my name engraved on it," she once told Tex McCrary and Jinx Falkenburg in an interview. "If I sneaked in for a chocolate sundae with pecan nuts and bogs of whipped cream on top—I used to dream about those things—I would always get the same story: 'Sorry, Mr. Mayer has left instructions about what you are to eat today—chicken soup!' That commissary changed managements, a whole new staff was brought in, it even burned down, but still, every noon, there was another damn bowl of chicken soup."

As her technicolor extravaganzas rolled off the MGM assembly line, the problem of weight assumed alarming, almost terrifying proportions. Rigid dieting would bring her small five-foot-two frame down to ninety-eight pounds for the filming of a picture. Then, in the brief days of rest which followed, the exhausted and ravenous star would eat with semidelirious abandon, only to go on another regime and, within a matter of weeks, drop the hastily acquired pounds which had never been given a chance to settle on her restless frame.

Hedda Hopper, visiting the set when Judy was filming a demanding dance sequence, watched with dismay as the haggard star, near collapse, pleaded "I'm too hungry," and asked for a rest. "Get on with it," said the dance director "and you won't feel hungry." His psychology, which skipped blithely back to the Dark Ages, did not work. To Judy, the tyrannical director became known as "the man with the bullwhip."

Sometimes, in a siege of dieting, the loss of weight would go too far. Suddenly, the thin, pale-faced star would reverse course and eat, not for neurotic satisfaction, but actually in a desperate effort to gain weight for a new film.

To help with the seesawing battle, a new tactic was introduced which created more problems than it solved—pills. Pills to take off weight and, at the other end of the cycle, pills to put it back on. At the same time, sedatives were a help in bringing on much-needed sleep, along with pep-up pills which gave temporary bursts of energy for the strenuous demands of film making.

Among the grubbier segment of the Hollywood press, rumor spread that the use of pills was turning Judy Garland, a symbol of youthful innocence, into a narcotics addict. In reply to their innuendo, Mike Connolly, columnist for the small but locally powerful *Hollywood Reporter*, wrote laconically, "Hollywood is the kind of place where, if you order aspirins sent up from Schwab's Drug Store, word immediately gets around that you're a dope fiend. Judy Garland, more than any other star, has suffered from this kind of gossip. Judy is no more a dope fiend than Lassie."

Although she was not a drug addict, it was with the heavy help of stimulants and sedatives that Judy completed a score of films, many of them strenuous song-and-dance extravaganzas, a good number enduring classics of their kind. Unaware of the behind-the-scenes battles of the popular star, audiences applauded these fabulous outbursts of celluloid gaiety which are as much a part of the history of Metro-Goldwyn-Mayer, or even the 1940's in America, as they are of Judy Garland herself.

After *Babes in Arms,* the youthful star, whose salary had risen from an initial $150 a week to $500, was signed to a long-term, seven-year contract. It brought her $2,000 per week for three years, $2,500 per week for the following two years, and $3,000 per week for the final two years. At producer Arthur Freed's insistence, she had been given co-star status with Mickey Rooney for the first time in *Babes in Arms.*

Strike Up the Band teamed Judy with newcomer Gene Kelly, and boasted a production group that was responsible for many of the era's most successful musical films: Arthur Freed assumed the producer's helm; Fred Finklehoffe—collaborating here with John Monks Jr.—was to write original screenplays or work on adaptations for many of the Garland vehicles; and in the director's chair sat Busby Berkeley, who specialized in the sweeping production numbers for which Hollywood films became internationally celebrated.

"Miss Garland is someone to reckon with," wrote New York critic Howard Barnes, of her performance as a vaudeville trouper in *For Me and My Gal.* "Of all the youngsters who have graduated into mature roles in recent years, she has the surest command of her form of make-believe." The film, which appeared in a wartime year of the early Forties, was set against the background of the First World War and packed a considerable emotional punch. It foreshadowed Judy's own later triumphal entry into New York's famed Palace Theatre, as it commemorated the heyday of the two-a-day, when troupers hopped trains to make a "split week" in Minneapolis and fought the often amusing battle of the big time against the hicks.

Presenting Lily Mars, in 1943, gave Judy an opportunity to play love scenes with rising star Van Heflin in her first semidramatic role. Booth Tarkington's romance told of a talented, stagestruck girl from Indiana who wants to be a great star and follows a theatrical producer to New York. "Beauty, poise and ability" characterized her performance in what the New York *Daily Mirror*'s Frank Quinn called a top-notch musical. For Judy, Quinn reserved the simple accolade, "the sweetheart of the screen," a title that all of America seemed to accept.

"Hold your hats, folks!" exclaimed the usually reserved *New York Times* later in the same year, "Mickey Rooney and Judy Garland are back in town. And if at this late date there are still a few diehards who deny that they are the most incorrigibly talented pair of youngsters in movies, then *Girl Crazy* should serve as final rebuttal." "Fast, funny, infectious entertainment," the exhilarated *Times* reviewer went on, "Judy sings and acts like an earthbound angel." Tommy Dorsey and his orchestra provided a big-band background for the songs of George Gershwin.

Following upon *Ziegfeld Girl*, in which she performed with glamour queens Hedy Lamarr and Lana Turner, and *As Thousands Cheer*, which provided her first really grown-up role, Judy turned out four major films in twelve short months.

Meet Me in St. Louis said *Time* magazine on November 27, 1944, "is a musical that even the deaf should enjoy." *Time*'s sister publication, *Life*, placed Judy Garland on its cover and declared that the film provided her handsomest screen role since *Oz*. The players benefitted from a first-rate script, based on Sally Benson's autobiographical *New Yorker* stories, which looked back lovingly to life in the days of the 1904 St. Louis fair. Judy sang "The Trolley Song," which would become one of the numbers most closely associated with her later career, as well as the title waltz and other period tunes. Her romantic interest was Tom Drake, the handsome basketball player next door, and her youngest sister was played by Margaret O'Brien, who gave one of the best performances of her child actress career. Responsible for the direction was Vincente Minnelli, a former stage designer, well qualified to recreate the charms of a city's bygone era.

Minnelli was considered one of the brightest young talents on the Metro lot, a difficult, demanding directorial genius who worked tirelessly to get the meaning behind the lines. Like Judy, he was a perfectionist. Between star and director, a professional rapport developed and evolved into a more personal emotion.

On June 15, 1945, Minnelli became Judy's second husband. This time the studio heartily approved the match, the union of two of its principals, and offered active encouragement. Judy had wanted to have the ceremony at the tradition-rich Little Church Around the Corner in New York, but when Louis B. Mayer expressed regret that he could not be present, the marriage took place in her mother's home in Beverly Hills, with Ira Gershwin as best man and L. B. giving the bride away.

After their honeymoon, the two lived in a home perched high on a winding road between Beverly Hills and Hollywood, with a magnificent panoramic view stretching into the far distance, and with rare porcelains throughout the interior from the eighteenth-century collection of Minnelli.

Minnelli directed Judy in her first straight dramatic role, opposite Robert Walker, in *The Clock*. Her performance was well received. Only a few months before the release of the film, Judy's former rival at MGM, Deanna Durbin, had also made her straight dramatic debut in a film called *Christmas Holiday*. Asked about her reaction to the picture, Judy told reporters that she thought Deanna was excellent, but that it was a role she herself would not have liked to play—too morbid.

And, indeed, the unending string of colorful, tuneful spectacles which featured Judy Garland all seemed to capture the joy and zest of life, the lilt and gaiety of a friendly world. "A pleasant thing with which to pass the time of day," said *New York Times* critic Bosley Crowther of *The Harvey Girls*, which chronicled the efforts of Fred Harvey to establish the first of his famous chain of restaurants in the frontier town of Sandrock, New Mexico. Although based on the book by historian Samuel Hopkins Adams, the film was longer on dancing, singing, and spectacular saloon brawls than it was on history.

Till the Couds Roll By was a colorful film biography of composer Jerome Kern, while the gifted Cole Porter provided the songs for *The Pirate*, which reunited Judy with Gene Kelly, with Arthur Freed as producer and Vincente Minnelli as director.

One of the happiest consequences of the Minnelli marriage was the birth of a daughter, Liza, on March 12, 1946. Unfortunately, a Caesarean birth weakened Judy, and when she got out of bed too soon, she fainted on the street. At a family conference, her retirement was decided upon, but this idea was later abandoned, and the work grind resumed.

Top-notch talent continued to predominate in the films which ended a fabulous decade in the history of Judy Garland at MGM. *Words and Music* was based on the lives and music of the composing team of Rodgers and Hart, and brought Judy together once more with Mickey Rooney.

After Gershwin, Kern, Porter, and Rodgers and Hart, there was little left for MGM's brain trust but to turn to Irving Berlin. And turn to Irving Berlin they did for the winning melodies in the screen classic *Easter Parade,* one of the most successful of all the Fabulous Forties musicals.

Unfortunately, the star of these joyous extravaganzas was ill, plagued by nervousness brought on by the tensions at the studio, the competition, the staggering work load, the desperate attempts to gain weight, to lose weight, and sleeplessness. A jumpy, irritable Judy dragged herself to work with tears in her eyes and muted resistance deep in her heart. As the relentless drain on her energies continued, that resistance occasionally turned on the director. And the director, unfortunately, was sometimes her husband.

"I was employed by the studio and Judy was now against the studio," Minnelli was later quoted as saying. "Judy was full of fears. I urged her to enjoy being the great star she was, and is, but she didn't know how to do that, and still doesn't."

Nervous collapses led to delays in the exacting production schedules at MGM, and severe reprimands from on high, reprimands which led to terrible feelings of guilt and increased anxiety, and so demanded more pills and medication to overcome them. Inevitably, Judy would sometimes arrive late for work. Arguments would start, tears, shouting, recriminations. At night, beset by insomnia, the exhausted star would relive the traumatic experiences of the long day.

As far back as 1942, Judy had tried to find a way out of her complex dilemma. A sensitive, sympathetic friend who saw the confusion and torture in her mental state privately recommended that she consult the distinguished psychiatrist Karl Menninger. Menninger sent her to a highly reputed colleague residing in Los Angeles. She had been seeing him only a short while when the MGM spy system went into sickening operation. Her mother, learning of the visits, took her alarming information to Louis B. Mayer. Mayer, in his own misguided fashion, thought of himself as Judy's studio "father," the one person who knew what was best for her. Best, to his mind, was stern discipline. The psychiatric sessions ended, and Judy was steered away from a possible avenue of hope and understanding.

The following year, however, she tried again, entering into psychiatry on the night of her twenty-first birthday. For years thereafter, she had her fifty-minute session each morning at the grotesque hour of six A.M., and then another at the end of the day when her fatiguing work at the studio was done. She does not appear to have been an easy patient, finding it extremely difficult to talk to her doctor, sometimes actually rehearsing what she planned to say.

"When I think of it now, no wonder I was strange," she wrote in her *McCall's* account of these years. "Imagine whipping out of bed, dashing over to the doctor's office, lying down on a torn leather coach, telling my troubles to an old man who couldn't hear, who answered with an accent I couldn't understand, and then dashing to Metro to make love to Mickey Rooney."

Psychiatry, for Judy, simply didn't take at the time. And the time stretched into five years of seven days a week at $50 an hour. Periodically, she became so ill that private sessions would no longer suffice. Haggard, harassed, she would enter a hospital and spend days of recuperation with others like herself, sensitive people for whom the pressures of life had become too great. The hospital, she discovered one day to her dismay, cost $300 a day. Even for a star earning $150,000 a picture, it didn't seem like a good idea to stay too long.

After a sojourn in 1947, she went back to work on her new film, *The Barkleys of Broadway*. Migraine plagued her, but the demands on her time continued as the studio asked her to do retakes of a number of scenes from a prior film. Again she was late for rehearsals, and even her husband, Vincente Minnelli, felt she was wrong. When she began missing entire days, Louis B. Mayer, himself under pressure for allegedly pampering the "ungrateful" youngster he had made into a star, took a drastic step. With a telegram he fired her from the picture.

Panic-stricken, Judy called her mentor, but Mayer was not there. She called her producer, but he was out of town. Anxiously, she waited to see if any one would get in touch with her. No one called, and Judy waited as though in quarantine, just as a dozen years later, one of the greatest sex symbols of the world, Marilyn Monroe, suspended by her studio, sat alone with nothing to do and plagued by sleeplessness, took a tragic overdose of sleeping pills.

Soon the newspapers brought further bad news. MGM had replaced the "temperamental" Judy with Ginger Rogers in *The Barkleys of Broadway*. There was no word of Judy's extreme exhaustion, or illness. All responsibility for the suspension was laid at her door. *The Barkleys of Broadway* turned out to be one of Ginger Rogers' finest efforts. Judy returned to her analyst.

Analysis had been a frustrating experience for her in the past. She has likened it to taking a huge dose of medicine for an illness one doesn't have. It was no different now. When, extremely distraught, she told her specialist she thought the whole thing was a waste of time, that she might as well give up the sessions completely, he reflected a moment before telling her she was free to do as she liked. Only, he warned her, if she left he would give her six months to live, since, he declared, she was, beyond any question of a doubt, suicidal. Reeling from this further blow, Judy has told of how she remembered his cold, cruel analysis, and thought about it often in the trying months ahead.

MGM now called her back to do Irving Berlin's *Annie Get Your Gun*. The role of the swaggering, gun-toting Annie of pioneer days was a much sought-after prize. It had been played on Broadway by Ethel Merman, and Judy had longed to portray the screen Annie. Unfortunately, she was a battered shell, sleepless for weeks, psychologically completely exhausted. She requested a postponement and was refused. Once more, she dragged herself through the unfailing California sunlight to the studio. Somehow, she did get the entire Irving Berline score onto records, an album that is now a collector's item. In a daze, she began the shooting. The role demanded a Western pioneer accent, and she tried gallantly to acquire one. Under better circumstances, this would have been a small matter, but now it topped an accumulation of difficulties anl miseries. Her old supporter, producer Arthur Freed, reported that she was repeatedly late for work. One day, she walked out at lunchtime, not to return until the following day. As difficulties mounted, MGM scrapped a small fortune in footage already shot and took Judy out of the picture, replacing her with Betty Hutton.

After a time, the studio cast its chastened star in another musical, *In the Good Old Summertime*, opposite Van Johnson. With personal tragedy drawing ever closer to its star, the film was described by *The New York Times* as a musical surrounded by "an air of gaiety and wholesomeness which defies description. . . . Miss Garland is fresh as a daisy and she sings a number of songs in winning fashion. In fact, her slightly amusing and free-wheeling interpretation of 'I Don't Care,' brought a burst of applause from the preview audience."

Judy had a new director, Robert Z. Leonard. Arthur Freed was nowhere in evidence, his place having been taken by Joseph Pasternak, the producer of Deanna Durbin's successful pictures for Universal, who was now to go on to a continuing career as the dean of MGM's technicolor musicals. A changing of the guard around Judy was clearly in evidence.

At home, her second marriage was slowly breaking up. Authoritative and commanding on set, Vincente Minnelli had a gentle, almost shy manner in a social situation. When Judy, her nerves taut with pressure and conflict, became emotional, he tended to withdraw. Rumors of separation became actual. Twice Judy left the house, only to return, convinced that the marriage could be saved. When a third separation ensued on March 31, 1949, the reluctant principals admitted their difficulties to the press. "I'm very sorry," Judy declared, "but it's true—we're happier apart. We tried very hard to overcome the difficulties of incompatibility."

"Yes, we have separated. I have nothing more to say," Minnelli commented in July as he prepared to move out of the sprawling mansion high up on Sunset Boulevard.

On May 28, 1949, Judy arrived in Boston with her manager, Carlton Alsop, who took her to Peter Bent Brigham Hospital for observation. "She feels better already," Alsop told the press. "Maybe all she needed was to get away from Hollywood for a

while. After all, she has spent almost her entire life on a movie
lot. She has made thirty pictures in thirteen years. She's a little
tired and she's under suspension." Officials at the hospital reported her suffering from no specific ailment, but obviously
overworked. It was announced that after treatment she
planned to go to New York for an extensive rest, there to be
joined by her husband, with whom she had effected another
reconciliation, and her three-year-old daughter, Liza.

At the Boston hospital, Judy slowly mended over a period of
eleven weeks. Her bill at Peter Bent Brigham was paid by
Louis B. Mayer. The incredible fact was that Judy Garland,
one of the greatest box-office attractions in the country, in the
top ten for 1940, 1941, and 1945, was broke.

Katharine Hepburn proved a thoughtful friend, offering
Judy the use of her estate in Connecticut as well as her apartment in New York. From MGM, however, came word that Joseph Pasternak wanted her for his forthcoming picture, *Summer Stock*. A revitalized Judy, feeling better than she had in
years, headed back to the scene of her troubles, only to have
them begin anew. She was told of how much she owed Metro
for taking her back. She was asked to be grateful to the studio
which had made her a star. Treated like a returning prodigal,
the deflated star threw herself back into the familiar routine.
Once more she was asked to lose weight. A new crash diet
brought on the old migraines. The rushes were bad, the studio
warned her. The confidence which had been built up in the
hospital was gradually worn away by attrition, and Judy again
began to be late for work.

"Delay with Judy is something she can't help," said her producer, Joseph Pasternak. "It isn't that she doesn't care. She said
to me, 'Why am I like this? I don't want to be. I want to
work.'"

Summer Stock was completed. A perfectionist even in this
critical period, Judy had worked herself to a shell, losing so
much weight—more than fifteen pounds—by the time of the
"Get Happy" finale that some observers thought the slim and

vivacious star who appeared on the screen had shot the closing scenes a year earlier.

Summer Stock was her final exhibition of exuberant film gaiety. *Life* reported: "The great song-and-dance actress makes this movie a personal triumph." The price of the performance was high; the reward, a brief rest in Carmel, from which she was called back to go into rehearsal for *Royal Wedding* with Fred Astaire. Insufficiently rested, a promised vacation of greater duration totally out of the question, she found the worst of her symptoms returning. After a particularly trying scene, Judy walked off the set. Four calls to her home went unanswered. When she failed to report for a Saturday dance rehearsal with Fred Astaire, MGM for the third time took her out of a picture, replacing her in *Royal Wedding* with Jane Powell. To her agent, come to protest the new suspension, Louis B. Mayer showed balance sheets which indicated that Judy's chronic absences and latenesses cost the studio a steep 20 percent extra in production costs.

With a rocky marriage to return to in the evening, Judy needed only the traditional straw to break her back. It came in the form of harsh, critical newspaper stories which made her the villain of the piece, calling her temperamental, uncooperative, harmful to the morale of her studio, asserting that her actions had cost MGM untold thousands of dollars, even hundreds of thousands.

On June 20, 1950, a shocked American public awoke to find that the evening before, from a disputatious conference attended by her business manager and her husband, Judy Garland had rushed into the bathroom, broken a water glass, and slashed her wrist with the jagged edges in a painful attempt at suicide. "Sing Hallelujah, c'mon, get happy!" she had sung in the gay finale of her last picture, which was even now showing in movie houses across the land. "You gotta sing all your cares away!" It would have taken the relentless sense of humor of a Judy Garland to see the irony of the situation.

As the news spread, journalists rushed to a sprawling mansion on Sunset Boulevard to which Judy had been removed from the more remote home on the hillside above the Strip. A well-known Hollywood publicist caught a glimpse of the thin, drawn star before the arrival of the mob. He described a scratch well covered by a quarter-inch bandage as the only evidence of the suicide attempt, and attributed this to hysteria more than to profound intent. No stitches were necessary for the wound, and her doctor called the episode "an attempt to get attention."

Now that Judy was clearly the underdog, the papers suddenly found stories favorable to her, even at the studio. Bit players and extras unwilling to give their names, told the United Press's Hollywood correspondent there wasn't an employee on the place who wasn't pulling for Judy. "They won't leave her alone until she drops dead," one was quoted as saying. "She'd lend you money if you needed it, and then act embarrassed when you came to pay it back," another stated. "If you were just down in the dumps, she'd knock herself out to cheer you up. And sometimes that's more valuable than money." Other colleagues from the lower echelons testified that they admired her, that she in no way lowered their morale, as the studio had charged.

"I couldn't have done more if she had been my own daughter," declared Louis B. Mayer, while from another source, curvaceous Jane Russell, of a strong religious bent, came a thoughtful offer of spiritual help.

It was too late, however, for support or sympathy at MGM. In a final conference with Mayer and other officials, Judy was released from her contract, which still had several years to run —"for her own best interest," read the press releases. When the debt-ridden star asked Mayer to lend her some money, he put in a call to the chairman of the board, Nicholas Schenck, in New York. Schenck refused the request, saying they were not running a charity institution. A reflective L. B. put down the phone to growl, "If they'd do this to you, they'll do this to me, too." His prophecy was fulfilled several years later when a swift toss of the dice sent the Hollywood Rajah, as Bosley Crowther dubbed him, spinning from his chariot. Now, the man who had guided her screen fortunes for more than fifteen years, who had bought her her first wristwatch, given her away in marriage, controlled her diet and much of her life, arranged to give his departing "daughter" a personal loan. With the memory of his firm handclasp in hers, Judy Garland walked off the lot where she had spent most of her brilliantly successful and bitter young days.

The curtain rung down on her career at MGM, the last shreds of self-confidence gone, she looked only for a place to hide. She found it at the Beverly Hills Hotel, where she checked into a seven-room suite and threw herself into an eating binge that stood a good chance of turning her into a balloon. In New York, she repeated this performance, but also walked the town, went shopping, cheered at World Series games, ate when and what she wanted. Her hair cut back in a trim, boyishly attractive style, she was seen by crowds who were drawn to her in a warm, friendly manner. Their concern appeared to comfort her. After a time, still plump and rather matronly-looking, she felt well enough to spend some time traveling and then to return to Hollywood.

Her arrival created not even a flurry of interest. There were no offers of film roles. No producer was willing to take a chance on the former reigning star who was considered temperamental, unpredictable, prematurely washed up. On the personal side, her marriage to Vincente Minnelli was in its final stages of dissolution. Judy was still hopelessly adrift.

At this difficult time, she met a young man-about-town named Sid Luft. A former Douglas test pilot, Luft had come to Hollywood as a technical adviser on films, spent eight years in marriage to actress Lynn Bari, who had recently divorced him, and the rest of his days as a theatrical producer and agent and as a dabbler in the sport of kings, horse racing. Like Judy, he was rootless and adrift in a town with which he was fed up but which he could not leave. When these two rebellious spirits met, Judy fell in love with the broad-shouldered former flier, whose direct, uncomplicated manner was in striking contrast to the more refined ways of those closest to her in the past.

In December 1951, she moved out of the house she had shared with Minnelli and the following February she started suit for divorce, citing the familiar Hollywood complaint, "extreme cruelty." The property settlement provided that Judy and Minnelli would share custody of their five-year-old daughter, Liza. With Minnelli, as with her first husband, David Rose, Judy remained on good terms throughout the succeeding years. The new man in her life, Michael S. (Sid) Luft, was not to fare as well.

At the beginning, however, their relationship was clearly good for both. Judy dropped her medical mentors along with some of the thirty pounds she had gained on her eating sprees. The two were often seen together at night clubs and, with time, Luft evolved into Judy's business manager and adviser. It was he who supported and developed an agent's idea of presenting her once more to the live audiences she had thrived upon as a child performer. For the occasion of a tryout, he chose a debut out of the country, at London's famed Palladium, one of the greatest and friendliest vaudeville houses in the world. It was an audacious and very clever bit of showmanship, and to Luft goes the credit for building up Judy's confidence as a woman to the point that she could begin to face the awesome hurdle of a comeback.

When, still in Hollywood, word spread that Judy was having nagging second thoughts about the London venture, Fanny Brice made a surprise appearance on her doorstep. "You're going to go over there and, with the voice and talent God gave you, you're going to make everybody proud of you," the celebrated Fanny lectured her younger compatriot. "It's time you stopped pampering yourself. Good Lord, girl, do you think you're the only person on earth who has problems?"

With money borrowed from her agents, Judy planed into the British capital in the spring of 1951, knowing that the eyes of

the entertainment world were on her, wondering whether a
twenty-nine-year-old former star, fired from her fat Hollywood
contract, considered unemployable in the film capital, and still
not looking anything like the vivacious, slim Judy of yesteryear, could make it back on her own. At dawn of the day of her
opening, she was still pacing her hotel room like a lost and
hopeless specter; and that evening, as she stood in the wings
waiting for her cue, she wondered whether the noisy crowd
was really friendly, or only curious, come to see the Hollywood
reject at the end of her road. The orchestra struck up the songs
of the overture, and Judy, like the cowardly lion in the *Wizard*,
brave because she could do courageous things when scared,
made her way with an effort to the center of the stage and
began to sing. Somewhat hesitatingly, she finished her first set
of songs, turned to bow to one side of the audience, and did
exactly what Sid Luft had earlier told her she wouldn't do. She
fell on her face. With no strength left in her half-paralyzed
legs, the slight turn had done it, dropped her to the floor,
where she sat mildly dazed, thinking that it was not a very
graceful way to end a comeback.

Looking up, she saw Luft leaning far out of a box, shouting,
"You're great, baby, you're great!" Unable even to half believe
him, she somehow found her way into the wings, where her old
friend and coach, Kay Thompson, also yelled encouragement
before giving her a shove that sent her flying back on stage. "I
bet no one ever made an exit like that before in this theatre,"
exclaimed the bewildered star.

The warm British vaudeville audience loved nothing better
than the unexpected. Judy's impromptu fall delighted them.
From the crowd came wave on wave of applause for the game
little woman who had come back from bad times to entertain
them. Deeply moved, Judy responded in kind. As she sang the
songs she had made famous, her strength, assurance, and poise
seemed to grow. Like a catharsis, she was singing the bad years
away, finding herself anew, being reborn. Almost an hour later
she brought her act to a close, and one of the wildest ovations

in the history of the tradition-rich Palladium greeted her. Adoring fans lined her path as she left the theatre. Judy Garland had come back.

The performance at the Palladium ushered in a brilliant new era in her career. After a number of successful appearances in England, she and Sid Luft decided on another giant step, a return to the United States for an American comeback. Audaciously, they booked Judy into what was once the greatest showplace in the land, the hallowed Mecca of vaudeville, New York's Palace Theatre.

In films like *For Me and My Gal*, she had celebrated the glories of this renowned house, where Sarah Bernhardt had played, and which had headlined the greats of the past, from Fanny Brice and Nora Bayes to Sophie Tucker and Al Jolson. *Variety* and all the world of entertainment were now asking whether Judy Garland could come back in this legendary shrine and restore vaudeville, at a $4.80 top, to the place it had held when the Palace, some nineteen years earlier, had closed its doors to the acrobats, trained seals, jugglers, song-and-dance men, and comedians who had made audiences laugh in every tank town of the nation before being called to appear on its big stage.

As the date of Judy's first appearance drew near, electricity filled the air. Billed as "America's greatest and most beloved singer—direct from her European triumphs," she was to be surrounded in her all-star variety show by a cast including the classic patter comedians Smith and Dale, veterans of forty years in vaudeville; Max Bygraves, England's newest star comedian; other familiar vaudeville units; and an attractive new ensemble known as "Judy's Eight Boyfriends." The entire evening was being staged by Charles Walters, who had directed Judy in *Easter Parade* and other successes, while at the piano was another face from Hollywood days, composer Hugh Martin.

On opening night, October 16, 1951, Duffy Square teemed with a tremendous crowd of Garland fans held in check behind solid police cordons. Inside the renovated Palace, splendidly redecorated in ivory, red, and gold, lights flashed and the sell-out crowd stared in wonder as the usherettes escorted to their seats the Duke and Duchess of Windsor, leading an audience of society figures ablaze with diamonds and jewels, and eclipsed only by such stars as Gloria Swanson, Jimmy Durante, Jack Benny, and Marlene Dietrich.

At eight-thirty, the red velvet curtains opened, conductor Don Albert waved his baton to lead the orchestra in the overture, and Judy's Boyfriends launched into a song about their star. Suddenly, behind them, appeared a flash of black velvet, a slim, radiant Judy Garland facing her first American vaudeville audience in a dozen years. A tumultuous burst of applause stopped only when she cupped her hands, yelled "Hello!" and began her program with a number that told of her long-time ambition to appear at the Palace.

The performance that followed is legendary. A keyed-up Judy sang the many songs that millions had applauded in her films and the melodies that others had sung before her but which she was to make her own—"You Made Me Love You," "Rock-A-Bye Your Baby," "The Trolley Song," "For Me and My Gal," "Come Rain or Come Shine." On a blacked-out stage, she did pratfalls with Charles Walters. In a handsome gown, she danced a step or two, and then stripped down to show the exquisite Garland legs. In a dashing tuxedo top, with long, black stockings and top hat, she sang "This Is My Lucky Day," before reverting to a chalky tramp makeup and baggy hobo costume for "A Couple of Swells." From time to time, she grabbed hold of the microphone in a gesture that was to become a trademark, and in asides to the audience she confided that she was still about ninety pounds too heavy, but feeling fine.

The versatile star had earlier delighted the crowd with impressions of Nora Bayes, Sophie Tucker, Fanny Brice, and other former Palace headliners. Now, with her amazingly broad repertoire near its end, she sat in the footlight trough, still clad in her hobo outfit, her chin cupped in her hands, and before a hushed audience, began the touching and unforgettable "Over the Rainbow." When she finished, the hard-boiled and worldly crowd sat in silence. Even the toughest, said columnist Earl Wilson, had tears in their eyes. Only after they had recovered did they proceed to systematically tear down the house, while for days afterward, at gatherings in New York, people gave emotional accounts of the evening, which they described as if they had witnessed a miracle.

"Judy Garland is in the great tradition of the two-a-day," wrote the man who had given her his name, Robert Garland of the *Journal American*. "There were shining show people in the good old days. There can be shining show people now. Witness Miss Garland. It is as if vaudeville had been waiting somewhere for her to come along. And she, in turn, for vaudeville."

"All the glory that once was the Palace's was restored in a matter of minutes last night when Judy made her surprise entrance," wrote critic Vernon Rice. "Two-a-day had come back with a smash." "When she sings them, songs stay sung," said John Chapman in the *News*. And Abel Green made the unanimous verdict official when he wrote in *Variety* of Judy's "simon-pure, stellar quality," and said that she could only brook comparison with the all-time greats, with Nora Bayes, Fanny Brice and Al Jolson.

Jimmy Durante and Al Jolson in the twenties had captivated audiences for hours with their remarkable stamina and virtuosity. The marathon performances of Judy at the Palace were in this tradition. For nineteen weeks she packed the house, performing before more than 800,000 patrons, breaking virtually every record the Palace could boast—Eddie Cantor and George Jessel had both had nine-week runs in 1931, Kate Smith had appeared in the same year for ten weeks. Judy, moreover, could have extended her engagement another nineteen weeks at will, according to the management of the theatre, which reported ticket sales still brisk after more than four highly profitable months.

For her last show on Sunday, February 24, 1951, many of the

first-night audience returned to bid farewell. At the end of the program, the crowd joined her in singing "Auld Lang Syne." Metropolitan Opera baritone Lauritz Melchior—in the audience in keeping with tradition because he was to follow her into the Palace—stood up halfway through the number, and then the entire house rose in a final tribute to the headliner they referred to simply as "Judy."

The record run at the Palace had provided the entertainment world with one of the most remarkable emotional binges on record. For other performers, private misfortunes and bad publicity had often been extremely harmful. With Judy, they only drew her closer to her audience. From the black nights and tortured days, a resurgent star had fashioned a triumphant new personality, the true Judy. Audiences that had loved her as the appealing, wistful young Dorothy of *The Wizard of Oz* and admirers who had applauded her exuberant and happy song-and-dance extravaganzas now formed themselves into a frenzied following for the Judy who was all these things, the little girl lost, the joyous adolescent, and something more, the complex woman with a telltale heart, pouring out her dreams and her great love in a torrent of song.

Columnist Sheilah Graham wrote that the public desire to do good which had been in evidence at the Palace appearances might never be generated again. Happily, it continued to manifest itself with extraordinary predictability.

After winding up in New York in February, the final step on the comeback road took Judy into the Philharmonic Auditorium in Los Angeles, where scalpers asked $100 a pair for tickets to the sold-out premiere performance. On April 26th, the West Coast version of the New York opening took place before a red-carpet crowd of West Coast society and film colony figures. The program carried the sentimental crowd back a long decade in their lives, back indeed to another era in Hollywood. At its conclusion, wild applause shook the rafters of the huge hall, sold out for its entire four-week run.

After the Los Angeles stand, on June 11, 1952, Judy married

her manager and producer, Sid Luft, in a simple, five-minute ceremony. The wedding took place near Hollister, California, at the home of a friend, a wealthy cattle rancher, where the couple spent the night. Both said they had planned marriage for a long time. The following day, Judy was already back at work in San Francisco, where her act had been booked into the Curran Theatre.

"Sid has done it for me," Judy had said after the Palace. "That's my fella." And Luft had declared, "I love Judy. I want to protect her from the trauma she once knew. I don't want her to be bewildered or hurt again. I want her to have happiness. She knows now what she wants and that's to be free to make her own decisions, not to be tied down to any studio. [Neither] I, nor anyone else, can force her to do anything she doesn't want to do."

These tender words of promise were beclouded only hours after the wedding ceremony when Luft was hailed into court by his former wife, Lynn Bari, who claimed that Judy had made $750,000 in 1951 and that Luft, as her manager, had received a good deal of it. She asked that his $200 monthly support payments for their son be raised to $500. In Superior Court in Hollywood, Judge Burke ordered Luft to double the monthly payments.

At almost the same time, Judy became the center of a legal action which was to have a profound effect on her. In an extraordinary move, her mother, Mrs. Ethel Gilmore, went to court to complain that her high-salaried daughter would not support her. Newspapers seized upon the "human interest" angle of the resurgent star's life. When the case fell through, Mrs. Gilmore took a job as a $60-a-week clerk at the offices of Douglas Aircraft, a move many observers viewed as an attempt to embarrass Judy, since Mrs. Gilmore was a capable piano and singing teacher.

The relationship between Judy and her mother had come many a twisted mile. Long years before, when Judy was beginning her career in Hollywood, stories would frequently mention the close relationship between the two, and, in particular, Judy's devotion to her mother. For long years, too, Judy took full responsibility for her own youth spent on the stage, exonerating Mrs. Garland of being a stage mother. "My mother is a strong-minded woman, but she was never a 'stage mama,'" she told Sheilah Graham. "During those vaudeville years, my sisters and I, while standing in countless wings waiting for our cues, used to hear other mothers threatening their children, saying things like, 'You go on out there or I'll break your head,' and it made us kind of sick. Nobody ever talked to me like that or forced me in any way. I drove myself—but it was my own doing."

Although no one has ever fully explained the causes of their later estrangement, a number of factors have been cited as contributing to trouble the mother-daughter relationship. When her mother remarried, becoming Mrs. William Gilmore, it was said to have been a psychological jolt for the sensitive youngster. In dealings with the studio, her mother unaccountably lodged herself on the side of the tyrannical rule of MGM, contributing to their spy system, seemingly pitting herself against her daughter. A further factor often mentioned as leading to the estrangement was her mother's handling of her finances.

During the Forties, the Gilmores moved to Dallas, where one of Judy's married sisters maintained her home. In July 1950, Judy's mother returned to Hollywood, taking an apartment within walking distance of her ailing daughter, who, at first, refused to see her. Rumors that Mrs. Gilmore did not approve of Sid Luft recurred in the press and were denied. When Judy returned to Los Angeles to appear at the Philharmonic, her mother went to the auditorium, but no meeting of minds took place, and the unsavory suit (which was soon withdrawn) hit the courts.

As an aftermath of the action, Mrs. Gilmore bared her soul to columnist Sheilah Graham, on July 19, 1952. Life on the stage or in pictures, with all the publicity, she stated, was not a normal life for a child. "If you have a daughter," she said, "don't let her sing or dance. We gave her everything she wanted. When she made her fabulous deal at Metro, I told her, 'Judy, think! You, Frances Gumm, getting $5,000 a week— aren't you thrilled?' 'Yes,' said Judy, 'but I always had everything I wanted.' "

Her daughter, she declared, had been spoiled, and this had warped her character: "Judy has been selfish all her life. That's my fault. I made it too easy for her. She worked, but that's all she ever wanted, to be an actress. She never said, 'I want to be kind,' or 'loved,' only 'I want to be famous.' "

Not only did she now not want any part of Judy's earnings, declared Mrs. Gilmore, but she wanted everyone, including the press, to forget her, as, she claimed, her daughter had forgotten her.

As Judy's contemporary at MGM, Lana Turner, had said, "It's a very difficult thing, growing up in public." An unpleasant remark is not easy to forget under ordinary circumstances. When that remark is carried in every major newspaper in the country and given its harshest editorial coloring, it may be impossible. Judy's quarrel with her mother took place under the bright glare of celebrity-conscious publicity. That notoriety could only aggravate it.

The harsh words were followed by an undeclared truce which in turn was followed not by a reconciliation but by a tragedy that cut all ties. On January 5, 1953, Mrs. Ethel Milne Gilmore, fifty-six, was found dead on the parking lot of the Douglas Aircraft Co. Due to begin work at 7:30 A.M. on her $60-a-week job as a clerk at the plant, she was discovered later in the morning, crouched on her hands and knees between two cars on the lot, the victim of a heart attack.

By one of those recurring thrusts of an ironic fate which characterize her life, Judy was rehearsing "Over the Rainbow" for a charity benefit when she learned of her mother's death. She heard the news with shocked disbelief. Sadly, she recalled that there had been disagreements between them, but said that plans had been set afoot to work out a trust fund for her mother, or to buy some income property for her, although, she stated, her mother didn't want to depend on her.

The attorney for Mrs. Gilmore confirmed that his client was proud and did not want to depend on Judy. "Mrs. Gilmore's arms were always open to Judy," he said. "They loved each other in their hearts."

It would be difficult to conclude that the relationship was anything other than complex. With her husband, Judy flew to Los Angeles to make the funeral arrangements that would draw a mournful curtain over a period in her life that had been labeled "comeback." She had thought she was well, but the loss of her mother tore open old wounds. For almost two years, she did no work, saw virtually no one. At the end of that period, she emerged to do what the majority of former child stars who stay in the business do—she staged another comeback.

Judy had long wanted to do a remake of *A Star Is Born*, the richly sentimental tear-jerker in which Janet Gaynor and Fredric March had scored a great success back in 1937. By now the almost legendary romance of a young actress headed for stardom and a once-great matinee idol headed down the road to oblivion had taken on a somewhat hackneyed quality. She proposed to give it new life by turning it into a musical.

Under an unusual agreement, Warner Brothers agreed to finance the production but stipulated that the entire cost of the film would have to be recouped before the star and her producer started earning their share, a provision which later warred against the often broke Lufts as the film's cost, budgeted at $2,500,000, soared to the vicinity of $6 million.

Even before filming began, Cary Grant, set for the leading male role, withdrew, saying he felt he wasn't right for the part. Veteran English actor James Mason replaced him. After a month's work, it was decided, over Judy's objections, that the musical drama should be filmed in Cinemascope. The change in process was a costly one both in time and money, since it meant scrapping the work that had been done and starting over. Next, arranger and composer Hugh Martin walked off the set when he disagreed violently with Judy about a key number. Five cameramen and four costume designers also walked off or were fired.

Reporting on the filming in the *Saturday Evening Post,* Cameron Shipp told of how Judy held up one major sequence for twenty-eight days. Unable to emote during the day, the volatile star insisted on working only at night. "She has accommodated the gossips by falling on her face, breaking contracts, walking out on pictures, and by collapsing in hospitals under the care of psychiatrists," Shipp declared in his critical account, while the *Hollywood Reporter*'s Mike Connolly wrote in a Sunday supplement that Judy "has unknowingly followed the old-time pattern of throwing her weight around. She wants things her way."

"I'm a little tired of being the Patsy for the production delays on this picture," Judy finally told the press in answer to these charges. "It's easy to blame every production delay on the star. This was the story of my life at Metro, when I was a child actress. When some problem came up that they couldn't lick, the delay, no matter who caused it, was always blamed on the star. Whoever was responsible figured that the star could get by without a bawling-out. They couldn't."

The film's director, the gifted George Cukor, commented with wry humor: "First they said it would never start; then that it would never stop; and finally they said the principals were battling. Judy used to amuse us by mimicking rumor-mongers worrying their heads about her picture."

The veteran Cukor, after six months of shooting, brought in a film which ran uncut for three and a half hours. Moss Hart had fashioned the screenplay, based on the earlier version by Dorothy Parker. Harold Arlen and Ira Gershwin contributed seven new songs.

"One of the grandest heartbreak dramas that has drenched the screen in years," said the dean of New York film critics,

Bosley Crowther of the *Times*. "No one surpasses Mr. Cukor at this sort of thing, and he gets performances from Miss Garland and Mr. Mason that make the heart flutter and bleed." "She sings the blues as though she were going to tear the place down," wrote *Herald Tribune* critic Otis L. Guernsey Jr. *Look* placed Judy on its cover, and for the eloquence and versatility of her performance, gave her its award for the best actress of the year. "In the past," read its citation, "she revealed extraordinary talents as a variety artist and actress potentially rich in both comedy and tragedy. These talents have grown to full maturity in this 'drama with music,' and give her a place with the genuine artists who are wholly products of Hollywood training."

Judy narrowly missed winning an Academy Award, which went instead to Grace Kelly for *The Country Girl*. Groucho Marx wired her: THIS IS THE BIGGEST ROBBERY SINCE BRINK'S. Even without an Oscar to make it official, Judy had climbed back to the top.

In early July, she began a seven-city West Coast tour with a dazzling performance in San Diego, where she asked the jubilant audience, "Do you think this kind of figure will ever come back?" For her appearance in Long Beach, long-time friend Frank Sinatra chartered a bus which brought Humphrey Bogart, founder of Hollywood's so-called "Rat Pack," Debbie Reynolds and Eddie Fisher, June Allyson, Betty Hutton and other stars from Los Angeles. At the end of the show, the elated Sinatra rushed on stage to hug Judy, who asked him to sing. "This I cannot follow," said the gallant Frankie, who again showed the chivalrous side of his nature when he later clouted a publicist for calling Judy Garland a "dame."

For a nightclub debut, Judy was booked into the New Frontier at Las Vegas. "In an air of expectancy as electric as the atmosphere attending the opening of a promising new Broadway musical," wrote *Variety*, "one of the greatest modern-day singers caught fire last night in the first nitery engagement of

her career." Once again, Judy was compared to Al Jolson as she sang for forty minutes out of the sixty-eight minute show, and broke every box-office record in the place, including an all-time weekly high gross of $71,643.

Judy launched her newest career, television, when she made her debut on September 24, 1955, with a one-and-one-half-hour "spectacular" to inaugurate the Ford Star Jubilee series. Before an audience estimated at forty million, the largest ever gathered for a ninety-minute TV program, she did a nostalgic reprise of most of her Palace show. "The greatest natural talent in show business," declared the *Journal American*'s usually caustic Jack O'Brien. "Tremendously appealing," said J. P. Shanley in the *Times*. Shanley warned, however, that her voice did not have the "crystal clarity of the past," and, "sometimes husky," reached for high and low notes with effort.

The following September, Judy returned for a second engagement at the Palace, where a gleaming gold plaque announced to visiting vaudevillians: THIS WAS THE DRESSING ROOM OF JUDY GARLAND WHO SET THE ALL-TIME LONG-RUN RECORD, OCT. 16TH, 1951, TO FEB. 24, 1952. RKO PALACE THEATRE. Once more, the red carpet was laid out, and once more the faithful, reading like a list from *Who's Who*, were on hand for the opening.

The second Palace appearance met a far more mixed reaction than the triumphant first stand. For many, Judy's performance was satisfactory. Other reviewers—especially the more knowledgeable students of Garland lore—found that she was not looking or singing her best. Weight was again becoming a serious problem; her movements were increasingly nervous, even mechanical.

While Judy Garland had soared back to the top, it was becoming apparent that her fortunes were beginning once more to tumble. Nothing is more characteristic of her turbulent life than this recurrent pattern of the roller-coaster ride. No star has been visited more often by fate, which has taken her many times for the swift ride to the top of the track, only to plunge her, sometimes precipitantly, sometimes more slowly, back to the bottom.

Trouble had begun at home, where the marriage to Sid Luft was in constant difficulty. With a great need for companionship, Judy found that her husband's work as her manager very often kept him from her side as he traveled to distant cities to make arrangements for her appearances, negotiating terms and settling the many problems involved in each booking. Furthermore, despite the great sums of money which she was earning, they were in constant financial straits.

In early February 1956, Judy sent attorney Jerry Giesler into court to file a divorce suit against her husband of four years' standing, charging extreme mental cruelty, a phrase as solidly established in cases of this category as "Till death do us part" in the marriage ceremony. She asked for an equitable division of community property and custody of their two children, whom she took with her. One day later, Judy and Luft reconciled, but within weeks another battle erupted.

In October 1957, Judy took her act to London, where she appeared at the Dominion. Husky-voiced, she coughed and sang her way through an eighty-minute program before a crowd that nevertheless stomped, roared, and whistled its approval of her less than top-notch performance. "Carefully rationed, atrociously dressed, and brilliantly reinforced," began a London reviewer, "she presents at first the melancholy sight of a star who has outgrown her myth. In the quick turn of her head, the upward glance of her eyes, one sees for a moment the little girl lost, trapped in someone else's body by time's practical joke. And then, as she warms up to the audience, one hears the sound of trumpets: the approach of a new Garland, lifting up her voice and making a great big, beautiful noise that cannonades around the cinema."

On November 19, Judy headed the bill for a royal command performance for charity at the Palladium, attended by the Queen Mother. She was presented to Queen Elizabeth II,

Mickey Rooney plays Gable to the Garbo of Shirley Jean Rickert in a Mickey McGuire Comedy of the early Thirties.

Above: Judy Garland, Mickey Rooney and Jane Withers in 1935. Below
Rooney, Ann Rutherford, Garland, Jackie Cooper and Marjorie Gestring i
1939.

Above: Deanna Durbin in *One Hundred Men and a Girl* (1937) with Adolphe Menjou, Leopold Stokowski and Mischa Auer. *Below:* Durbin on the set of *That Certain Age* (1939) with co-star Jackie Cooper.

Judy Garland and Mickey Rooney in *Girl Crazy* (1943).

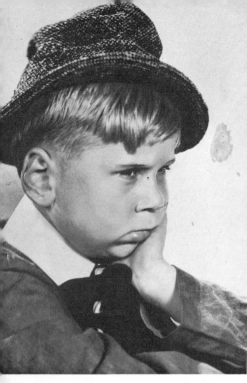

Above: Jackie Cooper in *Skippy,* his greatest success, and in the television series *Hennessey. Below:* Freddie Bartholomew as *Little Lord Fauntleroy* and with Spencer Tracy in *Captains Courageous.*

Freddie Bartholomew and his Aunt Cissy in 1935.

W. C. Fields, nemesis of children and child stars, with Gloria Jean in *Never Give a Sucker an Even Break* (1941).

Elizabeth Taylor in *National Velvet* (1944).

along with Count Basie, and another performer for whom the curse of calories appeared to be chronic, singer Mario Lanza.

In the United States, however, a concert tour had relatively poor grosses on the road. Illness forced cancellation of two Philadelphia performances, and also cut short a stand in Washington, D. C. Charges of temperament and unpredictability began to mount. As far back as 1955, *Variety* had reported that eastern and midwestern arena managers, in an unusual move, were asking for guaranteed indemnification against all losses should Judy fail to appear as per contract for any reason. Now these sentiments were more strongly in the air.

A recurrent squabble with CBS Television gained fresh fuel when columnist Maria Torre ran a piece that quoted a network executive as saying that Judy's concern about being overweight had brought on insecurities which made it difficult for her to perform. Judy promptly sued CBS, asking $1 million libel damages and $393,333 for breach of contract. During the suit, Miss Torre refused to reveal her source of information and was consequently tossed into jail, where she served a ten-day sentence, becoming the Joan of Arc of the columnists. Her colleague, Dorothy Kilgallen, mused, "I never thought I'd live to see the day when anyone would be tossed into the jug for saying Judy Garland has problems," apparently missing the reason for Torre's incarceration. Eventually, the suit was settled without an exchange of monies, but with the scheduling of new Garland TV spectaculars.

In March 1958, Judy again filed for divorce. A month later, when she was fired from a stormy engagement at Ben Maksik's Town and Country Club in Brooklyn, Luft flew to her side, and again a reconciliation was effected. "We're very, very happy," Judy said. "Everything is going to be all right now."

Four times in ten years, Judy filed suits for separation or divorce. "Sometimes it takes a few days, sometimes a bit longer, but they always make up," said her lawyer, Jerry Giesler. However, the relations between husband and wife were becoming decidedly acrimonious, with custody of their two young children, Joe and Lorna, increasingly the main bone of contention.

In April 1959, Judy began another concert tour that led to a week's engagement at New York's Metropolitan Opera House. No figure from the world of popular entertainment had appeared there since the days of Harry Lauder, the Scottish vaudevillian. En route, a forecast of what was to come could be noted in *Variety*'s sum-up of her Baltimore appearance. "Most spectacular personality to hit this town in years," said the trade paper. "Jolt of the engagement was Miss Garland's bulk."

Plump, puffy around the eyes, standing almost motionless in a dress styled for a Sophie Tucker or a Kate Smith, Judy Garland bowed into the Met, the inside of which she had never before visited, in the month of May. The unseeing saw nothing, and let their imaginations and memories take the place of perception. Even *Variety* called her a "whammo click," but could not refrain from saying that she looked a bit "Wagnerian," not unlike an "oversized kewpie."

In fact, Judy Garland was desperately ill and at the Met she gave what she herself has called "a terrible concert." In the middle of a performance she would feel nausea and dizziness. "Sometimes I felt as if I was performing in a blizzard. You are never so alone as when you are ill on stage. The most nightmarish feeling in the world is suddenly to feel like throwing up in front of 4,000 people."

It was, however, only on the next-to-the-last step in a disastrous decline. In the trying Fifties, Judy had worried too much, taken too many diet pills, too many tranquilizers, too many nerve tonics. She had quarreled with too many theatre managers and too many television officials, all the while carrying on a rancorous battle with her husband. Oppressed by almost every conceivable type of worry, not excluding constant financial harassment, she had abused her voice and her figure, turning into an awkward, ballooning caricature of the graceful Judy Garland of old. By the fall of 1959, she was unable to work at all, and in November she was admitted to the hospital. There she discovered that one more thing was wrong with her. For almost three years, she had been staggering about with a virulent case of hepatitis, a disease which can take a terrible toll of the most rugged constitution.

Sober-faced, the doctors came to Judy with their conclusions. For the rest of her life, all physical activity would have to be curtailed. Food and drink would be strictly regulated. She must learn to accept the fact that she was a permanent semi-invalid. It went without saying that under no circumstances would she ever be able to work again.

Startling as the verdict was, Judy's reaction was no less a surprise—she was immensely relieved. For twenty-five years she had worked too hard, and now she could no longer work. Responsibility was lifted from her shoulders. With a weak gasp she fell back, sank into the pillows, and let her tormented body relax.

For five months, she remained in the hospital, followed by four more months of rest at her home in Beverly Hills. Virtually everywhere else in the world, Judy Garland was in demand. In Hollywood, she was dearly loved, but not needed. She made her first public appearance in July to campaign for her friend John F. Kennedy.

Then suddenly, she boarded a plane and flew to London. Her hepatitis seemed to be a thing of the past, but the flight represented something far more important. For ten years she had had a series of phobias, a fear of going on stage, a fear of entering stores and cars, and, above all, a fear of flying. Now her resolute flight to London showed that her confused mental state was clearing up.

In the English capital, Judy's recuperation became complete. London, always extremely hospitable to her as a performer and as a woman, had become her favorite city. It gave her something she had not felt since leaving Grand Rapids, Minnesota, almost a lifetime ago, a feeling of stability, of having roots.

From director Sir Carol Reed, she received the loan of a house in the colorful Chelsea district. There was another reconciliation with Sid Luft, and soon he joined her in England, along with the children, who enrolled in an English school. Judy settled down to the life of a London housewife, walking the dogs she had bought, shopping in Mayfair, taking the children to Battersea Park and watching them acquire mild English accents. The interlude, which lasted almost a year, was one of the most pleasant in her life. By the fall of 1960, she was still comfortably chubby, but her sickly pallor was giving way to a healthful glow. The roller coaster was starting a climb.

One sleepless night, she left her bed to take a shower. The hot, steamy water poured down, relaxed muscles and nerves, and for the first time in many months, Judy began to sing, running playfully through old arrangements, occasionally testing to see what sounds her long-unused throat could bring forth. A half hour later, she woke husband Sid Luft to hand him a list of songs. In the shower, she had worked out the program that was to send the roller coaster shooting to a dazzling new pinnacle.

At the familiar Palladium, on August 28, 1960, Judy played her new show to a happy crowd. "It was a pistol," she herself declared. For two hours and fifteen minutes she sang her thirty songs, with only a short intermission. At the end, two thousand people united in a deep-throated cheer, far different from the high-pitched squealing and yelling of the rock-and-roll audiences.

From the English provinces, she went to Paris, where she gave two concerts at the 2,700-seat Palais de Chaillot Theatre. Returning to London, she was awaited by a visitor from New York named Freddie Fields. A former talent agent for the Music Corporation of America, young Fields had left that giant complex to set up shop on his own as agent, business adviser, and personal manager. The alert, witty young executive struck up an immediate rapport with Judy and became her manager, returning to New York and a whirlwind of activity on her behalf. He settled the three-year legal war with CBS, negotiated a promising new TV spectacular, signed Judy for a role in

Judgment at Nuremberg, her first Hollywood movie in seven years, and booked her for a fourteen-city, six-week concert tour designed to show the world that Judy Garland still had it, and, not so incidentally, to pay off her outstanding bills.

In February 1961, in Dallas, Judy gave her new marathon show for the first time before an American audience. A newspaper review the next day declared, "No entertainer has ever given such a show in Dallas." Two nights later, four standing ovations followed another dazzling marathon performance in Houston, where a stagehand, so enthralled by Judy that he unwittingly got rolled up in the curtain, struggled for ten minutes before his muffled cries for help were heard.

Looking trimmer and younger than she had in years, Judy came to New York in April and gave a concert at Carnegie Hall that was one of the most remarkable events in the history of show business and a shining highlight in her own highlight-studded career. Fortunately, a recording, *Judy at Carnegie Hall,* recalls for the faithful their emotional frenzy and hysteria of that memorable night, and serves as proof to the doubting Thomases that the incredible evening of April 23rd really took place. Without such corroboration, an accurate account of the proceedings might easily be looked upon as a fanciful exaggeration.

From the moment the superb thirty-nine-piece orchestra under Mort Lindsay struck up the overture, interweaving "The Man That Got Away," "The Trolley Song," and "Over the Rainbow," the applause of the capacity 3,165 spectators began to fill the famed hall.

Twenty-four programmed songs, two encores, and six standing ovations later, with still no letup in the applause, Judy was forced to say, "We just haven't got much more."

"Just stand there!" pleaded an admirer, and as the "Rainbow" theme filled the auditorium, a triumphant Judy Garland just stood there and shouted above the din, "Good night, I love you very much." Suddenly the aisles were mobbed with people. From the balconies they stormed down, rushing toward the stage, where they shouted and clapped and reached out to touch the hand of the great entertainer who had given a performance that would not soon be forgotten. And leaning over the footlights, Judy Garland reached out her hands, too, and happily touched the thing that had provided the most profound and enduring pleasure in her stormy life, the audience.

The lightning which struck at Carnegie miraculously struck again, sixteen times in sixteen cities. The high-priced *Judy at Carnegie Hall* album became the fastest-selling two-record LP in history, pushing the two-million mark in sales, winning a slew of Grammy Awards, and almost every other token of acclaim the recording industry can offer.

In the spring of 1961, Judy went before a Hollywood camera for the first time in six years, playing the role of a drab German housewife in Stanley Kramer's *Judgment at Nuremberg*. For her nine-minute role she was paid $50,000, far less than she usually received. It was a calculated move on the part of Judy and manager Freddie Fields. Abby Mann's screenplay took a thought-provoking, controversial second look at the question of guilt and responsibility in Nazi Germany. The film was an important Hollywood production, and an excellent opportunity to prove to producers that Judy was a stable, reliable professional actress.

"The actress I needed," declared producer-director Kramer, "had to have both a substantial dramatic quality and the ability to 'break' in front of the camera. To me Judy Garland seems an almost obvious choice, but most people forget she was a tremendous dramatic actress. And the quality she possesses isn't growing on trees. Apart from that, I happen to think she is the world's greatest performer."

The film was completed on schedule and without incident. By the end of the year, Judy had made close to a million dollars, and most wondrous of all, some of it was finally hers to keep. For the first time in her adult career, she was out of debt. To Freddie Fields and his associate, David Begelman, she confided that with all the millions she had made, she had never actually seen any of it. At one of their concert dates, the two appeared in Judy's suite with a large brown paper bag filled with bills—fives, tens, twenties. Running her hands through real money, an ecstatic Judy sent it cascading into the air in a delirium of joy and laughter.

The money was to go into trust funds for her three children, who, she declared again and again, were the most important thing in her life. When she was so ill that doctors told her she would never work again, it was for them that she determined to get well. "I have no ambition to be an actress," she said, "no ambition to be a singer. I have absolutely no drive. I just want to be a mother."

One testimonial to her love for her children is the fact that over the years she has constantly uprooted them to take them with her in her travels, feeling always that she should be near to give them a mother's affection and care. Another is the long, sad, debilitating fight she waged with husband Sid Luft for their custody.

The youngest, Joe, now twelve, has taken after both his parents, with an interest in machines emanating from his pilot father, and a love of music coming from Judy, while fourteen-year-old Lorna has all the characteristics her famous mother ascribes to an actress—"imagination, fiendishness, and curiosity."

Judy's oldest daughter, Liza Minnelli, was born in a trunk. At the age of sixteen months, she made a brief debut in *The Pirate*. In *Easter Parade* she was wheeled across Metro's back lot in a scene with the two most expensive bit players in the film, producer Arthur Freed and songwriter Irving Berlin. In addition to learning from being with Judy and performing with her, Liza studied dancing at the New York School for the Performing Arts, and also gave a moving portrayal of Anne Frank in a school production.

At twenty-two, she can already boast of a career of her own. She has appeared on television programs, in summer stock, and starred in a highly successful revival of the old George Abbott

hit, *Best Foot Forward,* at New York Stage 73. Her father, director Vincente Minnelli, flew in from Hollywood for the
opening on April 2, 1963, and the next night Judy sat in the
fourth row on the aisle to listen to Liza sing "You Are For
Loving" and the rousing "Who Do You Think I Am?" "She's a
heartbreaker," Judy said happily. "Liza's the first one to do
this. I never had a Broadway show." Technically, Stage 73 was
an off-Broadway production. In 1965, however, the name Minnelli shone brightly on a Broadway marquee as the star of
George Abbott's new musical, *Flora, The Red Menace.*

Years ago, when Liza was only three, Judy was asked if she
and her husband had any objections to their daughter's becoming an actress. "Objections?" interjected a surprised Judy.
"I've never thought for a minute that she would be anything
else. Her father and I could wish her nothing more wonderful
than the talent for a creative career of her own. She's only
three, but already she loves the studio. Until she is thirteen or
fourteen, she will have to confine her 'emoting' to pictures we
are handling. Then, if she still wants to be an actress, and I am
sure she will, she can work with other players."

And speaking more generally, she stated, "When actors say 'I
wouldn't think of allowing my daughter or son to go on the
stage or into the movies,' then something must be radically
wrong with them. They have found no happiness in their own
career, these people." For Judy, performing before an audience
has been one of the most intensely satisfying things in her life.
It is unlikely that she would deny the same experience to her
children, although she has often warned of its pitfalls and repeatedly said that she feels it would be wiser to begin a career
a little later than her own early start so that the children might
have more of the normal pleasures of childhood.

"If they approach acting," she has stated recently, "I would
want them to be aware of the responsibilities of a career and
the little hurtful things that can happen. They have to be
taught what true professionalism is—good manners at work,
thinking of other people, your co-workers in a production.

There are people who have been acting for years and have never achieved this. I may be many things people disapprove of, but I have always tried to be professional.

"So if they are talented, teach them and encourage them," she concluded, speaking of child actors in general. "If they are not talented, get them into another line quick."

Throughout 1962, Judy's line, acting and singing, was in constant demand. She continued to tour the country with her marathon performances, and the reception continued to be phenomenal.

There were successful nightclub and television appearances, and Stanley Kramer called her back to film *A Child Is Waiting* with Burt Lancaster. Her performance was well modulated and received praise from the critics. For Kramer, who had expressed unquestioning faith in her, Judy had the utmost gratitude. "I told him the other day," she said, "if he wanted to do a story about lepers, all he'd have to do is call me and I'd do a walkthrough for him." Late in the year she provided the voice for a svelte, silvery Persian cat named Mewslette in the film *Gay Purr-ee.*

I Could Go On Singing, the last picture Judy Garland has made, was adapted from a television play called *The Lonely Stage.* "She is a harrowing good actress," said Penelope Gilliatt in the English paper, *The Observer.* Some indication of the film's merit, however, could be garnered from the banal lyrics of the title song, "I could go on singing till the cows come home, and the roosters start to crow," written by Harold Arlen, who had done much better.

Near the end of one of Judy's concerts under the stars, a giant moth, attracted to the single beam of light that formed a halo for Judy as she sang "Over the Rainbow," fluttered blithely into her wide-open mouth. The crowd, lachrymose with the abidingly beautiful sentiment of the song, was unaware of Judy's discomfort. With the quick presence of mind of the professional, she tucked the fuzzy-winged creature behind her teeth like a piece of chewing gum, and sang the final twenty-eight bars without a flaw in the phrasing. The minute that the dramatic halo effect went dark, she spat, coughed, gasped, and stamped her feet in an attempt to maintain control under the trying circumstances. When the lights went back on, she stood before the throng, smiling through her tears. It would be easy to see a simile with Judy's life in that circumstance. Nearing the rainbow, ready to go over into happiness, she always seems to run into a crisis.

With the Carnegie Hall concert, she had reached the top of the roller coaster. While she stayed there for a little while, almost inevitably she was forced to look down. As early as July 1961, she had been stricken with a kidney ailment, and taken by ambulance to a hospital from her summer home in Hyannis Port, Massachusetts, near her friends, the Kennedys. In November, an ear infection forced her to cancel a Jersey City appearance. Several weeks later, acute laryngitis caused the cancellation of a San Francisco show, while the ear ailment turned up again in Toronto. "I am physically exhausted," Judy said, as she checked into Columbia Presbyterian Medical Center for "a short rest" in April 1962.

After a brief period of recuperation at the hospital, her disputatious marriage exploded into the headlines. On a Saturday she went to her husband's apartment at New York's Stanhope Hotel for long conferences with Luft, representatives of United Artists film studios, and other business associates. Staying with Luft at the time were the couple's children. The next day, Sunday evening, reporters gathered at International Airport to watch Judy board a Pan American flight along with the three children. Wearing slacks and sandals, she draped dresses and sweaters over her arms, testifying to the haste of her departure. To the wide-eyed press, a representative issued the following statement on her behalf: "I am leaving for London earlier than originally scheduled and my three children will accompany me as previously planned. This is in spite of attempts of my estranged husband, Sid Luft, to take my two younger children,

Joe and Lorna Luft, away from me. I have been informed by my attorney that Mr. Luft has threatened to have me declared an unfit mother. This threat is so without foundation as to be completely ridiculous."

In London, Judy declared that the marriage was over. "It lasted eleven years and it would take eleven years to tell what went wrong," she stated. "There's no chance of a reconciliation. We've tried them and they don't work." Almost immedi‑ ately she took legal action to have the children made wards of the British court.

Hearing of Luft's arrival in London to reclaim the children, Judy announced that she would not see him. Moreover, she hired around-the-clock guards for the children, and moved them from an English country home near Epsom to her London hotel. Successful in her efforts to have them removed from the jurisdiction of the American courts, she entered into behind-the-scenes maneuvering with Luft, who alleged they had been kidnapped. By August the air had cleared somewhat, and the British wardship was lifted. Judy, having received permission for the children to leave the country, headed for a Nevada vacation retreat.

JUDY GARLAND STRICKEN, HINT OVERDOSE read the headline in the New York *Post* on September 16, 1962. Found unconscious on the floor of a friend's home near Lake Tahoe, the star was rushed to the Carson-Tahoe Hospital. Friends reported that she had been distraught and nervous for weeks. Judy herself later stated that crash dieting without the benefit of medical supervision had resulted in a kidney attack which had felled her.

The following February, Judy tripped in her three-room suite at New York's Sherry Netherland Hotel, where she was found lying unconscious on her bed, at nine in the evening, by the hotel maid. Her younger children were absent, having gone off to see their sister, Liza, in *Carnival* at the Mineola Playhouse. Oxygen was administered and Judy was carried to Mount

Sinai Hospital on a stretcher, suffering cuts on her forehead and mouth. Doctors at first feared cerebral bleeding, but later released her after treatment for minor wounds.

On February 13, the embattled Lufts were once more reconciled, but the following month Judy again had recourse to a doctor in her suite at the St. Regis Hotel. Under great strain, she had flown to London for the premiere of *I Could Go on Singing*, then rushed back to give a party for daughter Liza, making her professional theatre debut. After the exciting activity, there was a sudden emptiness, a letdown which led to illness. Seemingly, the solitude of a hotel room could still evoke panic in the former child performer, even though the room was part of a suite in a princely palace like the St. Regis.

Inevitably, the mounting personal and professional pressures took their toll on Judy Garland, as usual impairing first her health and then her work.

At Harrah's Tahoe she had been forced to cancel a 1963 engagement after only one week, with her old-time co-star Mickey Rooney stepping in to sub for her. In March she stopped one of England's top TV shows, a live production of *Sunday Night at the London Palladium*, when she twice missed song cues and turned the wrong way leaving the stage, before the all-seeing live cameras.

An American TV special, a week later, was called "disappointing" by *Times* TV critic Jack Gould, and as the months wore on there was trouble in the taping of a thirty-two-show TV series for which James Aubrey, then president of CBS Television, had signed her earlier in the year in a much-heralded million-dollar deal.

For years, skeptics had been saying that the perfectionist Judy was too temperamental to carry off an hour television show every week, that she wouldn't hold up under the unremitting pressure. The courage she displayed in going on a demanding series was signaled by the real terror that the medium could evoke in her. "The other day I had to do a fifteen- to twenty-second trailer for the show. Now you'd think you could knock that off in a hurry. It took me ten hours. I was supposed to be relaxing next to a piano. I was so nervous I was holding on! I had a few words to say, but I couldn't get them out. I stutter like the dickens, anyway. Finally, they asked me if I wanted an idiot card [an industry term for a prompting sheet held behind camera]. I got very incensed."

The Garland humor was again evident when she told of some of her other problems with the medium. "If you sing as loud as I do, you can hardly hope to look good to a camera a few inches away from your face while you are doing it . . . seven cameras glaring at you from all angles, and only a tiny red light to tell you which to look at, probably the one behind your back."

To launch the series, Judy reached far into her past. "I can't do the first one with anybody but Mickey," she said. "He's my partner." *Life* reported the nostalgic encounter, as onto a CBS set in Hollywood sauntered a balding, thickset, but youthful-appearing Mickey Rooney, to be followed moments later by an anxious Judy, nervously puffing away at a cigarette. "Mommy!" Mickey shouted happily. "Sweetheart!" returned Judy, and the fabled pair fell into an embrace that seemed to wipe away the long and violent years.

During the taping of the show, Rooney kept up a series of running gags and quips that broke up the cast and delighted Judy, dispelling all suggestions of the tension which so often hangs over a Garland performance. For the final taping, the elite of Television City gathered in the studio. When it was over, the hard-boiled professionals paid tribute to the two veteran troupers with a tremendous ovation. Mickey took Judy's hand. "This is the love of my life," he said. "There isn't an adjective in the world to express my love for Judy. She's Judy, and that's all there is to say."

When the highly touted series finally made its debut on September 29, it fell victim to the vicious ratings game, running behind the NBC competitor, the top-rated *Bonanza*, and fighting to outrate ABC's *Arrest and Trial*. The candid Judy commented; "You know, I used to watch *Bonanza* all the time, and if my show doesn't get better, I'll go back to watching *Bonanza.*"

At CBS, talent chief Michael Dann and president James Aubrey announced that they wanted to change the show's format. In an extraordinary statement, Dann outlined his views: "We're trying to give Judy a program with a weekly thread to make her more acceptable in the hinterland. In the second thirteen weeks we decided that she should never appear in sketches and never play any character but herself. And she'll be singing more medleys, more standards. Songs are her goodies, her babies. We told her what we think and she's listening. She's far too insecure about TV to exercise her own judgment. She knows we know what's good for her."

This type of pronouncement could make even a steel-nerved performer insecure, and at the CBS executive offices a nervous, ninety-seven-pound Judy crossed and recrossed her legs as she heard of the plans to increase her appeal to the hinterland, which had insatiably gobbled up her every effort for a quarter of a century. "I'm the original take-orders girl," she declared. "CBS knows more about television than I do. . . . If [they] said dye your hair blond, I'd do it."

Judy followed orders, and the show continued to be a disappointment. "Since show's premiere, the singing has been outstanding," wrote *Newsweek*, "but merely talking, even walking, Judy seems uncomfortable, and on occasion, as she tugs at her ear, or brushes her forehead, almost unnerved."

In late January 1964, exercising an option in her contract, she sent a letter to Jim Aubrey saying she wanted to drop the show, ostensibly because its Sunday nine-to-ten slot kept her from her children. After a run of twenty-six weeks, at $30,000 per show for the star, the Judy Garland Show hit the screens for the last time on March 29th. Ironically, the taped programs which appeared after the decision had been made to cancel emphasized Judy's singing in rousing production numbers and were highly praised. They also picked up in the ratings.

Corporate decisions are hard to change, however, and the show was replaced by hastily devised substitutes and reruns.

Shortly thereafter, Judy left the country to extend her concert performances to the far corners of the world. At Melbourne, Australia, a dramatic series of incidents inaugurated an entirely new and highly original chapter in the life of Judy Garland. On her previous tours, she had been accompanied by her managers, Freddie Fields and David Begelman, debonair young men with whom she had an easy rapport. Because she considered them precociously bright, she nicknamed them Leopold and Loeb, and they in turn invented a Judy Garland kit for her—one long eyelash, a tear-soaked handkerchief, a used Lifesaver, a baby fan, and a tiny bottle of Liebfraumilch, virtually the only drink Judy dared touch after her bout with hepatitis. When the going got rough, these two knew how to smooth things over with laughter and wit and a great managerial capability. Unfortunately, neither of them accompanied Judy to Australia.

For her Melbourne concert, the star arrived an hour late, to be met by an impatient crowd of 70,000 who greeted her with shouts of "You're late," and "Have another brandy." "I love you too," Judy replied, but the Aussies were not in the mood for humor. After fluffing several notes in her first songs, she tried again to joke, toying with the mike in the gesture many of her fans know and love. "Sing, sing," shouted the hecklers. "Get on with it." While most of the crowd was won over with old favorites like "For Me and My Gal" and "You Made Me Love You," the heckling went on. After forty-five minutes, an exhausted Judy walked off the stage and the orchestra was left to play the "Rainbow" theme to the angry, shouting crowd.

Nursing a sore throat, clearly in bad voice, she had nonetheless tried to carry on and give a performance. The manager of the tour, Karl Brent, stated that she would have stayed and sung all night had she been given any warmth or encouragement. "I didn't like it," Judy said sadly. "I sang a song called

'I'll Go My Way by Myself,' put the microphone down, and got the hell out of it."

From Melbourne she flew to Sydney where she gave a concert without incident, and then to Hong Kong. From that city, ABC correspondent Stanley Rich sent a cable which was swiftly translated into headlines in America. Judy Garland was unconscious, in critical condition in a local hospital where doctors had administered oxygen, worked over her for two hours, and finally brought her out of a fifteen-hour coma. Outside, a typhoon was roaring, with ninety-mile-an-hour winds battering the city.

On May 28th, a new figure appeared in Judy's life, a young actor named Mark Herron, whom the press described as her traveling companion. "Her condition is awful," Herron was quoted as telling a reporter. "She is very bad, very bad. The doctors won't tell me anything." In a sobbing voice, he asked the reporter to call Freddie Fields right away.

Next day, the relieved Herron again spoke to the press. "She's much, much better today. I talked to her a little while today. She can't talk much. But she was smiling. It looks like she's going to be all right." Reports of an overdose of sleeping pills were denied, as were reports that Judy had suffered a heart attack. Once again, exhaustion, it was said, had felled the star.

Her physician, Dr. Lee Siegel, flown in from Hollywood, characterized her ailment as pleurisy, a chest inflammation usually accompanied by high temperatures and difficulty in breathing. Siegel prescribed an extended rest and held off delivering a piece of bad news to Judy. Her sister, Mrs. Sue Cathcart, forty-eight, had died two days earlier in Las Vegas, Nevada, leaving Judy and her sister, Mrs. Virginia Thompson of Dallas, as the only surviving members of the old vaudeville team known as the Gumm Sisters.

On June 11th, the incredible saga of gung-ho Judy in old Hong Kong took a bizarre new turn. To an incredulous world came the news that she had married Mark Herron. It was not explained how this could have happened at a time when she was still legally married to Sid Luft.

Recovered to an astonishing extent from her most recent illness, her weight back up to ninety-eight pounds from a frail seventy-eight only days before, Judy made an appearance at a Hong Kong night club with Herron. An account of the event in the New York *Daily News* said that Judy, flushed and clearly enjoying herself, indulged in an old habit, joining in the entertainment and singing "Over the Rainbow" for the delighted crowd. "We've been married five days now," she declared, pointing out the matching jade rings worn by Herron and herself. "I'm very happy."

In a telephone interview from Hong Kong, Herron confirmed reports of the marriage, although he appeared remarkably vague about when it took place, or where. "We were married about six days ago—I don't know what day it was," the actor was quoted as saying. "It was on board a ship. We had rented it for the day. We were just anchored in the harbor here in Hong Kong. It was sundown. I don't know the name of the ship. A very nice Chinese fellow stood up for me. I don't know his name."

Vague as he was about the matter of the ceremony, Herron's memory was excellent when it came to minor details, such as Judy's wedding outfit. "She wore a tan suit," he declared, "and she looked just lovely. We're both very happy and excited."

Less elated were others involved in the proceedings. Flabbergasted would more accurately describe their reactions. Judy's New York lawyer, Irving Erdheim, said that he'd have to check to see if a Mexican divorce from Sid Luft had come through. Manager Freddie Fields simply stated, "It's impossible. Judy isn't divorced from Sid Luft yet." And one of her press agents, Guy McIllwaine, gasped, "It must be a gag."

For those of little faith, a further surprise was in store the following day. From Hong Kong's Mandarin Hotel, where Judy was staying, came word that she had been married to Herron a second time in a traditional Chinese ceremony with candles and josh sticks. The earlier ceremony, it was reported, had taken place on June 6th aboard the 18,000-ton Norwegian cargo ship *Bodo*, three miles off the Hong Kong coast, where a Captain Naavik had performed the wedding ritual, with the crew as witnesses.

With mystery trailing behind, Judy and Herron now sailed on board the liner *President Roosevelt* for Tokyo. Back in Hong Kong, the marine department stated it could find no record of the *Bodo*, on which the first ceremony presumably took place outside Hong Kong territorial waters, and a government spokesman said that in any event it was only a widely held myth that ships' captains have the authority to marry people. As for the second ceremony, the spokesman declared, the colony's law had long recognized Chinese-style traditional marriages as being for Chinese only, and even local residents were no longer relying on the ancient form based on worship for ancestral tablets. On board ship, Judy dismissed repeated questions about the marriage certificates by saying they were "locked away."

After a few days in Japan, Judy clarified the circumstances surrounding the puzzling twin marriage ceremonies. "Mr. Herron and I were blessed in Hong Kong by a Buddhist priest for my recovery from a serious illness," she stated in an interview reported in the *Daily News*. "We were blessed for our life together, but we were not married. We are engaged to be married and will be married later." Together, she declared, they might do a play in London.

For the legions of Judy's admirers who wondered about Mr. Herron, there was not much to go on. A graduate of theatre groups in Los Angeles and Arizona, the tall, dark, slender actor, in his late twenties, went to Europe in 1963 and took a bit part in Federico Fellini's film, 8½. When Fellini came to Hollywood the following spring for the Academy Award ceremonies, he told Herron that he would like to meet Judy Garland. Through actor Roddy McDowall, Herron arranged the meeting. As a consequence, he himself met Judy and accompanied her when she began her Australian tour. While early reports described him as her traveling companion, the press gradually added the titles of tour manager and bodyguard.

In her volcanic forty-three years, Judy Garland has already lived a good number of the cat's traditional nine lives. Her handmaiden, Fate, may have singled out the obscure young actor to play a leading role in yet a new chapter, and perhaps he will help her to reach still another crest of achievement. In the past, with the odds heavily against her, she has shown a startling ability to come back and confound the chartmakers. But then, when it comes to Judy Garland, it may be just as well to throw away the charts.

6.

LITTLE LORD BARTHOLOMEW

One of the most highly applauded roles of English-born boy actor Freddie Bartholomew's career was that of the hero of Frances Hodgson Burnett's celebrated tale, *Little Lord Fauntleroy*. As Cedric Errol, he incarnated the carefully etched portrait of an American boy brought from the wilds of nineteenth-century Brooklyn to the hallowed halls of Dorincourt Castle, there to take up his burden as Lord Fauntleroy, heir to the grizzly and gruff old Earl of Dorincourt. His graceful dignity and measured youthful spirits, it was said, fitted him perfectly for the role. In private life, Freddie Bartholomew made somewhat the reverse trip. From a lower-middle-class upbringing in England, he was transported to the wilds of Hollywood, there to take up the mantle of youthful stardom on the Metro-Goldwyn-Mayer lot, but like Little Lord Fauntleroy, not before overcoming a series of obstacles that necessitated his calling for help from the denizens of his humble birthplace. If anything, Freddie's struggle to come into his rightful inheritance was even more grim than that of his fictional counterpart. Rarely has a child performer been so relentlessly exploited.

In the opening reel of his own saga, Freddie first saw daylight in a smoky factory section of London, on March 28, 1924. His father, Cecil Llewellyn, was a minor government employee, a veteran of World War I who had had one leg shot away serving with the Canadians during the Battle of the Somme. Freddie's mother, Lillian Mae, was a small, intense woman who already had her hands full with two daughters, Eileen, three years old, and Hilda, one. When Freddie's grandparents and aunt offered to take him under their wing, she let him go.

Freddie was three when he moved in with Mr. and Mrs. Frederick R. Bartholomew in their comfortable little country home at Warminster, Wiltshire, one hundred miles from London. His father's sister, his Aunt Myllicent, also lived in the modest house called Carlton Villa, and it was she who took charge of Freddie. She soon noticed his easy ability to read and memorize and, although she had had no dramatic training herself, she decided to prepare him for the stage. She taught him a faultless, precise diction. She emphasized poise and good manners. She acquainted him with many of the short pieces from the classic repertoire.

Soon after his arrival at Warminster, Freddie recited a poem at an entertainment. Thereafter, he was readily available for benefits and concert parties, as well as for walk-ons in films which happened to be shooting on location in the area. He appeared briefly in *Toyland, Fascination,* and *Let's Go Naked,* hardly a budding career, but enough to make his elders reflect on the financial promise of his young professional life. Accordingly, they signed an agreement dividing the potential future spoils. Aunt Cissie, as Myllicent was familiarly called, was to receive the first $2,500 earned in any year plus one third of the remainder. The grandparents were also to receive one third of the remainder in exchange for providing the boy with an education and support. The last third was to be put into a trust for the little wage earner himself. No provision was made in the agreement for any monies to go to the parents, and father Cecil, who had signed the agreement, had neglected even to inform his wife of the move. As a consequence, she was at first properly outraged. On considering the matter, however, she did not raise much of an outcry. The times were bad, with a depression lurking over the country, and it looked pretty much as though the principals to the agreement were splitting nothing into three different portions. When Aunt Cissie announced in 1934 that she would like to take Freddie to the United States to visit relatives in Scarsdale, it seemed a good idea all around, and both parents gave their consent.

As it happened, Aunt Cissie did not come back at the end of two months, nor at the end of four, nor at the end of six. When word did reach the smoke-shrouded home of the London Bartholomews, it was startling news indeed. Their little boy, their little Freddie, was an American movie star! Moreover, he was earning not little piles of pennies, but pots of pounds. For his first role, the lead in *David Copperfield,* he had signed a seven-year contract running from $175 a week to $500 a week. After the success of his second film, *Anna Karenina,* in which he had skillfully portrayed Greta Garbo's son, a new contract was drawn up giving him $1,000 per week. Further successes in *Professional Soldier,* with Victor McLaglen, in *Oliver Twist, Lloyd's of London,* and *Little Lord Fauntleroy,* had again boosted the salary figure. Here, indeed, was a howdy-do.

More disturbing still was a second bombshell dropped in their midst. In October 1935, Myllicent Bartholomew went to a California court, declared that she had had exclusive care and custody of her nephew for eight years, and asked the court to make her the legal guardian. The notice from Judge Thomas P. White which the London Bartholomews received told them that they had twenty days in which to appear in the American court to contest the action. Since the mails bringing them the notice had taken fifteen days, they were hard put to take swift action, finally settling on a written affidavit which they sent to the court. It declared in no uncertain terms that they opposed the guardianship; that Aunt Cissie had not told them what she was up to when she had left England with their son, a virtual contract from MGM in her pocket; and that they had had no intention of parting with him permanently. "Trickery and deceit," they declared, had been used to deprive them of their son. The judge decreed that a written affidavit could not take the place of a personal appearance in court and awarded Myllicent Bartholomew the legal guardianship of her nephew. He did, however, stipulate that the parents had six months in which to present formal and legal opposition to the guardianship.

Only a few days before the end of the time limit, in early April 1936, the newspapers were suddenly ablaze with the impending arrival in America of the parents of child star Freddie Bartholomew, come to these shores to claim their own.

On April 8th, three hours before the scheduled debarkation of the Bartholomews, their New York attorney issued a statement purportedly coming from his clients. It repeated their earlier charges and quoted Mrs. Bartholomew to the effect that her husband was a badly wounded war veteran whose disability had caused them to turn temporary custody of Freddie over to the grandparents and aunt, never, however, with the intention of such separation being permanent.

Lest there be any misunderstanding on the delicate point of finances, Mrs. Bartholomew was quoted as saying, "My visit here is not actuated from a monetary standpoint, nor do I wish to deprive his Aunt Myllicent of any of the rightful and proper benefits which may accrue to her as a result of his success. I do not desire to embarrass my boy's career, but feel that his love and affection should not be weaned away from his parents." Mrs. Bartholomew further announced her intention of proceeding to California where she would try by amicable settlement to reestablish her parental rights, and, failing that, go to court.

It was the only contact the lawyer was to have with his elusive client for some time. When he had cabled Mrs. Bartholomew that he would meet her, he had received a curt and somewhat mysterious return cable saying, PLEASE REFRAIN FROM MEETING BOAT. WILL TELEPHONE YOU ARRIVAL HOTEL. As a result, he was not at the dock to welcome Mrs. Bartholomew, a dark-haired woman of medium height, in her middle thirties. Mr. Bartholomew was also absent, having remained in England due to lack of funds and ill health. The missus, however, swiftly outlined their position as she debarked from the North German Lloyd liner *Europa*.

Since leaving England, neither Freddie nor his aunt had written to them, she declared. Their own letters and cables had gone unanswered and phone calls had been refused. The resulting embarrassment was particularly disturbing to their two daughters, Eileen, now fifteen, and Hilda, fourteen. "When they tell their friends that Freddie Bartholomew, the now famous juvenile movie star, is their brother, they just laugh and advise them to tell it to the marines and do not believe he is any relative of ours," she related.

As for herself, it was a mother's heart that thumped away beneath her breast. "No one can love a child like his mother," she declared. "I am anxious to see Freddie and take him into my arms again. I shall not be deprived of my own flesh and blood." The money, of course, should not be completely overlooked. "My husband and I believe we deserve a small share of his income, but we want him because we love him."

Her strategy for regaining custody of the boy had a definite flair for the dramatic. "I will fight all the way to Washington," she told reporters. "I'm sure the President's wife will understand me because she's a mother, too." Her endeavors had already won the sympathy of Frances Perkins, Secretary of Labor, with whom, she said, she had been corresponding. Having delivered herself of these statements, she departed, ostensibly for the Waldorf-Astoria, her stay there having been arranged by a former officer in her husband's regiment whom she told of having met on the boat.

The Bartholomews' New York lawyer was not very happy with the way things were going. Instead of the phone call which Mrs. Bartholomew's cable had promised, he now received a brief note from his erstwhile client. "Before seeing you *re* the legal aspects of my case," it stated, "I have decided to

visit Washington and accordingly am traveling there tonight.
You will hear from me in a few days. Meanwhile, please do
nothing." The note was written on Hotel Pennsylvania stationery. The injunction to do nothing was not obeyed. A call to the
hotel, however, revealed no clue to the mysterious behavior of
Lillian Mae Bartholomew. Similarly, at the Waldorf-Astoria
neither the principal in the case nor her friend from the boat,
whom reporters identified as a prominent London broker,
had registered. "I have been given the big double cross," the
lawyer summed up the matter.

The strange turn of events, most notably the disappearance
of Mrs. Bartholomew, caused as much consternation in England as it did in New York. In London, a worried Cecil Llewellyn Bartholomew cried out that his wife had been kidnapped.
The earlier cable, he asserted, did not "sound at all like her."
Through his English attorneys he sent a 146-word cable of his
own to their New York associate, imploring him, RELAY THIS
URGENTLY TO ALL LOS ANGELES EDITORS. His wife, he declared in
the cable, was scheduled to arrive on the 15th at the Hotel
Biltmore in Los Angeles. Evidently referring to his former
army associate, he declared his wife had been TRAPPED AND
TRICKED BY UNSCRUPULOUS PEOPLE AND RESTRAINED FROM COM-
MUNICATING with him. While she was not supposed to discuss
any aspect of the case during the boat trip, he feared that he
had influenced her against him during that voyage. Signif-
icantly, the broker had also disappeared from sight. The cable
urged editors to implore every father and mother with love
for their children to give Lillian Mae the following message:
FOR THE SAKE OF EILEEN AND DIMPS AND ALL YOUR FRIENDS WHO
HAVE HELPED US IN OUR FIGHT FOR FREDDIE, GO AT ONCE TO THE
POLICE AND ESTABLISH CONTACT WITH US. WE ARE ALL FRANTIC
WITH WORRY OVER HERE. LOVE AND TRUST. CECIL.

In addition to giving the message to Los Angeles editors, the
attorney gave it to all New York editors. He then called up the
Missing Persons Bureau of the Police Department and asked
for their help in finding his missing client. At the bureau, the

call elicited little excitement. "It is just a case of a lawyer looking for a client," a spokesman laconically told the press.

Meanwhile, at the Biltmore in Los Angeles, no one had heard of Mrs. Bartholomew. "Lily would not change her plans voluntarily," her husband commented. "There is no reason for her to dodge . . . the only person she was supposed to contact and the only person she knows in the United States."

Three days after her disappearance, the elusive Lily, whom one begins to suspect of having read a good many detective stories, strolled nonchalantly into the British Consul's office in Los Angeles and derisively branded the nationwide search for her as "publicity." Having traveled under an assumed name, she now brought a new firm of lawyers that she had engaged into the fray. Already on the scene, waiting to meet all comers, were the legal forces retained by Aunt Cissie. From New York came the lawyer who was still representing the absent father. If, as the principals in the case declared, love of little Freddie Bartholomew had motivated their actions, these legal minions were later to make it clear that they expected to be fully reimbursed.

For the moment, Aunt Cissie felt she needed additional non-legal support and sent a call for help to Freddie's grandparents. In due time, these two stalwart figures, Mr. and Mrs. Frederick Robert Bartholomew, set sail for America on the Cunard liner *Aquitania,* for a "vacation." When they arrived on April 15th they were greeted by swarms of reporters. "I'm not talking," Frederick Bartholomew explained to the assembled hordes. "I just came here for a holiday. Well, yes, I do hope to see Freddie. But I can't talk." With a violent tug at his arm, his wife reiterated that cautious point. "We didn't come here to see you," she declared aggressively. "Certainly not. We're on a holiday and we will not talk." Then to make sure that the point stuck, she marched her husband off the West 14th Street pier in New York and disappeared into silence.

On April 18th, Lillian Mae Bartholomew filed a court petition asking for the removal of Aunt Cissie as guardian of her son, charging he had been taken out of England under false pretenses. At no time, she stated, had she relinquished her rights to his guardianship, which had been taken over by Myllicent Bartholomew for her own profit, an action which made the latter not a fit and proper person to retain control. In a surprise move, the action was opposed not only by Aunt Cissie and the grandparents, but by Freddie's father as well. Affidavits denying Lillian Mae's arguments were read from all three, and several days later the Superior Court postponed action on the motion to set aside the guardianship until June 6th.

The continuing activity caused father Cecil Llewellyn to take a leave of absence from his job with the Ministry of Agriculture to join the exodus for Hollywood. En route he was quoted as saying, "I think my son's affairs should be handled by myself, and that is why I have come to America, why I am flying out to Hollywood." Obviously now more closely allied to his sister than to his wife, he stated: "I will stay with my sister when I get to Hollywood. I left my home on twelve hours' notice. I've sold my home and I left my two daughters in school in England. I want this matter straightened out. I will stay right here in America with my son if necessary, to see to it his welfare does not suffer."

The object of all this torrent of love and concern, twelve-year-old Freddie Bartholomew, was reported to be "on vacation." Louella Parsons confided to her readers that Aunt Cissie had spirited him out of the city to spare him unnecessary publicity and anxiety. Louella also testified to the devotion of Freddie and his aunt, who had been father and mother and brother and sister to him all rolled into one. Aunt Cissie herself said nothing, while MGM, fearful of antagonizing any of the parties involved, also maintained a discreet silence.

Shortly before the court was to hold a hearing on Lillian Bartholomew's petition to set aside the guardianship of Aunt Cissie, the relatives met and came to a surprise understanding that made further legal action unnecessary. Out of Freddie's approximate monthly earnings of $4,400, 10 percent was to go to the parents, and 5 percent to each of the two sisters. Aunt Cissie was granted approximately 10 percent per month for support and maintenance of herself and Freddie, whose personal custody the pact allowed her to retain. The remainder of his earnings were to go into a trust fund to be administered for him by the Union Bank and Trust Company in Los Angeles.

For a time, there was talk of the Bartholomews bringing their daughters to America and settling in Hollywood so that they could be near their son. After the division of Freddie's earnings, however, his parents together with the grandparents sailed for England.

If the tragicomic mess appeared to be over, in reality it had only just begun. First there was the sad business of the batteries of lawyers who had hovered over the contending clients. Their charges consumed over $26,000 of Freddie's earnings, an amount which later prompted Superior Judge Ben Lindsay to speak of a "travesty of justice."

Even more dismaying was the continuing series of lawsuits which now developed as a result of the original action. Aunt Cissie sued one contingent of lawyers to whom she had promised to pay a sum which was $200 more than her ward had in the bank at the time. A series of countersuits resulted from this move, which was complicated by further suits from agents who claimed percentages of Freddie's earnings. Pressured by her own needs and spurred on by more lawyers, Aunt Cissie quarreled with MGM to increase the young star's salary. In August 1937, the battle erupted into court before Judge Emmet H. Wilson, the guardian stating she wanted a raise from $1,100 to $3,000 a month, the studio contending that they had offered a flat $2,000 a month to be paid into Freddie's estate, an offer which Aunt Cissie had rejected, demanding that $1,500 be paid into the estate, the other $1,500 to be paid directly to her. Eventually, a compromise was worked out, but not before Freddie had been suspended, lost pay for "nonperformance," and been replaced in several important pictures. A similar train of events was to repeat itself at a later date, as one series of lawsuits bred another.

Earlier in the year, a Los Angeles court had allowed Aunt Cissie to legally adopt Freddie, an action which his parents once again contested. For a second time, the Bartholomews descended on Hollywood trying to regain custody, declaring that the aunt was poisoning their boy's mind and taking control of his estate in violation of the earlier out-of-court agreement. The adoption was upheld, but the suits and countersuits continued. At one time, the two sisters, whom the elder Bartholomew declared to be "way ahead of him in looks," sued their brother for monies they alleged were owed them and never paid.

In February 1938, Freddie, now fourteen, sent his attorneys into court to plead for an exemption from the payment of 10 percent of his income to his father. If forced to make the payment, his attorneys pleaded, he would have just about $2,000 left to show for five years of film work, and possibly be forced to go into debt. His assets, they asserted, included his 1938 earnings of $100,000, plus a bank balance of $18,800. His obligations included $67,000 in federal and state taxes, $15,000 in attorneys' fees, $9,800 in living expenses, $5,000 in agents' fees, a total of $96,800. In addition, there were pending claims by two agents for $39,000 and $4,700. After hearing the testimony, Superior Court Judge Clement D. Nye excused Freddie from sending the percentage payment to his father, the exemption to cover the year 1938 only, however.

By the fall of 1939, the harassed performer went into court once more and through his aunt sought an injunction which would declare a dozen or so actions still pending against him as being without merit. The fifteen-year-old Freddie stated that he had been able to save hardly a dime from his considerable earnings, that lawsuits filed against him had so far cost him a staggering $83,000 in attorneys' fees, and that these actions kept him in court so much that he did not have time to perform properly in movies. The extraordinary fact of the matter was that he had been in court an average of twice a month since he had come from England in 1934.

That Freddie Bartholomew was able to continue his career despite the savage onslaughts against his time and spirit is altogether amazing. That he was able not only to persevere, but to persevere with marked success is a profound tribute to his ability. Critic after critic paid homage to his talent as displayed in *David Copperfield, The Devil Is a Sissy, Captains Courageous, A Yank at Eton,* and many other films. "Freddie is one of those boys who, until this last generation, were typical of English boyhood," wrote Ruth Woodbury Sedgwick in an effusive *Herald Tribune* article, "that boyhood which first made England, and then went out and made an empire. You cannot define their quality without pilfering from the language of old ballads: they were manly, gentle, brave, true, full of honor and love of God." Considering Freddie Bartholomew's splendid, stoic demeanor during the trials, one is inclined to agree with the passionate praise of his admirer. To his Aunt Cissie, he maintained a steadfast loyalty. Toward his parents, a dignified reserve that never turned to cruelty or vindictiveness. To his work, he continued to bring a full devotion.

On January 13, 1943, Freddie was sworn into the United States Air Force, shortly after receiving his first citizenship papers. At eighteen, he had turned into a gangly six-footer. It was perhaps just as well that the call to service cut short a career which had lost its momentum and was no longer pointed in any meaningful direction.

Two years later, the returning soldier, like many other veterans, found that things at the old stand were no longer the same. He had outgrown his accustomed roles, and he was considered a bad risk by the movie moguls who remembered the legal hassles with MGM that Aunt Cissie and the lawyers had so often staged. After launching a theatre group on the West Coast, Freddie came east to tour with road companies as actor-director, and to hit the vaudeville and nightclub circuit.

Along the way he married twenty-eight-year-old Maely Daniele, who had been doing publicity for the coast group. A daughter was born early in the marriage—which ended in the early Fifties.

Although he had an important TV role in a production of *Outward Bound* in 1949, neither a substantial television career nor a call to Hollywood developed. With virtually all of the million dollars he had earned as a child star dissipated by the unholy procession of twenty-seven costly lawsuits, Freddie turned to regular employment as associate director on New York television station WPIX. His second marriage, to Eileen Paul, a fellow employee of the station, took place in December 1953, and two more children were born.

In 1964 Freddie Bartholomew returned to Hollywood, but not to make a film, nor to stage a comeback. Now a forty-year-old advertising executive with a major New York agency, he had come west to look at his company's filmed TV shows. At a party at *Rifleman* star Chuck Connors' home, he indicated that his stay would be brief, that he wanted to hurry home because his oldest daughter was about to start her first year in college. His children, he said, associated him "in some vague way with stars like Clara Bow and others of a long ago day." And to further attempts to churn up nostalgia, he softly replied, "I have many happy memories of Hollywood, but I much prefer what I'm doing now." For some of those present, the still perfect and precise Bartholomew diction recalled the past. For others, however, perhaps for most, it sounded very much like the suave, assured voice of Madison Avenue.

7.

EDNA MAE DURBIN, ALIAS DEANNA

Little twelve-year-old Edna Mae Durbin did not want to become a movie star. As Deanna Durbin she did not enjoy her decade of fame as a movie star. And today, as a happily married woman of forty-three, she vows that she will never go back to being a movie star. In the annals of child performers there is none who took success with such reluctance and even disdain. To Deanna Durbin, fame was an unwelcome intruder, the glamorous life a bore, success a cooked-up trumpery. When the right time came, she slammed the door on Hollywood with a bang that was heard halfway around the world.

Today she lives a quiet life of anonymity in a sleepy little village about a half hour's drive from Paris. The slim, girlish figure has turned somewhat corpulent. The brown hair, once parted in the middle in a style imitated by adoring youngsters all over the western world, is combed straight back, sometimes hidden by a kerchief. The lilting soprano voice, as beautiful as ever, now brings pleasure not to millions, but only to Deanna herself, her two children, and her husband, a French film director. To the villagers, Deanna is known as Madame David, a woman with a famous past who loathes publicity. She and her

family live in an old two-story farmhouse surrounded by a high
stone wall. A garage across the way notifies them when unknown visitors appear to be prowling about, but even under
ordinary circumstances Madame David does not answer the
phone or the door, nor grant interviews to the reporters who
persist in wondering if she plans a comeback. Monsieur David
has explained the desire for privacy to the villagers, who respect it to a truly remarkable degree, content to serve Madame
in their shops, which she frequents each day like the other
housewives of the neighborhood, seeking out bargains,
scouting about for the best cut of beef to serve to her family.
One reporter who inquired about the former star was told by
two of the local denizens that they had never heard of Deanna
Durbin. A third referred them to another location some thirty
miles away. Among the good people of her little village, one
might easily gain the impression that Deanna Durbin had
never existed.

Indeed, the really improbable elements in the story of the
girl born to the name Edna Mae Durbin, on December 4, 1921,
in Winnipeg, Canada, are those which form the chapter called
"Hollywood." Although, for reasons of her father's health, her
parents moved to Los Angeles when she was little more than a
year old, the proximity of the film capital had virtually no
effect on the thrifty, reticent, unassuming couple, good conservative middle-class English people who had migrated to Canada from their homeland city of Manchester not many years
before. British understatement was the order of the day, a far
cry from the flamboyant folkways of Hollywood. James Durbin, an obscure railroad-shop worker in Winnipeg, turned to
real estate in California. His wife, Ada, kept a neat, well-or-
dered house. Neither Edna Mae nor her sister Edith, two years
older, were drawn toward the hoopla of Hollywood premieres
and the favorite sport of the local youth, autograph collecting.
Edith did, however, admire her sister's lovely voice, already
quite full at ten, and told her she would help pay for singing
lessons. Edna Mae was delighted and dared sometimes to

dream of a far-off opera career. Meanwhile, she went to Bret Harte Junior High School, where she formed many happy childhood friendships, and earned spending money by serving as cashier in the student cafeteria.

While the Durbins were quietly and happily minding their own business, the restless natives of Hollywood were busily and noisily minding theirs. At Metro-Goldwyn-Mayer, someone decided that the life of the great opera singer, Madame Schumann-Heink, would make a wonderful movie. Word swiftly went out to the vast network of MGM talent scouts to find a young girl who could play the role of the renowned diva in her early years. To the neighborhood school where Edna Mae Durbin and others were giving a recital came scout Jack Sherrill. He listened to Edna Mae sing "Drink to Me Only," took her to the studio, and smiled knowingly as she was signed to an optional contract which could be renewed or dropped every three months for a year. Unfortunately, within two months, Madame Schumann-Heink died, and unaccountably the powers at MGM decided that this event also washed out the picture, which they had tentatively—and somewhat ludicrously—entitled *Gran*.

As a consequence, the little girl whose name they had changed to Deanna and whose birthdate they had stealthily moved up one year to make her seem younger, wandered about the studio for weeks with nothing to do except draw her paycheck. "I didn't belong at all," she later said. "It's the most dreadful feeling in the world."

Finally, she was put into a short with another youngster who wandered aimlessly about the lot, a pudgy girl named Judy Garland. The film was called *Every Sunday*. Studio officials took one look at it and decided to drop the option on Deanna's contract. Several weeks later, as a result of the move, they feared for their jobs if not for their lives. The head of the studio, Louis B. Mayer, returning from a vacation in Europe, screened the short and instructed his underlings to team the two youngsters in a feature film. When he heard that Deanna's option had been allowed to lapse without his knowledge, the turbulent L. B. put on a dramatic display that easily rivaled some of the more violent scenes from the studio's films. It was, however, too late.

Agent Sherrill had taken his protégée to one-time Metropolitan baritone Andres de Segurola to coach her fast-developing soprano. "She flats less often than Jeannette MacDonald; her diction is better than Grace Moore's," declared the reputed maestro. Fortified by advanced training and kind words, Sherrill presented Deanna to Eddie Cantor, who listened to her sing "Il Bacio" and signed her up for his popular Wednesday night radio program.

Much bigger things loomed on the horizon. At once-prosperous Universal Studios, sad notes were being sung. While few stars graced the payroll, quite a number of relatives of top executives were drawing fat salaries. Red ink splashed over the company accounts, dividends had been passed several times, and only a series of outmoded horror films were listed on the schedule of forthcoming productions. Finally, a group of New York bankers took over a bankrupted studio.

Into the midst of the new regime walked two strange figures recently arrived from Europe, a pint-sized Hungarian producer named Joseph Pasternak and a German director named Henry Koster who had not yet fully mastered the English language. They had been hired by the old regime of "Uncle" Carl Laemmle, film pioneer, but now ex-head of Universal. His successors asked Paternak and Koster to withdraw as gracefully as possible. When the stubborn foreigners refused to go, they were reluctantly given a bit of office space and allowed to languish, or so it seemed to them.

One day they were startled by a summons to the office of the company's new president, Charles Rogers, and even more widely awakened when they learned that what he would expect from them was a rousing good story idea. Chattering in German, they put their heads together and were immediately visited by inspiration. They would do a story about a girl! Nonsense, *two* girls. Three! Later, when Rogers asked them for a proposed plot line, Pasternak boldly announced that it would tell of three smart girls. There was a period of painful silence, during which the Hungarian producer hoped that the fruitful mind of his German colleague would bring forth an elaboration of the theme. When nothing came to break the heavy quiet, he told the uncomfortable Rogers not to worry about details, they would get all that down on paper, and present it to him later.

Remarkably enough, from this threadbare outline, scriptwriter Adele Commandini fashioned a delightful screenplay. Before it was finished, the two elated Europeans, happy to be at work, albeit on a low-budget picture, cast about the lot to find the physical embodiment of their lead roles. The picking, they found, was lean. In a moment of despair they thought of changing the story to have it revolve around three smart boys. Once more, however, fortune intervened, in the person of Rufus LeMaire, a former MGM executive who had just come over to Universal as casting director. LeMaire recalled two youngsters from the MGM lot who might be worth looking into, especially since he had heard that the option of one was about to be dropped. Both, moreover, were girl singers, and by now the story of three smart girls had turned into a musical.

When Pasternak viewed the screening of the first youngster, he jumped up with delight and yelled "That's it!" In every way, the girl had what he wanted, a good voice, a sweet face, spontaniety. Too bad, declared LeMaire. The girl's name was Judy Garland and she was the one whose contract MGM had decided to renew. The deflated Pasternak started to walk out, but LeMaire called him back. Convinced that lightning could not strike twice in so short a period, Pasternak sat glumly in the projection room—glum, that is, until he heard the crystalline soprano of the second youngster and saw her simple, natural charm and beauty reflected on the screen. Once more he jumped happily to his feet, and once more, fame reached out its hand for Deanna Durbin. The fourteen-year-old English born youngster took the hand pretty much as Joan of Arc had taken the flame: grim-faced.

"It looked hopeless," the now-defunct *Collier's* said in summing up her first, frigid meetings with executives at Universal. "When she came in with her mother to talk to Koster, it was even worse. She never said a word; she refused to talk when spoken to; she was obviously scared stiff." In an attempt to get their projected screen test underway, the puzzled Koster asked his potential new leading lady to leave the room, enter again, and sit down. Instead, to his increased bewilderment, she broke down and began to sob. "I don't want to be an actress," she cried. "You're all torturing me."

It was a strange beginning to a spectacular film career. The canny Pasternak saw through the tears to the golden treasure that had been unveiled before him. "When God gave us Deanna," he declared, "my world changed from humdrum to wonderful. I still pinch myself to make sure it's true." The filming of *Three Smart Girls* was postponed two weeks while Koster visited Deanna at home, bringing her tasty cookies that his wife had baked, coaching her gently in the rudiments of film making, and gradually breaking down her reserve.

As the early footage rolled in, it was readily apparent that Pasternak and Koster were justified in their attentions. The plot had Deanna playing the youngest of three sisters who make it their duty to keep a portly pater out of the clutches of a blonde gold digger. Using methods lifted from romantic films, pulp novels, and their own feverish imaginations, the three smart girls succeed in foiling their adversary, who is forced to look on as the youngsters steer their erring father back toward the wife he divorced ten years earlier. On screen, Deanna came across as simple and unaffected, pretty, with a reserved but notable charm, and an altogether glorious voice. The small budget for the film was upped from $150,000 to twice that amount as her role was repeatedly padded to give her more exposure. When the finished product was unveiled to the public in 1936, the verdict was unanimous: The floundering Universal Studio had come up with a sensational new star.

In *The New York Times*, Frank S. Nugent delivered a typical encomium. Deanna's manner he found "agreeably artless," her voice "velvety and bell-like," and perhaps most pleasing of all was "an ingratiating impudence which peppers her performance and makes it mischievously natural." Audiences throughout the land were in complete agreement as they sent more than $2 million pouring into the coffers of a revivified Universal, which hastened to put the gilded newcomer into her first official starring vehicle.

One Hundred Men and a Girl, at producer Pasternak's insistence, introduced the long-hair theme into a story that dwelt on the current economic depression. As the enterprising daughter of an unemployed trombone player, Deanna goes straight to Leopold Stokowski, noted maestro of the Philadelphia Symphony Orchestra, talks him into forming an orchestra of one hundred unemployed musicians, and sails merrily on her missionary way to get a radio sponsor for the new assemblage, feats which *Life* found were pretty much to be expected from the girl who had single-handedly lifted an entire film studio out of the red. While one exhibitor magazine proclaimed that the film had "made" Stokowski, there was universal acclaim for the delightful Deanna.

By now a formula for success had crystallized, and for the better part of the next decade, at the rate of two a year, it was repeated with only minor variations. Deanna played the part of a nice, wholesome girl growing up in a pleasant atmosphere. With a certain appealing impudence she faced the problems that came her way, solving them with spirit and imagination. Several times during the course of the action, she would lift her lilting soprano voice in song, judiciously mixing classical selections with popular refrains. It was all very entertaining, all very light. "They appreciate a picture that entertains them, that doesn't give them any problems," Pasternak said of the cinema audience.

It was Pasternak, too, who fought back the forces that wanted Deanna to grow up too fast, to become prematurely sophisticated. The story lines he secured for her were appropriate to her age, and left her always the same, the sort of good, wholesome youngster that others of her age might look up to.

The 1938 duo of films was *Mad About Music*, and *That Certain Age*, in which Deanna was allowed a girlish crush on an older man, Melvyn Douglas, while a quiet, unassuming boyfriend, in the person of Boy Scout Jackie Cooper, looked wistfully on. The following year came *Three Smart Girls Grow Up* and *It's a Date*, with Deanna vying with her mother, but only temporarily, for the affections of Walter Pidgeon. Finally, in 1940, a satisfied America saw Deanna receive her first screen kiss from newcomer Robert Stack, an event which received almost as much attention in some newspapers as the war in Europe. *First Love* was the subtle name of the epic, which was followed by *Spring Parade*, a Viennese costume musical.

In 1941, Deanna's screen maturing was continued with a film called *Nice Girl?* The story had Deanna accompanying suave Franchot Tone on a long automobile trip to New York City. While absolutely nothing happened in the course of that much-publicized ride, the daring producers felt it justified adding a suggestive question mark to the title of the picture. After *It Started With Eve* a captivating comedy with Charles Laughton, Pasternak left Universal for MGM, and Deanna Durbin's career henceforth was guided by other hands, not always as skillful as his.

The Amazing Mrs. Holliday and *Hers to Hold* in 1943 were not entirely successful in their attempt to give her more mature roles. The following year, *His Butler's Sister*, which marked a return to the old formula, was well received, but it was followed, not too happily, by a straight dramatic role with Gene Kelly in *Christmas Holiday*. "It is really grotesque and outland-

ish what they've done to Miss Durbin," wrote an irate Bosley
Crowther. "Imagine a sweet schoolgirl performing the role of
Sadie Thompson in *Rain*.

Can't Help Singing, in 1944, was an airy, outdoor musical
with a great many songs by Jerome Kern and E. Y. Harburg,
and very little plot. *Lady on a Train*, in 1945, had Deanna
playing in a mystery. *Because of Him*, in 1946, continued to
show up her severe limitations as an actress, and by the time
For the Love of Him appeared, in 1948, it was apparent that
she was rapidly losing her girlish charm and that the end of the
road was in sight. When her contract with Universal was up,
the still highly paid star went for a vacation to Europe, never
to return to the studio she had caused to prosper.

For the frenzied following which had banded itself into fan
clubs called "Deanna Durbin Devotees," some 300 scattered
around the globe, it was a terrible blow. They could still sub-
scribe to the *Deanna Journal*, which cost only 50 cents a year,
but what would the journal now have to report? And if there
were no more films how could they go to see them twice,
another requirement of membership? Of course, A. T. Held, of
Columbus, Ohio, the champion Deanna viewer, could go back
to *Mad About Music*, which he had seen a record 144 times,
but what would the champion collector, Loraine McGrath of
Lynbrook, Long Island, do to increase her scrapbook collection
with its record 1,500 stills?

And if Universal was now on a sounder footing with a stable
of prominent stars and a backlog of worthy properties, what
would happen to the manufacturers of Deanna Durbin dolls,
and dresses, and ribbons, and toys? What new style would the
beauty parlors invent for the teen-age girls who had aped
Deanna by parting their hair in the middle and combing it
back over the temples?

Moreover, what would happen now to the Harvard sopho-
more who had jumped off a bridge into the Charles River in
protest when Deanna had announced her first engagement?

Of all the people who were concerned about the disappearance of a great star from the spotlight, the one who probably cared least was Deanna Durbin. As a child living next to Hollywood, she had thought that autograph collecting was a lot of poppycock. She was too sensible to change her mind when the pointless scrawled signature in demand was her own. The whole Deanna Durbin fad always struck her as somewhat false, trumped up, and she considered herself its first victim.

"It's not that I didn't like acting. I did, although the kind of picture I made didn't place much demand on acting. What I didn't like was the publicity, the invasion of my private life. A person needs to have an identity of his own. When you're a star, it's virtually impossible. That's something I could never get used to."

She despised the publicity gimmicks her studio and reporters thought up. She was supposed to collect fuzzy toy animals "like pink teddy bears and purple and yellow monkeys." She was supposed to collect stamps. And on and on. The truth of it was that Deanna Durbin didn't collect anything. She missed her friends from Bret Harte Junior High and the simple pleasures they used to have. She wanted to go ice skating and to the corner drugstore for a soda. When, already a star, she tried both, mobs of people swirling about her caused her quietly, but determinedly, to withdraw.

Similarly, she tried going out occasionally with young men, but the ensuing publicity was so overwhelming and exaggerated that she stopped. Again the studio's attitude was a big factor in pushing her into this withdrawal. Louella Parsons, whose prose style seldom turns to metaphor, came up with a startling but accurate one to describe Universal's reaction to rumors of Deanna's impending marriage after one of her infrequent dates. The gossip, reported Louella, caused more excitement among the frightened heads of the studio than Hitler's march into Vienna.

The public, the studio, everyone, it seemed, did not want a mature Deanna. They wanted her to remain simple and charming and unspoiled. Deanna was the symbol of perpetual youth, of innocence, and even a kiss might spoil the image, to say nothing of the calamitous possibility of real romance.

When her parents, and the public, and the studio finally allowed her to go out on her first unchaperoned date, the coltish Deanna quickly bolted into a premature marriage. The man was Vaughn Paul, young assistant director on the lot, son of the studio manager. The wedding, on April 18, 1941, at the Wilshire Methodist Episcopal Church, was one of the great social events of the time, attended by many screen notables, as well as virtually every studio technician Deanna had ever worked with.

Writer Adela Rogers St. John was quite carried away by the young couple. "Deanna Durbin and Vaughn Paul bowled me over," she wrote. "For they have achieved something so rare and lovely that every man and woman will recognize it, every boy and girl will know it by name. It is like a song once heard and lingering on forever in memory. Young love . . . first love . . . clean and strong and perfect. . . . Neither of them has ever been in love before; neither even thought he was in love. Nor will they ever be again." The divorce took place two and one half years later.

"It is with deep regret that Mr. Paul and I have found it impossible to continue our marriage," began Deanna's dignified announcement of the breakup. "As a result, I am taking legal steps to have the marriage terminated. Our marriage was embarked upon with all the sincerity and hope that should go with marriage. But circumstances which neither of us have been able to solve now make it imperative for us to part to assure our mutual welfare and happiness."

The best Deanna could do to drum up grounds for divorce was to say that Paul continually criticized her film efforts. A year later, however, she put the blame squarely where she felt it belonged, on her unreal, abnormal upbringing in the film colony. "I hibernated all my life, and when I married Vaughn Paul, it wasn't any different. I was sheltered, everyone thought for me, and at the age of nineteen I stepped from that cloistered girlhood into a marriage that gave me the same sort of protection. Every girl should be allowed to think for herself. If I'd had other previous romances I might not have married the first man I was permitted to go out alone with and to see. That would have saved his unhappiness and saved me from a marriage that should never have taken place." Indicative of Deanna's rebellious attitude toward Hollywood was the fact that throughout their days of wedlock, Paul called her by her given name, Edna Mae.

In June 1945, Deanna tried a second marriage, this one with Felix Jackson, a man twenty years her senior, who had helped write several of her early screenplays and produced a number of her later films. Their daughter, Jessica Louise, was born the following year, but in January 1947 the couple separated. "It's no more Hollywood for me and no more marriage," Jackson wrote to Deanna's friend, Anne Shirley, from New York. A divorce followed.

Deanna had wanted to leave Hollywood during the height of her triumph, but someone told her that the best thing she could do to contribute to the nation's wartime effort was to go on making films. Deanna had stayed, continuing to make her two pictures a year, less successful ones, as noted, but financially rewarding, bringing her $300,000 a year near the end—a total of more than $2 million over a decade. By the late Forties, however, her last contract had run out, her second marriage had ended, and Deanna fled from the land of the pink teddy bears.

The girl Lawrence Tibbett had called "the modern Jenny Lind" was still only twenty-seven years old when she arrived in Paris. To her graceful five-foot-five silhouette, she had added a few pounds that took her over the 116 which characterized her days of film stardom. Her lovely auburn hair, her startling blue eyes, her dazzling white teeth, were still part of a screen image familiar to millions, and Frenchmen recognized the pert, oval face, the attractively short lower lip, the softly rounded chin that had figured so prominently on the screen. Impossible for them to know that the effervescent beauty who had sung and acted her way through a score of joyous musical films had been one of the loneliest adolescents in Hollywood, that as queen of her lot, she had sat in cool, dignified detachment working away at needlepoint between scenes, living out a life decreed for her by studio censors. "The point is that she still doesn't want to act," *Collier's* reported at the time of her greatest fame. "She has no love for it, wants babies, and will someday stop at the end of a film and never return to the studio."

The prophecy now came true, and dispatches from France started filtering back to Hollwood that told the story of the breakaway. Deanna was refusing film offers unconditionally, whether they came from her old mentor, Joe Pasternak, or from singer Mario Lanza, who was persistent in his efforts to get Deanna to co-star with him in a picture. She was living in a modest flat in Paris for which she reportedly paid less than $100 a month. She was continuing to study voice, and also learning to speak French.

One day word came that Deanna was getting married, and in due time news arrived of the simple civil service that united her with French film director Charles Henri David on December 21, 1950. David had directed her in *Lady on a Train* and they had known each other for more than nine years. He was forty-four, she twenty-eight. Giving up her flat in Paris, Deanna moved with her husband to an isolated town on the fringe of the Vosges mountains. Here, their son, Peter Henry, was born, in 1951.

The following year, the couple paid a visit to Madame David's parents, the Durbins, still living in North Hollywood, not in the large mansion with a swimming pool which they had inhabited in bygone days, but in a more modest dwelling better suited to their needs. "I don't want to go back to making pictures," Madame David said in reply to the inevitable question about a possible comeback. "And I wouldn't recommend it as a career for youngsters. It's hard enough to grow up without getting into the kind of life where your friends are adults instead of children."

While reporters were still blinking their eyes in disbelief, she removed any lingering doubts about her meaning. "I'm not a ham. I never have been, although I could never get people to believe it," she stated. "I started when I was thirteen. I was caught in the whirl until I quit three years ago at twenty-seven. That's a big hunk out of my life. Sure I had a lot of fun and I enjoyed things I otherwise wouldn't have had. But I also missed out on a lot of the joys of girls who lead normal lives." Describing her present life of anonymity, she concluded almost defiantly, "I'm one child star who grew up to be happy." With that Deanna Durbin returned to the obscurity of life with the 1,486 inhabitants of her French village.

Once the world has taken a poor mortal, willingly or unwillingly, from a workaday routine and placed the halo of fame around his head, that world is reluctant to let its hero go. The film offers continued. The reporters continued to lurk about the old farmhouse with the high stone wall. Finally, in 1958, Madame David, once more refusing an interview, wrote a letter of explanation and authorized it for publication. The objectionable elements in her past were now brought out in detail.

"My fans sat in the dark, anonymous and obscure, while I was projected bigger than life on the screen," she said in her letter, which was quoted by Garvin Hudgins in a New York *Post* account. "Fans took home an image of me and studio press agents filled in the personal details. They invented most of them and before I would resist, this worldwide picture of me came back stronger than my real person and very often conflicted with it. How could a young, unformed girl fight this publicized image of herself while still groping for her own personality? I was a typical thirteen-year-old American girl. The character I was forced into had little or nothing in common with myself—or with other youth of my generation for that matter."

Having described the unreality of her screen image to her-self, the discordances it awoke in her, she went on to take a caustic look at her fans, outlining her belief that it was her contemporaries' parents rather than the youngsters themselves who were her admirers. Unable to manage their own children satisfactorily, they took refuge in her screen image of perfec-tion, an image bearing little relation to reality: "Just as the Hollywood-produced pinup represents sex to many dissatisfied people, I represented an idealized daughter to the millions of frustrated fathers and mothers. They could, with their tickets, purchase twice a year new stocks of sweetness and innocence."

And in delineating the closing phases of her career one could again detect a note of acerbity, of exasperation with the working of Hollywood's dream factory: "The time came when I ceased to be sweet and innocent. The war and especially the postwar period for a while shattered a lot of make-believe and unchecked platitudes. My pictures, written for me like so many variations on the theme of the concocted Durbin personality, were a series of failures. To this, more than anything else, I owe my luck of being able to jump off unharmed. Yes, I was lucky. Deanna Durbin was dead, and my own life really began. . . . For any past pleasure I gave to movie fans I am sincerely happy," she concluded, "but I want to become dissociated once and forever from that young Deanna Durbin with whom I may still have some vague exterior resemblance, but who never had any similarity to me, not even coincidentally."

Today, even the exterior resemblances are disappearing as the portly Madame David wanders in and out of the local shops or putters about the garden behind her walled domain. The language she speaks is French. From time to time, the family goes on a trip. The happiest in recent memory took them to London. "It was wonderful," said Monsieur David. "Why Deanna strolled across Piccadilly Circus and not a soul noticed her." Her children are growing up. Jessica is eighteen, and Peter, thirteen, is turning into an excellent pianist, much to the delight of his music-loving mother. "I get a tremendous kick out of singing to help him practice," she recently said. Her own voice remains limpid and beautiful, seasoned by the years and by a daily hour of practice. She loves to sing, but now, she says, "I sing only for myself and I sing the songs I want, not what I'm told to sing."

About a year ago, Joe Pasternak paid a call on his former protégée and star and tried to coax her once more into a comeback. When she declared that she was very happy, he jokingly feigned regret. "I wish you weren't," he said, "because then you'd make another picture for me." Nevertheless, after his departure the usual spate of stories appeared, claiming that Deanna Durbin was planning to return to the screen. Her old mentor was going to cast her in "a good story, a happy picture, with a lot of good songs and a lot of zip." Reporters rushed once more to the tiny hamlet near Paris for confirmation, only to be met by Monsieur David with the word that his wife had agreed to read any scripts Pasternak wished to send. She would not, however, act in any of them. Not now. Not ever.

Deanna Durbin, as Madame David had said, was dead.

8.

THE MICK

"Getting married is like batting in a baseball game: when the right one comes along, don't let it go by. So when you find the right girl—and I've found her—there's no sense in waiting. I've never had time to wait for anything. Right from the start everything has come with a rush. I guess that's why 'Do it early' has always been my rule."

In these terms, Mickey Rooney, who as Andy Hardy was the reigning all-American boy of the screen, outlined his homespun philosophy of marriage at the symbolically crucial age of twenty-one. On January 10, 1942, he put the doctrine into practice by marrying Ava Gardner, a nineteen-year-old starlet only a few months removed from a tobacco plantation in North Carolina where her job, as she candidly avowed, was to pick the bugs off the tobacco plants and drop them into old coffee cans.

Hollywood was startled when the Mick, as he was and is known in his field, announced that he had found the right girl. Not that he wasn't known as a ladies' man. At an early age he had discovered the unique appeal of the opposite sex. If shooting began on a film with the Mick still absent, those in the know usually sent scouts to look for him on whatever adjoining set happened to abound in pretty girls. It was, rather, his confirmed bachelorhood, his energetic playing of the field, which had made marriage seem unlikely.

"Me go steady with someone? Why that's romantic suicide," the teen-age star told a reporter in a typical interview on the subject of his love life. "No, thanks. So don't ask me which girl I like best, because I don't. I just like girls." A familiar sight on Hollywood Boulevard was Mickey speeding along in a smart roadster, the top down, a cute girl at his side, several reserves in the rumble seat. The powers at MGM would listen with dismay to accounts of his forays into the Cocoanut Grove and other nightclubs, fearing that the carefully built-up screen image of the clean-cut, clean-living Andy Hardy might suffer from the real-life adventures of box-office star Mickey Rooney. Once, he had reportedly donned a Western Union outfit and crashed into a series of glamour queens' dressing rooms delivering spurious telegrams. His dates with such beauties as Lana Turner and Linda Darnell were hot publicity items. In 1941 alone he had pursued and was reported engaged to an entire gaggle of girls, eleven by count.

The statuesque Ava had been in Hollywood less than three months when Mickey married her at a little Presbyterian church in Ballard, California. Blue-eyed, with soft, dark brown hair, the bride was poised and beautiful. The short, chunky, athletic groom resigned his bachelorhood with traditional trepidation, nervously wiping his brow and exclaiming, "My, my," as the ceremony unfolded.

"I love Ava," Mickey's mother, Mrs. Nell Pankey, was reported to have said a few days before the wedding. "She's a grand girl, and naturally I want Mickey to be happy. But I give the marriage three weeks before it's over." The dire prediction was somewhat off in its time estimate, but the marriage of America's talented boy actor and his first bride did travel a blistering pace toward dissolution, a pace which paralleled the hasty trip to the altar.

After six months, a stormy argument presaged the end of the union, which was formalized when the young couple separated in September of the year. In suing for divorce, Ava claimed that in eight months of marriage, her husband's community property had a value of $200,000, of which she was entitled to half. She also asked for alimony commensurate with his $5,000-a-week salary.

In later years, after Ava had gone on to great fame as a screen sex goddess and to two further unsuccessful marriages, to Frank Sinatra and to Artie Shaw, she declared that Mickey had been wonderful, "but a child." In similar terms, Mickey reminisced, "You know something. I can hardly remember my marriage to Ava. We were both kids—but let's talk about the future instead of the dear dead past."

Mickey married his second wife, Betty Jane Rase, on September 30, 1944. If his courtship of Ava Gardner had been startlingly swift, that of seventeen-year-old Betty Jane could only be described as whirlwind—less than a single week. Recently inducted into the Army, he was stationed in Camp Sibert, Alabama, when a news reporter introduced him to the tawny-haired, blue-eyed beauty who had placed fifth in the Miss America contest at Atlantic City. He married her a few days later at the home of an army officer stationed at Birmingham Air Base. Not until after the ceremony did Mickey hurry to a telephone to give his mother the news, while to reporters he indicated that for the new bride, a lyric soprano who had been preparing for opera and screen work, there would be no career, a belated indicator that career conflicts had plagued his earlier marriage.

Three weeks after the ceremony, Mickey was sent to New York for embarkation overseas, and did not see his wife again until his return to the United States in March 1946. Meanwhile, their son Mickey Jr. was born in his absence.

Apparently, the precipitate marriage lasted as long as it did largely because of the extended wartime separation. From March 1946 until October, the couple were together, but on October 29th, Betty Jane left her husband and returned to Birmingham to have their second baby, Timothy, born the fol-

lowing January. After several trial separations and reconcilia-
tions, the marriage ended in divorce in May 1948, with Betty
Jane testifying in court that being married to the explosive star
was like living in a combination all-night restaurant and Coney
Island, a variation on Ava Gardner's reported assertion that it
was like living in the current of an electric fan and being
unable to reach the switch.

"This one's going to last. If it doesn't, there's something
wrong with me," Mickey announced as he embarked on a third
marriage—to actress Martha Vickers—on June 3, 1949, only a
few days after the interlocutory divorce decree from number
two became final. On this occasion, the courtship period lasted
two months before the unpretentious wedding ceremony in
North Hollywood. The wedding band, engraved with the
words, *Today, Tomorrow, Always, I love you,* was placed on
the bride's finger by a crew-cut, nervous Mick, who chewed
gum incessantly and broke his chain smoking only for the duration of the ceremony.

At the end of the following year, the third Mrs. Rooney announced that she would file for divorce. "We found out we
didn't have enough in common," she stated. "My interests are
centered in the home and Mickey's are not. He doesn't like the
restrictions of marriage. He will be happier free." In September 1951, she was granted a divorce, with alimony payments of
$2,000 a month to start, scaled down to $300 per month by
1959. She was also granted custody of their son, Ted, Mickey's
third child.

Once again, the interlocutory decree—a provision of California law that states a divorce does not become final until one
year later—had barely reached its term before Mickey rushed
back to the altar at Las Vegas's Wee Kirk of the Heather. His
fourth bride, on November 18, 1952, was Elaine Mahnken, a
tall, red-haired model. A recent graduate of Compton Junior
College, she was nine years Mickey's junior. They had met at a
Hollywood party two months before flying to Las Vegas.

First reports indicated that Elaine, never a member of the

show-business world, had calmed down her high-flying husband; he stayed at home more and gave up smoking and gambling. Unfortunately, having the Mick in the house apparently had drawbacks as well as advantages. When Elaine sued for divorce in February 1959, she charged that their home was in "a constant uproar. I guess we're just not temperamentally suited to each other," she said in a classic summation.

"Marriage is like life," was Mickey's profound comment. "You're never sure you'll awaken tomorrow morning." Life certainly favored the young divorcee at this juncture. Superior Judge Orlando H. Rhodes approved a $381,750 property settlement. In addition to their $100,000 home with its furnishings, Elaine was granted alimony payments of $1,750 per month, having asked for $2,353 on the basis of annual earnings of $350,000. Total alimony payoffs for the all-American boy now amounted to a cool $1 million, according to journalistic statisticians.

The drain on the family exchequer did not prevent the Mick from putting a ring on the finger of a fifth Mrs. Rooney, Barbara Thomason, a twenty-two-year-old starlet, who was Miss Muscle Beach of 1954. On this occasion, the veteran husband incurred the wrath of the law when he slipped across the border to Mexico for nuptials that took place several months before his California interlocutory decree from Elaine Mahnken became final. While Judge Rhodes, who had granted the decree to number four, said he would look into the Mexican ceremony, it was later revealed that Mickey, reportedly with Elaine's consent, had also obtained a "quickie" divorce south of the border. No charges were brought.

"I've known Barbara for two years," he declared at the time of the marriage announcement. "As a matter of fact, I courted her longer than any of the others. The others were a little hasty. They were unfortunate."

The couple's first child, a daughter, Kelly Ann, was born in late 1959, to be followed by another daughter, Kerry, in 1961, a son, Kyle, in 1962, and still another girl, Kimmy Sue, in 1963.

"I believe in lots of children," Mickey said. "Maybe it's because I was an only child. After all, you should leave something behind when you leave this earth."

"What both of us want now is a happy, normal home life," he told an interviewer. "I guess you could say that's all I ever wanted really." In seventeen years, he had made five tries at marriage, after courtships that lasted three months, a week, two months, again two months, and finally a longer acquaintanceship of two years.

One of his friends once said that Mickey Rooney knew more about show business and less about women than anyone he'd ever known. The friend probably didn't know many child stars, for Mickey's pattern—five marriages and four divorces before the age of forty—was pretty close to par for the course. Together, the eight major stars treated at length in this book have accounted for a total of twenty-four marriages. Most of them, moreover, are still relatively young, with many years left to go before the final tally is taken.

For these stalwart eight, the search for a so-called normal life through the convention of marriage has led down a bumpy, uncharted road. The romantic visions they have had of a happy hearth have many times gone awry. Perhaps they were building up illusions about what a normal home life consists of. Perhaps they had seen too many movies. Certainly, they must sometimes have felt, they had *been* in too many movies. "Hollywood is the most difficult place to stay married in," Mickey has declared. "That's the price we pay for all the fame and money. An actor's life is not his own. It belongs to the people who applaud him. But it's worth the price. Without the public interest, I wouldn't have anything you would want to write about."

One of the things about Mickey that has been written about endlessly is his height—or lack of it. As with many other child performers, during his early career reports circulated that he was a midget. The reports were untrue, but Mickey was always pint-sized, an expression—along with the fact it described—

that clung to him through his adolescence. For a time, he engaged in vigorous exercises, but these were of no avail in terms of height. The Mighty Mite remained a solid, chunky youngster five foot, three inches short, with disproportionately short arms and a big head.

Like countless other short men, Mickey compensated for his lack of height by drawing forth an enormous energy which he consumed in a restless, dynamic, compulsive activity that included his spectacular career as an actor, a spirited athleticism, and the vertiginous pursuit of tall, attractive women.

His first wife, Ava Gardner, who towered over three inches above him, obligingly took off her shoes for wedding shots and slouched gracefully when posing with the Mick. His second, Betty Jane Rase, was already a little taller than Mickey's five foot three when they married, but she was only seventeen and still growing. When her husband returned from a year and a half of overseas duty with the army, he discovered that she had added three long inches to her stature. Martha Vickers, wife number three, also was taller than her husband, and the Mick just about came up to the shoulders of number four, lanky Elaine Mahnken. When Betty Jane once asked him why he preferred tall girls, she received a typical Rooney quip in reply: "I like them better than short ones." Unquestionably, the Rooney ego took a happy bow each time he proved that a certain type of little fellow could make the grade even with a big, tall beauty.

Not until Mickey's fifth marriage, to tiny Barbara Thomason, did he stop trying to prove his point. "She's short," he declared, perhaps with some sense of relief. "She's only five feet two. We see eye to eye on everything. " Perhaps it was a sign of his psychological coming of age.

There were great career advantages to being short, and Mickey was aware of them. "Most boy actors reach an age where they start growing and reach what they call the gangling age. Then they have to quit," he later explained.

"I didn't grow that way. I've been able to grow up in pictures."
As a result of remaining short, Mickey was able to play an
adolescent Andy Hardy until he was well into his twenties.

Andy Hardy, however, was only one of the countless roles
that the indefatigable Mickey played, on screen and off, in his
unceasing efforts to prove that he could reach the top. Right
from the start, as he said, everything came at him with a rush.
The start took place at 57 Willoughby Street in Brooklyn, on
September 23, 1920, when Ninnian Joseph Yule III was born to
a pair of vaudevillians, dancer Nell Carter and her husband,
Joe Yule, a burlesque comic. Little more than a year later,
Baby Joseph was playing the vaunted Palace, the ultimate goal
of every vaudevillian, bouncing out of a hatbox to impersonate
the new year. Obviously, the special nature of the act limited
its run. One night not long after, a more substantial debut took
place. Sid Gold and Babe Latour, a well-known vaudeville
team, were beginning their act with a sentimental melody
called "Pal of My Childhood Days." The veteran troupers were
expecting to hear sniffles, but instead came a quick burst of
laughter. Out of the corner of his eye, Sid Gold saw a remarkable sight. At stage left, the impish figure of little Joe Yule had
drawn the attention of the audience. He was standing on his
head. After murmuring a few unquotable words to his partner,
Gold took command of the situation. "Well, sonny," he said, "I
suppose you can sing this song better than we can?" In a loud,
clear voice, the tiny two-year-old sailed through the tearjerker,
skillfully imitating the gestures and intonations of the astonished Gold. When he had recovered, Gold added the impromptu appearance to his act.

Since the elder Yules separated when their only child was
very young, and divorced when he was four and a half, it was
with his mother that the boy performer made his way around
the country. It was she who learned that a tearjerker called *Mr.
Iron Claw* was having trouble in Chicago because the show's
midget, Heinie Hanley, had fallen ill with indigestion brought

on by eating too much cheesecake. Nell Carter told the management her three-year-old Joe could play the part. She won him the role.

The following year, the vaudeville season produced a run on midgets. Given a special work permit by Governor Alfred E. Smith, the child actor was doing a song-and-dance act in New York when someone remembered his appearance in *Mr. Iron Claw.* As a result, Joe was again cast as a midget in *Not to Be Trusted,* and in the film *Orchids and Ermine,* which starred Colleen Moore and called for him to hold a big black cigar in his mouth throughout. The cigar was made of dark chocolate. One day, in an attempt at realism, he chewed off the end and vigorously spit it out, sending two small teeth flying toward the camera along with the chocolate cigar end. The roles led to the later speculation that the Lilliputian performer actually *was* a midget.

The trouper's life in the East was a hard one for young Joe Yule and his mother. Their bookings were uncertain and infrequent and the pay scale low. In an attempt to improve their lot, Nell Carter started moving west, stopping in Kansas City to visit relatives and buy a jalopy that took them to California. There she found a job managing an auto court, and tried to get her boy into the movies.

Their big break came when Joe was chosen out of more than two thousand applicants to incarnate the role of a Fontaine Fox cartoon strip character called Mickey McGuire. For the audition, his mother had to dye her blue-eyed offspring's light-brown hair black. "I remember how sore his ears were," she said. "I'd spilled some dye on them and I tried to get it off with soap and water and finally with cuticle remover. It was that or starve."

Over a period of six years, more than seventy Mickey McGuire short-reelers were turned out. Joe Yule Jr. became, almost literally, Mickey McGuire. By 1932, however, the market was saturated. The series was dropped, and cartoonist Fox took legal steps to make sure his young star would no longer call himself Mickey McGuire. Out of work and out of a name, the despondent eleven-year-old looked up at his mother. With a wink, she suggested that he call himself Mickey *Looney*. "Nope, *Rooney*," said the Mick, as he was already known, and the idea held.

As Mickey Rooney, he took once more to the vaudeville circuit with his mother. The time was 1932, with the country in the grip of a searing depression. An unsuccessful tour came to a bleak end with mother and son once more in Hollywood, making the wearying rounds of the casting offices, picking up bit parts in literally scores of films, but never a contract, never a role that seemed to lead anywhere.

The part that finally kicked off Mickey Rooney's big-time career was that of gangster Clark Gable's kid brother in *Manhattan Melodrama*, a film that also teamed William Powell and Myrna Loy for the first time. The following year, 1935, brought a meaningful role as the pesty kid brother in *Ah, Wilderness*, a film version of the Eugene O'Neill comedy, and then a much-applauded venture into Shakespeare, as Puck, in the celebrated Max Reinhardt production of *A Midsummer Night's Dream*.

By now, Mickey had a studio contract. In the next two years, Metro-Goldwyn-Mayer discovered that his career carried veins of purest gold which they proceeded to mine with semi-hysterical speed and delight. First came *The Devil Is a Sissy*, which also starred Freddie Bartholomew and Jackie Cooper. The film was the pilot in a series which pitted a frank, pugnacious American boy against the more cultivated, refined English schoolboy. Every cliché about the differences between Britishers and Americans was brought out in these films, which included the memorable *Little Lord Fauntleroy*, *Captains Courageous*, *The Devil Takes the Count*, *Lord Jeff*, and *A Yank at Eton*.

An even richer vein was struck in 1937 when MGM dusted off an old play entitled *Skidding*, by Aurania Rouverel, and converted it into a low-budget film called *A Family Affair*. *Skidding* had opened on Broadway in 1928 and played for eighteen months—a hit, but even so, hardly a sound indicator of the fabulous success the Rouverel characters were to have as the protagonists of the Andy Hardy series. During the next six years, fourteen Andy Hardy epics rolled off the MGM production line. A modest investment of $4 million grossed well over $20 million for the studio, and the Hardys became the first family of moviegoing America.

A Family Affair could properly be termed a sleeper. MGM didn't really know they had struck it rich until exhibitors began calling for additional pictures about the small town, Carvel, Idaho, where the screen Hardys lived and thrived, content with the pleasures and problems of their simple, honest lives. Lionel Barrymore played Judge Hardy in the initial effort, but when he was uavailable for a follow-up, Lewis Stone was cast in the role, which he carried through the entire series. Fay Holden played Mrs. Hardy, Cecilia Parker their daughter Marian, Sara Haden was Aunt Milly, and Ann Rutherford played Polly Benedict, the girl next door.

The unquestioned star of the series, however, was the high-flying son of the household, Andy Hardy, played by Mickey Rooney. "That gnomish prodigy, that half-human, half-goblin man child, who is as old in cinema ways as Wallace Beery and twice as cute, inexorably dominates the Hardy series as Pearl White used to dominate *The Perils of Pauline*," wrote Bosley Crowther.

Mickey has told of his doubts and anxieties when first assigned the role of a typical small-town adolescent. Born in a theatrical trunk, his youth spent on stage and backstage, he was desperately trying to feel his way into the part, when one day he arrived late on the set, delayed by a football game, his face sweaty, his sandy brown hair tousled, shirttails flying. "That's it, that's Andy Hardy!" his director told him before Mickey could eradicate the natural, realistic quality which was to distinguish his portrayal of the role.

Nothing very remarkable happened to the Hardys as they lived out their genial lives in Carvel, and the soft-sell sagas which MGM fed to the exhibitors were sometimes hard to tell one from the other as they flashed on the screen—*Judge Hardy's Children, Out West with the Hardys, Love Finds Andy Hardy, The Hardys Ride High, Andy Hardy's Double Life, Judge Hardy and Son, Andy Hardy Gets Spring Fever, Andy Hardy Meets Debutante, Andy Hardy's Private Secretary, Life Begins for Andy Hardy, The Courtship of Andy Hardy, Andy Hardy's Blonde Trouble. . . .* The unassuming titles seemed to reflect the tame goings-on.

In a typical outing of the typical U.S. family next door, *The Hardys Ride High*, the Judge is led to believe he will inherit a Detroit auto fortune of $2 million. Eventually, he learns that the inheritance will not come through, but meanwhile Andy has a chance to perform his various routines, aptly described by Bosley Crowther in these terms: "Mickey in a top hat, trying with the most successful non-success to be a man of the world; Mickey turning down cigarettes and strong drink, fleeing madly from the blandishments of a chorus girl; Mickey being a little man at last and admitting with a catch in his voice that honesty is better than millions, these are the high spots of *The Hardys Ride High* and if they leave you in low spirits, you must be pretty low yourself. A veritable beast in human form."

In addition to making audiences privy to the excitement of Andy Hardy's high school adventures, his family problems, and his courtships, the series occasionally probed deeper into the American way of life. In *Life Begins for Andy Hardy*, there was an edifying set of sermons about what to avoid in the wicked city of New York. In *Andy Hardy Meets Debutante*, a rousing bit of patriotism demonstrated that the series could keep abreast of the war years. Andy brags about knowing a celebrated society girl, but when he goes to New York to try to meet her, he finds obstacles lining his path. On hearing him bemoan his lowly state, that of a nobody, the Judge takes him to New York University's Hall of Fame to show him a lot of other nobodies who became famous as a result of the opportunities our form of government gave them. The series' progenitors never left any doubt that to their way of thinking, the basic U.S. character was good, the American way of life the best in all the world.

The head of the studio, Louis B. Mayer, attracted by these themes, took a highly personal interest in the Hardy epics and poured some of his brightest young stars into the proliferating episodes. In addition to Mickey and Ann Rutherford, the series was a training ground for Judy Garland, Lana Turner, Virginia Weidler, Donna Reed, Kathryn Grayson, and Esther Williams.

Mickey's own performances, while they drew a great deal of praise, rated an almost equal amount of criticism for what many viewed as overacting, mugging being the term most frequently applied to his exaggerated facial expressions and heavy use of gesture. To the charges, Mickey pleaded a qualified guilty, declaring that he deliberately played the role broadly because he believed Andy Hardy to be the type of American boy who would wear his emotions on his sleeve, an immature high school kid who imagined that he was mature until he got into trouble and was forced to run to his dad; a type, Mickey felt, who would then be too proud to cry, and consequently would screw up his face into a near caricature.

Box-office business must have made much of the criticism seem trivial, especially when Mickey and his Metro mentors struck pay dirt still again with a modest little film called *Thoroughbreds Don't Cry*. For the first time, Mickey was paired with young Judy Garland in a musical. While their scenes together were relatively brief, the magic that was distilled when they met was a highly potent brew. It led MGM to pair them in a series of brilliant musicals that had the American public kicking up its heels and shelling out dollar bills as though the depression had been a mirage.

When the versatile Mick wasn't doing a female impersonation of Brazilian bombshell Carmen Miranda or otherwise dancing and singing up a storm, he found time to do variations on the theme of the all-American boy—as a diamond-in-the-rough in the moving *Boys' Town*, which won an Academy award for Spencer Tracy; as the mischievous, carefree Huckleberry Finn in Mark Twain's classic tale of childhood along the Mississippi; as the incarnation of one of the nation's real-life heroes in *Young Tom Edison*; and in William Saroyan's *The Human Comedy*, as Homer McCauley, the telegraph boy who discovers that people are beautiful and that in everyone there is good. In a memorable instance, he departed from native characterizations to play an English boy in *National Velvet*, Enid Bagnold's touching story of youngsters and animals, which featured a vibrant, affecting performance by that airily beautiful child actress, Elizabeth Taylor.

As late as 1937, Mickey Rooney was still quite low in the popularity ratings, placing 104th in the *Motion Picture Herald*'s annual poll. A year later, his meteoric star had spun him into the number three spot, trailing only Shirley Temple and Clark Gable. For his performances in 1938, Mickey, along with Deanna Durbin, received an Academy Award miniature trophy —midget Oscars for the outstanding juvenile players of the year. By 1939, he had edged out Shirley Temple to become the new number-one box-office attraction, a spot he held for three consecutive years, 1939, 1940 and 1941, after which he remained in the top ten for four more years until his entrance into the United States Army.

Counting the almost fourscore Mickey McGuire films, the numerous bit parts of his early years in Hollywood, the splendid MGM features of his and the studio's golden years, as well as the comeback efforts since his return from the army in 1946, Mickey Rooney has made a total of close to five hundred motion pictures. This figure becomes all the more impressive when put into the perspective of his total life. The screen formed only one part, though an extremely important one, of his incredibly diverse and cyclonic days.

In addition to his films and romantic involvements, the Mick found time for scores of personal appearances and radio broadcasts, writing many of the scripts himself. At the studio, he organized his own football team, the MGM Lions. He organized his own swing band, taught himself to play the piano, the drums, the xylophone, and virtually every other instrument of the band, even though he had never had a music lesson in his life. At ten he composed his first song, presciently entitled "That's What Love Can Do to You." For boy singer Bobby Breen he wrote another prophetic song called "I Can't Afford to Fall in Love," which Breen sang on the Eddie Cantor radio program, and in succeeding years he continued to compose melodies which were published and recorded by singing star Vic Damone and others. A more ambitious work, a symphony called *Melodante*, was performed on a national radio show by the Ford Symphony Orchestra. For his film work, Mickey speedily and expertly learned tap dancing, and for his private pleasure, he took to sports with a vigor that President Kennedy's physical-fitness experts would have heartily applauded. In addition to managing his football team, he became an accomplished swimmer, and, under the aegis of professional champion Big Bill Tilden, a junior tennis champion. After a year's practice, he shot golf in the middle seventies. He was a demon at badminton and table tennis, and somewhere along the way he also found time to enter the poultry business, to invest in a prizefighter, and to buy a racehorse which he named Bing Crosby.

"Mickey Rooney is about the busiest youngster in the world right now," wrote the Los Angeles *Times* in 1934. With each succeeding year, he became busier, and to a great extent, his private life paralleled his screen development, leading him at one point to state quite forcefully, "I *am* Andy Hardy. I feel right playing Andy." Mickey *was* the brash adolescent with a penchant for mischief, he *was* the country's leading puppy lover. On screen and off, he *was* pugnacious and cocksure, although often conventional and naïve, wisecracking and sometimes smart-alecky, but with an underlying immaturity and frustration. Superficially glib, he could display a profound and abiding generosity.

The wide-ranging set of characteristics gave him his legions of admirers, and a not insignificant number of detractors. While Hollywood hostesses danced a jubilant jig when the screen's Wunderkind accepted an invitation to a party, his buoyant presence assuring its success, newspaper and magazine reporters, whom he sometimes led down the garden path, were not always kind in their references to the box-office leader. According to a writer in *The New York Times*, the irrepressible Mick had more enemies than any actor in history, and a columnist once wrote that if Mickey Rooney were murdered, they'd have to hire a thousand extra cops just to question the suspects.

While a shy, reticent young child star like Judy Garland was cowed by the authoritarian regime at MGM, with its rigorous professional demands and spy system that kept tabs on the private lives of its inmates, Mickey's irrepressible nature was more of a match for the powers at the studio. To Mickey, the stern patriarch of the lot, Louis B. Mayer, was "Uncle Louie," with whom he joshed and whom he tried to wheedle into letting him try his hand at directing. Similarly, MGM's top stars were taken in stride by the Mick, not always to their complete satisfaction. Spencer Tracy and Lionel Barrymore, "Uncle Spence" and "Uncle Lionel," were not enthusiastic at the prospect of appearing in films with their scene-stealing "nephew." They had taken note of how, while their colleague Wallace Beery emoted, the young child actor would unobtrusively wipe his nose on his sleeve in stealthy imitation of Beery and quietly walk off with the footage. If Mickey eventually won them over, it was not without considerable effort, an effort greatly advanced by the fact that in actuality Mickey had great respect and admiration for these screen veterans.

His foremost idol was Clark Gable, whom he imitated at every turn. When the King took to wearing loose wool sport coats and vest sweaters, his young admirer followed suit. When Gable turned up with a felt hat with a brim turned back, the Mick swiftly rushed out to buy one. Somewhat incongruously,

Mickey adopted the Gable swagger, the standard Gable prop, a pipe, and the Gable vocabulary with waitresses—casual salutations like "Honey" or "Toots." Shortly after buying a smart green roadster, Gable found that Mickey was also driving around in one. "Someday I'll play a dirty trick on that kid," he finally declared. "I'll start wearing a sarong and riding around in a hearse."

Along with his exhibitionism and youthful pranks, the young Mick found time for genuine friendship and generosity. Judy Garland has said that she doesn't know what she would have done without Mickey Rooney to help her through her days at MGM. By being thoughtful and kind, he made that troubled star's life more bearable, and with his enormous professional know-how he contributed to her acting skills. Kathryn Grayson, Lana Turner, Ava Gardner, and Esther Williams were other young performers that he has been credited with helping to guide and instruct. If their physical beauty tends to make his motives appear less than totally disinterested, it is worth noting that he also found time to play a role in Red Skelton's success, drawing that engaging comic's talents to the attention of Louis B. Mayer, who brought Skelton to MGM.

Periodically, Mickey's ceaseless activity took its toll, and then his aggressive and cocksure manner would wilt, much like that of the screen's Andy Hardy, leaving a bewildered adolescent on the verge of collapse. "It isn't worth it," the Mick told a reporter during one of these moods. "Besides, I'm too tired to care. It's all work and no play. Home and in bed every night after dinner. That's me. That's fame."

At the height of his success, the all-American boy tried to enlist in the army. After an initial rejection due to a heart flutter, he was accepted in 1944 and sent overseas. In Europe, he traveled more than 150,000 miles to put on jeep shows before two million G.I.'s. His tireless efforts won him the coveted Bronze Star.

On his return from overseas, he threw himself once more into compulsive activity, but the twenty-six-year-old Mick was to find the climate of the country, and consequently the tenor of his life, greatly changed. Fresh from the cataclysmic experience of a savage and cruel war, the nation seemed to feel that Andy Hardy had outworn his welcome, that his problems were unrealistically simple, his attitudes naïve. Mickey Rooney, moreover, was too old for the part.

Ironically, this had been his complaint long before leaving for wartime service. "Nobody treats me grown-up," he said in 1938. "I get no adult consideration. Pretty soon I'm going to have to start yelling around here for fewer pictures. And better ones, too. So, if you hear I've gone temperamental, that's why." On duty overseas, he had had more hard thoughts about how his studio had treated him—or, as he increasingly felt, mistreated him. Particularly galling was the fact that during much of the three-year period when he was the top box-office draw in the country, he had received a salary less than the studio paid some of its better supporting players. As a result of his various dissatisfactions, he obtained a release from his regular MGM contract when he returned, an angry young man, to Hollywood.

"He had too much success without any hard knocks," Joe Yule Sr. used to say in voicing his one regret about his illustrious son's career. Mickey took his dad from the Follies Burlesque Theatre in Los Angeles and helped him secure roles in a number of his films before the elder Yule died in 1950 at the age of sixty-one. By that time, he had lived to see his boy take a good number of hard knocks, all of which the scrappy young veteran survived. Too old for Andy Hardy roles, Mickey was nonetheless considered too youthful for the strong dramatic parts he wanted. In 1947, he scored one of the few successes of his postwar career in *Killer McCoy*, which told of the rise of a tough kid up the fistic ladder; but MGM, for which he made the picture under a contract calling for a reduced output, was itself going rapidly downhill at this period, with Louis B. Mayer putting his boundless energy into building up his racing stable rather than the studio. When more roles of the Killer Mc-

Coy type were not forthcoming, Mickey set himself up with Sam H. Stiefel, a former Philadelphia exhibitor who had been his business manager, to produce films as an independent. The concern made a number of very bad pictures before dissolving. Meanwhile, Mickey had taken to playing the horses, to high living, and to a pair of ricochet romances. Said the Hollywood pundits as they sadly shook their heads, the Mick was washed up.

The pundits were wrong. With the game spirit of the long-distance runner, Mickey Rooney continued doggedly to ply his trade. Out of the running for the important films, he turned out a series of low-budget quickies, including one with Francis, the talking mule; he performed in night clubs; he starred in a television comedy series called *Hey, Mulligan!* which lost out in the ratings game to the popular *Jackie Gleason Show*; then he turned to television guest shots. Finally, after many a long, dry summer, a really good role came along.

"In a tense ten minutes of gambling frenzy, Mickey Rooney has lifted *The Bold and the Brave* above ordinary war movies," *Life* wrote in 1956. In the film, the Mick played Dooley, a happy-go-lucky G.I. whose dream is to have "the most beautiful restaurant in Jersey." On the eve of battle on the Italian front, he gets hot at a fabulous crap game that continues through an air raid, under blankets, by the light of a lantern. His face pure greed, he wins $303,300, later surrenders it to a moralizing sergeant, attempts to retrieve it, and dies. For his dynamic portrayal Mickey was nominated for an Academy Award.

A short time later, he enjoyed an even greater success, in the Playhouse 90 production *The Comedian*. As a monstrously cruel and egotistic TV comic, he gave a gripping, biting performance. Columnist John Crosby, at the height of his power as a reviewer, wrote, "It was such a professional job that only the old pros will fully appreciate how good it was, the great detail that went into it, and the range of acting it encompassed." "Extraordinary, remarkable," said Jack Gould in *The New York*

Times. Look gave him an award, and around the country, prominent figures in the entertainment world took note of the fact that Mickey Rooney had made a comeback almost as startling as that of Frank Sinatra. CBS-TV signed him to a five-year pact, and film offers came his way. The future looked promising once more.

"It's finally gotten through to me that you learn in this business by listening," he said. "And you learn that you can't take the business for granted. The business can take you for granted, but you can't take the business for granted. That's the trouble with being a kid star. It all falls into your lap and you figure the big red balloon is going to be flying over the fairgrounds forever. Then all of a sudden a hawk with a sharp beak comes along and pow! there goes the balloon."

The trouble with being a kid star, as the Mick put it, was that it meant a delayed maturity, a naïveté in almost all fields except the professional, but most notably in love and finances. Despite a comeback that sent him once more into the big money orbit, the newspapers in June 1962 reported a startling story: the former box-office star had filed a petition of voluntary bankruptcy in the federal court, listing assets of $500 and debts of almost half a million dollars. The horses, four former wives, the government, and bad business deals had combined to take their toll, and the Mick, who had earned more than $12 million over the years, was broke. The irony was all the greater because his mother and the studio had carefully invested much of his money in trust funds which supposedly he could not touch until certain stipulated age periods. To enable him to pay $90,000 in back taxes, however, the court let him dip into a trust fund established in 1940. By the trust's provisions, he was not to have had the money until he reached sixty.

Typically, an avalanche of new activities soon blotted out the star's financial plight and drew attention to his continuing career. *Variety* reported: "Mickey Rooney whips into 1964 plotting more activities than any other two Hollywood personalities." Over the weekend, he had winged to Houston to pre-

pare for the opening of a Mickey Rooney School of Entertainment, one of eight franchises scheduled to bow within eighteen
months. He had formed a new corporation called Hilarity, Inc.,
which planned to make three films utilizing the talents of a
repertory company of ten top comics. Not too surprisingly, the
three scheduled films—*There's No Place Like Rome, The Big
Snatch* and *Follow That Kite*—were all originals by an author
named Mickey Rooney. The orbiting Mick was also planning
an independent production of *Love and Let Love*, with his
former child co-star, Judy Garland, and a film called *The Five
Leaf Clover*, to be filmed in Ireland, with Pat O'Brien. In addition, there were nightclub dates, a stand at the London Palladium with Bobby Van, a television series for ABC called *The
Mickey Rooney Show*, as well as a new organization called
WE (World Entertainment) Country Club in Woodland Hills,
with membership limited to showfolk. "Each time I shake hands
with Mickey Rooney it's like walking head-on into an eighty-
mile gale," wrote Hedda Hopper, testifying to the ebullience
of the personality that could put so many irons into so many
fires at one time. Mickey added one more impressive iron to
his fires in mid-1965 when he announced his imminent Broadway appearance in a play entitled *The Gift Horse*. Charac-
teristically, he was not only to star, but also to direct.

Meanwhile, there were more Rooneys than the Mick appearing on the entertainment scene. Mickey Jr. was fashioning
a career as a rock-and-roll singer. Timmy had made his debut
in a TV production with Mickey and Donald O'Connor. And
Teddy Rooney was becoming an actor much in demand on TV,
starring as Huckleberry Finn on Shirley Temple's *Storybook*,
performing on Playhouse 90, and appearing in guest shots on
the *Jack Paar Show*, where Mickey, too, made a well-publi-
cized appearance, storming out of the studio when Paar told
him abruptly, "I think you're loaded," a remark that began one
of the many famous Paar feuds.

Teddy also appeared in films—with Doris Day in *It Happened to Jane*, and with his dad in an attempt at a revival of

the old Hardy series, *Andy Hardy Comes Home*, in 1958. For the filming, a gray, balding but still exuberant Mickey returned to his alma mater, MGM, for the first time in many years. "It gives me a strange feeling to be back at this studio," he said. "I still expect L. B. Mayer to be walking down the street, to see Joan Crawford or Clark Gable or Spencer Tracy. But they aren't here anymore. None of the old gang is here anymore." For the renewal feature of the series, Mickey once more played Andy Hardy, now an attorney returning to his hometown. Teddy played Andy Hardy Jr. Cecilia Parker, Fay Holden, and Sara Haden were brought back, while flashbacks showed scenes with Andy's old girl friends. It didn't work. Just as none of the old gang were there to welcome Mickey Rooney back to the studio where he had been the top box-office draw, so now there were few of the audience left to welcome Andy Hardy back to the screen.

Mickey was happy, however, to see a new generation of Rooneys entering the field of entertainment and he turned his energies elsewhere when the Hardy revival idea was dropped. Energy remained the keynote of his being, its strength and perhaps its limitation, for that energy could at times be somewhat aimless. After a vaudeville appearance at the London Palladium, one reviewer felt that the weakness of Mickey's postwar act was not that he did too little, but that he half-did too much. He seemed to tire of his tricks before he had them properly started, and too swiftly went on to something new. For the music hall, more than colossal verve was required. That verve needed to be carefully channeled, concluded the reviewer.

In the Mick's early films, a good director could guide his energies. And he has continued to respond to skillful supervision, turning in excellent performances in recent years in films like *Baby Face Nelson*, *Operation Mad Ball*, *The Bridges of Toko-Ri*, *Breakfast at Tiffany's*, and *Requiem for a Heavyweight*. Without direction, however, he could flounder and dissipate his strength, not only professionally, but in his private life as well. Responsive company would turn him into the life of the party, with his running antics, his ready quips, his rich store of anecdotes. Left to himself, he was nervous and tense, jumped up and down a good deal, let his mind skip aimlessly from subject to subject, or engaged in conversation that turned easily to philosophical platitudes. "Life is like a roulette wheel; we spin it and hope for the best, and just do the best we can and hope everything comes out happily," he once told Sheilah Graham.

A dynamic, restless, generous personality, the Mick was less effective when he slowed down and started probing beneath the surface. Like the screen Andy Hardy, with whom, to his dismay, he continued to be compared as the years wore on, his was a life full of sound and fury, but signifying what, it was sometimes difficult to tell. In this respect, his lot was not unlike that of other former child stars who found it difficult to establish perspectives in lives that started with the focus so far off center.

"Mickey didn't actually have much childhood," his dad often reminisced. "At the age of one and a half we had a doctor give him a thorough checkup, and he told us Mickey had the mentality of a ten-year-old. And by the time he was three, Mickey was earning a living on the stage." On stage as a baby, his parents separated, his home the restless road of the vaudevillian, the pint-sized kid from Brooklyn developed an indomitable spirit that shot him to stardom of the highest magnitude. After falling from that high perch, he doggedly clambered back up, but never again to the top, never again to the heady, rarefied air he once had breathed as the boy wonder of the land. And reflecting on the joys and sorrows his experience had brought him, he felt that perhaps it was all for the best. "I don't want to be on top any more," he recently said. "It's too tough a position. I want to be happy." May the Great Casting Director grant him his wish.

9.

JACKIE COOPER

"Don't put your daughter on the stage, Mrs. Worthington," Noel Coward admonished humorously in one of his most delightful patter songs. Former child star Jackie Cooper has used capital letters and the utmost seriousness in expressing the same sentiment: "I advise ALL parents to keep their children home—where they belong." Deanna Durbin, Jane Withers, Shirley Temple, and many others less prominent have all voiced extreme caution about putting their children into the limelight, but none has expressed his misgivings more forcefully than Cooper.

The burden of his complaint is that early success inflicts a distortion of values on the child star, leaving him confused and deflated once his brief days of glory are over. That brevity, moreover, is inevitable not only because youth passes swiftly, but because the child actor is rigidly and fatally typecast. "When you are successful, nobody wants you to change—you never get any dramatic lessons," he explained to Edwin Miller in *Seventeen.* "I made movies like *The Champ, Skippy* and *Treasure Island.* They were altogether different kinds of pictures. But the characters were tailored to fit the personality— me. Kids don't act. So-and-so speaks in a particular way, this one has a cute smile, that one is a natural for sad, underprivileged roles. If they want a certain look, they hire the child actor who goes with it."

For repeating the set pattern, the child performer receives exaggerated applause. This can be extremely dangerous, especially when the acclaim starts dying down: "You find that nobody cares any more. No one makes a fuss about you. . . . You feel that something is wrong, lost. You keep asking yourself, 'What am I doing that's wrong? Why don't people like me any more?' It's a terrible time, and hardly anybody is prepared for it. Most parents of theatrical kids aren't prepared to help the kids over it when the time comes and certainly the kids themselves don't know what to expect."

Not only is the child actor suddenly deprived of the attention and admiration which he has come to take for granted, but he finds himself in an alien world facing problems for which he has almost no background or preparation. "Nobody taught me to grow up. I wasn't given an ounce of responsibility. I didn't know the value of money, and I didn't know how to handle it," Jackie said in another interview. "Not only didn't I know how to get along with people my own age, I didn't know how to deal with adults either, except to let them treat me as a kid. It was a real vicious circle."

Jackie Cooper has made the adjustment to what he calls "the tough competition of the adult world" with remarkable success, although certainly not without enormous effort. Following a familiar pattern, his parents were entertainers, his mother a vaudeville pianist, his father an orchestra leader who died when Jackie was still very young. Two other relatives played important roles in his early career. It was his grandmother who took the three-year-old boy to casting offices and got him his first job in a slapstick comedy with Bobby Clark. The salary was $2 a day plus box lunches for himself and his chaperone. An uncle, director Norman Taurog, cast him in several Lloyd Hamilton comedies, which led to appearances in eight episodes of the Our Gang series. Neither grandmother nor uncle was responsible for the jump to stardom which shortly ensued.

Jackie's own tear ducts pointed the way; a crying scene in a Gang picture led to his being cast in *Skippy*.

The film, based on Percy Crosby's cartoon strip, was released in 1930 when Jackie was eight. For his directing effort, uncle Norman Taurog won an Academy Award. Jackie narrowly missed an Oscar for his portrayal of the leading role, losing out to Lionel Barrymore. Although it was the closest he ever came to winning a major award, the success of the film, which he made under loan to Paramount, brought him a swift and remunerative fame. MGM bought his contract from Hal Roach for $150,000 and signed him up at $1,000 a week. With his mother acting as his manager, his film income was to rise to $2,500 a week at the end of the seventh year of the new contract.

At Metro, Jackie was teamed with Wallace Beery in the sentimental effort called *The Champ*. Highly favorable box-office receipts led to further appearances with the gruff veteran in *Treasure Island, O'Shaughnessy's Boy,* and *The Bowery,* and to roles in almost fifty MGM features, most of which had the winning youngster with the familiar bee-stung lower lip crying his eyes out as he faced, and usually overcame, adversity. A typical reviewer of *The Champ* had marveled at "the sweet and touching scene at the end of the picture in which the brave little son of the dead prizefighter finds comfort in his mother's arms." Several years later, another reviewer reported, "Jackie Cooper's tear ducts, having been more or less in abeyance for the past few months, have been opened up to provide an autumn freshet in *Peck's Bad Boy*." Tears were decidedly the order of the day.

The monotony of his well-received characterizations was only one of the factors which later dismayed the adult Jackie, who felt that it kept him from really learning his craft. "I wasn't a great actor, even as a kid," he was to say. "I was simply an attentive youngster who could take direction. Great directors make great child actors." With his mother managing his finances, he also remained in ignorance of this cruel aspect of life, content to appear in a sleek little polo coat for personal appearances which brought in $7,500 a week above his film earnings. His education was largely a matter of tutors, except for one brief semester in high school at fifteen. His friends were other celebrities. Although he survived the awkward age in films, appearing in adolescence in *Seventeen* and a series of Henry Aldrich films, he was ill-prepared in almost every way for the outside world that was shortly to beckon.

In 1942 he went into the Navy, and served for three years, island-hopping in the South Pacific, where he played drums with Claude Thornhill's band. On entering the service, he viewed himself as "a pretty spoiled kid." He feels his experience in the Navy cured him of much of the disorientation occasioned by his career as a child star. Forced to compete, to stand on his own without his mother or a director to guide him, he found his own painful way. Difficult as these years were, Jackie was grateful for the lessons they taught him.

Returning to Hollywood after the war, he made two mediocre films with former silent star Jackie Coogan—*Kilroy was Here* and *French Leave.* "B's" like *Stork Bites Man* brought him no satisfaction, and although he was offered a lucrative contract to make Westerns, he turned it down. His future, he sensed, lay outside of films. He attempted a part in a play, *Sleep It Off,* which folded in Chicago. Despite its failure, he made an important decision: to go on to New York to venture a career on the stage. Summer-stock appearances seasoned him sufficiently to open on Broadway in *Magnolia Alley* in 1948. The play was panned, but excellent personal notices brought him to the attention of Joshua Logan and Leland Hayward, who signed him for the national company of *Mr. Roberts.* As Ensign Pulver, he toured the country before creating the lead role in the London production of the play. In October 1951, he returned to Broadway in *Remains to Be Seen,* co-starring with Janis Paige. The play was one of the hits of the season, enjoying a profitable run in New York before taking to the road.

Along with stardom on Broadway, Jackie Cooper was also forging a successful career in television. After appearing on almost every major network show, he went into his own series, *The People's Choice*. In addition to starring as Socrates "Sock" Miller, he directed a show featuring Cleo, the talking basset hound, which had four years of popular success.

For a time, Jackie's efforts went into a projected series based on his youthful characterization of Skippy, but when the networks failed to buy the idea—in part because he refused to play the role of Skippy's father—he became the star, entrepreneur, and co-owner of *Hennessey*. That series spanned three years on television, and Jackie received a citation from the American Medical Association hailing him "for portraying a Navy doctor who is a dedicated physician with unflagging good taste and a depth of understanding that has brought credit both to the medical profession and his own."

During the past decade Jackie has produced, directed, and starred in a long skein of TV shows. Early in 1964, contracts were drawn for him to head up production for one of the giant packaging firms of the industry. As his own unit was moved over to this new employer, Jackie Cooper effectively became one of the tycoons of the booming television industry.

Two marriages—one to June Horne, a director's daughter, in 1944, the other to television actress Hildy Parks, in 1948—ended in divorce, both unions plagued by "career conflicts." A more successful marriage began in 1954, with Barbara Kraus, a young advertising agency employee with no film background nor career ambitions. A son by June Horne, Jackie Jr., was awarded into her custody at the time of the divorce. With Barbara, Jackie has added two more children to the household.

"The movies ignore me now," he recently said. "I'd say that it's because I've got a kid-type face and don't fit in with the Hollywood conception of what a leading man should look like." Five foot nine and weighing 170 pounds, Jackie Cooper still has the bee-stung lower lip over which torrents of tears once flowed in his child star epics. While the films are no longer interested in the adult Jackie, for a time they cast a luring eye at Jackie Jr., living in Hollywood with his mother.

People would stop him on the street, reminded of a little boy they had seen in films long years ago. Occasionally it was a producer who made inquiries. His mother was polite, but moved on. His father, she would declare, "hopes I don't let little Jackie be a child star." Indeed, for that fleeting wisp of glory, the moment has now already passed.

10.

WHERE ARE THEY NOW?

It is not surprising that a young nation should take youthful entertainers to its heart. From its earliest days, the screen reflected its environment by glorifying child stars, signaling those of stature by tailoring material to suit their needs and fashioning a publicity halo around their tiny heads.

Baby Doris, born Doris Baker in 1908, had played the leading role in a wide array of film dramas by the time she was six. "Listen," she once said to a newspaperman, "my hair is real light. But Mama had a beautiful dark wig with long curls made for me. And when a director wants a little girl with light hair, I can play the part. And when a director wants a little girl with dark hair, I just say, 'Oh, well, but I got a wig.' And he hires me right away." With the help of what her interviewer described as a "mighty alert mother-manager," Baby Doris played the little True Blue girl in *The Heart of Maryland*, the lead in *Little Orphan Annie*, and appeared in photoplays for a dozen other picture companies. Although it was said that constant association with grown-ups had not made her affected or unnatural, an editorial of the time mused: "One can't help wonder whether Baby Doris wouldn't be just a wee bit happier with a rag doll and a kitten than as the petted star of the 'canned film' world."

Legal authorities took to task the parents of Baby Helen, Baby Doris's contemporary, in 1915. Born Helen Badgeley, in New Rochelle, New York, in 1911, the petite artiste became known the world over as the "Thanhouser Kidlet," after the company for which she starred in such epics as *Her Big Sister*, *Little Mischief*, *A Dog's Love*, *Helen Intervenes*, *The Baby and the Boss*, *Fires of Youth*, and many more. Like Baby Doris, she had begun her career in vaudeville, where her "I Don't Care" song, her imitations, her fund of rattling good stories, and her yodeling—which, it was said, would make a Swiss mountaineer turn green with envy—had built up a loyal following. In between films, the demure and dimpled entertainer continued her road appearances, and it was in Atlanta, on March 25, 1915, that she ran afoul of the recently enacted child labor law. Her stepfather and the local theatre manager were arrested and brought to court. The defense, in trying to show that Baby Helen's act did not constitute labor under the provisions of the law, called the performer to the stand as their main witness. "Do you find your work hard or irksome?" attorney Van Astor Batchelor asked the tiny star. "Beg pardon, sir?" lisped Baby Helen. "You don't dislike to work on the stage do you?" repeated the defense. "Certainly not," replied the witness. "But I'd dislike it if Mama wouldn't let me. I'd rather be on the stage than anywhere I know." The testimony, plus the fact that she earned $250 a week, led the court to the conclusion that Baby Helen was an artist rather than a laborer. She was allowed to finish her engagement on condition the theatre book no children under fourteen in the future.

Bright stars in their time, Baby Doris and Baby Helen are now largely forgotten, along with most of the other top-rated child performers of the silent era: Essanay's Mary McAlister, who starred in *The Kill-Joy, Pants, Do Children Count? Sins of Ambition*, and other important films of their time; Bobby Connelly, Vitagraph star for whom the Sonny Jim and Bobby Connelly series were especially written; the appealing Fairbanks Twins, Madeleine and Marion, who later became a top song-and-dance team on Broadway; Fox stars Jane and Katherine Lee, billed in vaudeville as the "Baby Grands" before they hit the screen in their first co-starring vehicle, *Two Little Imps*, in 1916; and Andy Clarke, who had his own series, the Andy Series, with Edison, at the time of World War I. Clarke later worked in the production phase of films as assistant director before becoming inactive in the field. His death in 1960 brought forth brief obituaries in the New York papers which gave little indication of the stature he had once enjoyed in the industry.

Similarly, the shadows of oblivion have largely obscured Yale Boss, a comedy favorite whose impersonations delighted audiences at the turn of the century in Edison vehicles; Wesley Barry, the freckle-faced favorite who played important roles in many films before his advancing years forced him into insignificant supporting parts; and Baby Marie Osborne, who emerged briefly from fame's penumbra to become the stand-in for Ginger Rogers, and then turned to a new career in the studio's wardrobe department.

Jackie Coogan's female contemporary, Baby Peggy, began her career at the age of two under the aegis of Julius Stern, president of Century Comedies, who was also responsible for the "discovery" of Brownie, the studio's popular dog star. In one of Brownie's canine epics she played a featured role before graduating to starring vehicles such as *The Flower Girl, The Darling of New York, Whose Baby Are You? Editha's Burglar,* and *Captain January.*

Even more swiftly than the Kid, she outgrew the precocious roles which had brought her fame and almost a quarter of a million dollars. Peggy was only five when she left the screen in the early twenties and, with her parents, retired to a Wyoming ranch. With the stock market crash at the end of the decade, the family lost the ranch and most of the money she had earned. Under her full name, Peggy Montgomery, she later tried to make a comeback.

"One of my chief obstacles now is that many people in

Hollywood think I'm trying to cash in on my name," she declared in 1936. "There is no foundation for that. All the years that I've been out of pictures I've been working hard preparing myself for real work." At eighteen, Peggy still had the glowing coal-black eyes which had intrigued an earlier generation, but the film medium had turned from silent to sound and demanded new skills. Memories of the past, Peggy maintained, only made things more difficult for her.

"I'd like people to forget the past and look at me as I am now," she said. "All I want is a chance to test my abilities in pictures. If I can't make good in sound pictures, I'll be among the first to find out. And believe me, I'll try something else right away. All I ask is that they forget Baby Peggy. I'm grown up now." The grown-up Peggy, trying to recoup the fortune lost during the 1929 crash, was offered only bit parts, and gradually drifted from the scene. Eventually, she settled in Mexico with her second husband, and turned to an entirely new career as a writer of books and magazine articles.

Never a top star, but an important player in fourteen films, including early talkies like *Tom Sawyer* and *Huckleberry Finn* with Jackie Coogan, winsome Mitzie Green left the screen to return to the vaudeville circuit where she had debuted in infancy as a prop for her parents' act with the Gus Edwards revue, her salary at the time a tidy two cents a week. At seventeen she enjoyed a full-scale triumph as the star of the Rodgers and Hart Broadway musical, *Babes in Arms*. A prosperous musical-comedy career followed, but for seventeen years Mitzie stayed away from films, candidly admitting she was scared. "It seemed different when I was grown-up," she stated in explanation of her long absence. Marriage to Hollywood director Joe Pevney eventually brought her back to the screen, at his urging, with a small part in a 1951 Abbott and Costello movie. The stage and nightclubs, however, have dominated her latter-day career.

Of all the child stars of the silent screen, Madge Evans easily made the most graceful transition to an adult career. As Baby

Madge, she had played vaudeville before turning to films, where she made *Sign of the Cross* at the age of three and became the Shirley Temple of an early era of silent pictures. By 1920, the awkward age had forced her temporary retirement, but a series of good roles on the New York stage led her back to Hollywood, and a highly successful career in talking pictures. Marriage to playwright Sidney Kingsley in 1939 brought about a virtual retirement from the screen. She occasionally makes an appearance on television.

Just as the great child stars of the Thirties treated in this book have had widely varying careers and lives as adults, their contemporaries of somewhat lesser prominence have met diverse fates. Cora Sue Collins, who played many leading actresses as a child—the baby Garbo in *Queen Christina,* the young Norma Shearer in *Smilin' Through,* and so forth—has dropped from view, as has Sybil Jason, the little English-born actress Warner Brothers groomed as a rival to Shirley Temple and starred in *Little Big Shot.* A custody fight between her parents and her uncle, in 1938, revealed that her total assets amounted to a scant $3,500.

Universal's entry in the "Another Shirley Temple" sweepstakes was Juanita Quigley, better known as Baby Jane. After her debut as Claudette Colbert's daughter in *Imitation of Life,* the studio tailored *Straight From the Heart* to the needs of its clever three-year-old starlet. Although signed to a longterm contract, Baby Jane's career was relatively brief.

Virginia Weidler was Paramount's answer to Fox's Shirley Temple and Jane Withers. A feature player in such well-remembered films as *Laddie, Freckles, Young Tom Edison,* and *The Philadelphia Story,* she ended a fourteen-year film career in 1943 and headed for the New York stage. Her career on the boards never caught fire.

The Mauch Twins, Bobby and Billy, delightful stars of *The Prince and the Pauper* and other films, played on Broadway in *Winged Victory* in 1944, but never scored as adults in motion pictures. Today, they have moved behind the scenes as expert film cutters. Freckle-faced Jackie "Butch" Jenkins, who stole many a scene from Mickey Rooney in *The Human Comedy,* long ago vacated his position of film prominence for a business career, while Johnny Sheffield, a frail, four-pound incubator baby who grew up to fame as the muscular "Boy" in the Tarzan series, left films in the Fifties to register as a premedical student at U.C.L.A.

Husky-voiced Baby Rose Marie, better known in radio, where she was billed as "the darling of the air waves," made a few films as a child and later went on to Broadway success as the female lead with Phil Silvers in *Top Banana.* Today, married with a family, Rose Marie is well known to television audiences as the secretary on the popular *Dick Van Dyke Show.* Many of the followers of that medium are probably unaware that she once sang at request performances for Presidents Hoover, Coolidge, and Franklin Roosevelt. "I've been around so long that when I talk of entertaining the troops, they think I mean the First World War," she once said. Her views on her own background are firm. "If I had my life to live over again, I would never be a child star because the hard knocks, when you become of age, are too great."

A similar sentiment comes from former boy singer Bobby Breen, once the standby of the Eddie Cantor radio show, and the star of *Rainbow on the River, Let's Sing Again,* and other Thirties films: "I'd be reticent about a show business career for my son. Too tough. Why push the boy into this highly competitive business and give him a lot of complexes and things?" Today, the still-youthful Bobby maintains an active pace fulfilling vaudeville and nightclub dates.

Leon Janney, First National star of *Penrod, Penrod and Sam,* and other talkies, has frequently added his voice to those who feel that child stardom can be painful. Janney continues to play character roles in films and on the stage.

Jackie Searle, the sissy who made screen life difficult for Jackie Cooper and others, earned $27.60 a week as a riveter at the Lockheed plant in 1941 before the Army commandeered his services. "Not nearly enough has been said of Jackie Searle's vast and incomparable skill at playing disagreeable and properly punished children," wrote critic Richard Watts Jr. at the time of Searle's screen successes. "He is certainly one of the most complete and satisfying actors on the screen." Unable to find roles after youth had flown, Jackie came back from his war service to find the Hollywood studio's still uninterested in him. As a result, he went into business, becoming the owner of a company which manufactures cases, mostly for sewing machines. Today, at forty-four, a married man with two children, he occasionally appears on television, usually in the role of the heavy. His screen career throws an interesting light on the financial rewards of all but the top child players. His highest annual income during the time when his name was a household word was no more than $8,000. His average annual earnings in Hollywood were a mere $4,000.

The son of Sheik Abraham, elephant trainer for the Maharajah of Karapur, twelve-year-old Sabu was discovered by Robert Flaherty in India, where the director had gone to film *Elephant Boy*. Flaherty made him the star of the picture, and its great success led to the boy's appearance in *The Thief of Bagdad, Jungle Book, Song of India,* and other exotic adventure films. During World War II, Sabu entered the United States Army as a private, returning as a heavily decorated veteran, and becoming an American citizen some years later. With his brother, to whom he was deeply attached, he entered the furniture business during a postwar lull in his career. His untimely death of a heart attack came in the early Sixties when he was thirty-nine.

Donald O'Connor, a vaudeville entertainer at two, entered films as a juvenile, playing Bing Crosby's kid brother in *Sing You Sinners* in 1938, and then going on to co-starring roles in films with Gloria Jean and others. It was, however, his postwar role on television's *Colgate Comedy Hour* which finally brought his fullest measure of success both in that medium and in films which resulted from his new-found popularity.

Near the end of the Thirties, another baby star also made her Hollywood debut, ten-month-old Sandra Henville, better known as Baby Sandy. Actually, the baby needed for a Bing Crosby film, *East Side of Heaven,* was supposed to be a boy. Sandy had worked two days before the studio discovered its error. By that time, her versatility was so manifest that she remained in the film and stole most of its scenes. Although a case of measles delayed one of her pictures, Sandy rose in popularity so swiftly that *Life* put her on its cover, a dainty little miss with a seductive spit curl and a neat white dress. *Little Accident, Sandy Takes a Bow, Sandy Is a Lady,* and other episodes of the Sandy series found favor with the public. The studio cast her again as a boy in *Unexpected Father,* and in 1940, *Parents* magazine named Sandy its Baby of the Year. Babyhood past, she gracefully retired from the screen. Today, the former child charmer is married and lives in California, where she has, however, no connection with the film industry.

Just as the popularity of Jackie Coogan and Our Gang had led studios to develop a plethora of child performers in the silent era, so Shirley Temple and Louis B. Mayer's MGM stable of child stars dominated the field in the epoch of the talkies. Twentieth Century-Fox was never able to find a successor to Shirley, but at Culver City, Mayer continued to pursue with phenomenal success his policy of grooming child actors. If Elizabeth Taylor—whose brief childhood career encompassed *National Velvet* and *Lassie Come Home,* along with small parts in *Jane Eyre* and *The White Cliffs of Dover*—was the most spectacular product of the studio in the Forties, there were other notable young players under contract at MGM.

English-born Roddy McDowall's sensitive portrayal of the little Welsh boy in *How Green Was My Valley* won him critical praise and a substantial following. In the early part of the decade, Roddy secured his position with two animal pictures, *Lassie Come Home* and *My Friend Flicka,* both of which had numerous sequels. His career went smoothly until he moved into adolescence. Because he looked younger than his age, directors continued to cast him in his familiar "lovable young boy" role until he was in his twenties, so that eventually he began to feel he was making bad imitations of Roddy McDowall movies. Resolutely, he left Hollywood for New York and the East Coast, where he fashioned a completely new career on the stage in classics by Shaw and Shakespeare, and later in contemporary plays like *No Time for Sergeants* and *Compulsion.* With a new grasp on his métier as an actor, he returned to Hollywood and finally won the type of varied characterization he had been seeking: Octavian in *Cleopatra,* a cameo role in *The Longest Day,* a murderer in *Shock Treatment,* and the disciple Matthew in *The Greatest Story Ever Told.* Save for the temporary period when he was dissatisfied with his roles, Roddy admits to having thoroughly enjoyed his life as an actor. In recent years, he has added a gratifying second career as a celebrity portrait photographer to his achievements, his work appearing in *Life* and other publications. Despite these manifold activities, there are those who appear to have lost track of the former child actor. "Some dumb woman came up to me the other day and asked, 'Are you doing anything interesting any more?' " he recently related in an interview. "This is the terrible sort of depressing thing people do, just because you're no longer box office, in quotes, or no longer the shining light of the moment."

Another MGM graduate, Dean Stockwell, has voiced more profound criticisms of the drawbacks of early life in Hollywood, where he made almost thirty films between six and sixteen, among them, *Anchors Aweigh, Gentlemen's Agreement, The Green Years,* and *The Boy With the Green Hair.* "As a child actor, you're never accepted," he related to Joe Hyams. "I had no friends, except my brother, and I never did what I wanted to do. I had one vacation in nine years. I went fishing." To another interviewer, he said, "The life of a child star is so fraught with responsibility that it frustrates normal interests and associations with other children. . . . It's a miserable way to bring up a child, though neither my parents nor I recognized it at the time."

After his boyhood career, Dean enrolled as George Stockwell at the University of California, but found himself ill at ease. "I was unhappy and couldn't get along with people," he says of this period. "I still can't function in any group on the group's terms. . . . So I decided to try acting again because I had nowhere else to go. I wasn't sure I could. I didn't know anything about acting."

To learn the rudiments of his craft, he came east to study. After auditing one lesson, he walked out of the Actors Studio in New York, although he has been called a Method actor who scorns the Method approach. "Acting is a great and important art and demands all the dedication, intelligence, and talent that an actor can give to it. At least that is my approach to it," he has stated. In New York, his performance in *Compulsion* was highly praised for its steely sensitivity. It led to other stage work, and then, in 1957, back to Hollywood, where his appearance in a film today is often a sound indication of its merits, since he has no hesitation in rejecting roles which he feels lack substance. "Acting is my business, my work. I love it, even when I'm miserable," he says. Despite his continuing professional success, there is a wariness about the intense young actor that always puzzles interviewers. "He still remains suspicious and somewhat rebellious," wrote Sidney Skolsky in a 1963 interview. "He is convinced that people hated him when a child. . . ."

Still another MGM graduate of the Forties was Margaret O'Brien, whose wartime film, *Journey for Margaret*, led her to stardom—an Academy Award in 1944, a $2,500 weekly salary at nine, and top-ten box-office rank in 1944 and 1945, when she made such winning films as *Meet Me in St. Louis* and *Our Vines Have Tender Grapes*. A 1949 role as Beth, in *Little Women*, was one of her last before adolescence reduced the demand for her services. Sensibly, she turned to television and the stage, always expressing the view, however, that life as a child star had been pleasant and left her with no regrets. On one occasion *Time* reported on a meeting with Jackie Coogan at a television studio. "The two cinemoppets of yore," as the Luce reporter called them, "heartily agreed that a child actor's life can be altogether jolly and not a bit traumatic."

Peggy Ann Garner, having made her film debut at six, earned an Academy Award at thirteen for her portrayal of Francie in *A Tree Grows in Brooklyn* in 1944. While her adult career has been somewhat less prestigious, Peggy Ann has likewise remained well disposed toward her past, of which she has said, "I'm grateful that I've had a career. Now I have no smoldering desire to prove anything to anybody."

Jane Powell, almost an adolescent when she began her career as an MGM singing star, moved easily from teen-age roles to young adult starring vehicles, but Gloria Jean, née Schoonover, found studio doors closed to her once she had passed adolescence. In 1960, she became a restaurant hostess across from Republic Studios in Hollywood. "I want to get my career going again," she told a reporter. "The size of the parts doesn't mean a thing. I'll do anything. I just want to get back in the business." Two years later, she was again quoted in the press, still hoping for another chance. "I just got a raise at the restaurant," she said, "and now I am working lunches. Now I think things will start to break because that's when the people from the movie and TV business come in." Today, Gloria Jean, who had followed in Deanna Durbin's footsteps at Universal, starring in a score of movies—*The Underpup, A Little Bit of Heaven, If I Had My Way,* etc.—with Bing Crosby, W. C. Fields, and other bright names, has still not found the key to the comeback trail.

Equally disheartening, perhaps more profoundly so, has been the recent fate of Bobby Driscoll, who won an Academy award as the best child actor of 1949 for his performances in *The Window* and Walt Disney's *So Dear to My Heart.* Frequent brushes with the law have dogged the difficult days of the one-time child actor, a $500-a-week breadwinner at twelve. "I really feared people. The other kids didn't accept me. They treated me as one apart," Bobby has said of his days of supposed glory. "I tried desperately to be one of the gang. When they rejected me, I fought back, became belligerent and cocky and was afraid all the time." Married and with a family, Bobby attempted a business career as a clothing salesman, but the effort failed. With a screen role once more in the offing in 1958, he told a reporter, "I have found that memories are not very useful. I was carried on a silver cushion and then dropped into the garbage can." The comeback effort in 1958 led nowhere.

If the sentimental, somewhat simple-minded sagas which Shirley Temple enacted in the Thirties met the needs of that depressed period, the more mature stories in which child actors performed in the Forties—wartime dramas like *Journey for Margaret* and evocative studies like *The Boy With the Green Hair*—reflected a more searching spirit in that decade's film makers and their audience. With the breakup of the studio system in the late Forties and Fifties, child stars—with a few notable exceptions, like Brandon De Wilde and Patty Duke in the Fifties, and English child actress Hayley Mills in the Sixties—became almost a vanishing breed. For independent producers there was no longer an incentive to engage in the long process of buildup accorded child performers of the past. And while Patty Duke scored a success in the stage production of *The Miracle Worker* and repeated her role in the award-winning film, she then went on to forge a career in a new medium, television, whose ability to develop child stars is also questionable.

If the structure of film making had changed in the last decade, certainly the audience, too, had once more changed its character. With the nation's accelerating urbanization, the emphasis had, at least in part, shifted away from the family film to productions which appealed to the ascendant teenagers of the cities. This youthful market appeared to find most of its idols in its own general age group.

Where the child stars of yesterday once ruled the popular imagination, today's Beatles and Frankie Avalons hold sway. A somewhat frantic young public accords them hero worship. Publicists sing their praises. Amateur psychologists study their backgrounds and contemplate the effects of their sudden glory on their future years.

"If you took 176 other kids and followed them through their lives, I believe you would find the same percentage of them have troubles in later life," Our Gang producer Hal Roach stated in a 1959 interview: "There are many of the Gang who have turned into happy and respected citizens, including doctors and lawyers here in Los Angeles." The adult careers of his better-known alumni, who span several decades of film making, provide another sobering barometer of what happens to former child performers.

A half dozen of the youngsters who appeared in the series over the years have retained some prominence on the entertainment scene, including Jackie Cooper, Johnny Downs, Eddie Bracken, and Nanette Fabray.

Darla Hood turned to singing on TV and for a time was a member of Edgar Bergen's entertainment act, while Jean Darling won a role in the Broadway musical *Carousel* in 1945, and later starred in *Hilltop House*, a daytime radio serial.

Mary Kornman, the Gang's first love interest, played grown-up roles in a number of films before retiring into marriage with cameraman Leo Tovar. Similarly, Virginia Lee Corbin, also a baby star in her own right, made a comeback as an adolescent in 1929, turned ingenue, then left the screen to marry a New York stockbroker.

As Roach indicated, a number of Gang graduates turned to other professions, including medicine and the law, while some, like little Dickie Moore, continued in the theatre for a time before going into other fields—in Moore's case, to a related post as executive secretary of Actors Equity in New York, and then into the television end of an advertising agency. Perhaps the most unusual career in later years was that followed by Gang mischief-maker George Wendelken, a onetime "Freckles," who became the "Searchlight King" of New York, owner of a caravan of trucks equipped with units capable of shooting beams of light fifteen miles into the sky at film premieres, supermarket openings, and the like.

Tragedy stalked several members of the Gang, whose screen mischief never exceeded the bounds. Squeaky-voiced Alfalfa, master of the bug-eyed double take, left the screen when age crept up on him to become a hunting and fishing guide in northern California. After drifting from job to job, including a stretch as bartender, he was slain in 1959, in a scuffle over a $50 debt owed him by a former partner in a bear-hunting scheme. "Justifiable homicide," reported the coroner's jury, and the slayer of Carl Switzer—the thirty-two-year-old former child actor's real name—was released.

Froggy McLaughlin, of the spectacles and the incongruously deep voice, was killed in a motor-scooter accident a number of years ago near Huntington Beach, California. Don "Fats" Law ran a clothing store in Meadsville, Pennsylvania, managing a theatre in the years before he died, at thirty-eight, of an intestinal disorder. Clifton Young, a tough kid of some of the early comedies, died in a Los Angeles hotel fire in 1951. He was thirty-four. Police said the fire began when he fell asleep in bed with a lighted cigarette.

For a good many of the Gang, the going in later life was just plain rough. Chubby Spanky McFarland, ringleader and featured player, operated a gas station, sold hot dogs, was an oil promoter, and made a personal-appearance tour of the Midwest before finally landing a job on a TV station, in the late Fifties. Like his other ventures, the television job didn't work out, and a weary Spanky told the United Press, "I'm trying to work out a nightclub act." Jay R. Smith, the original Skinny Kid, left the Gang in 1928, tried in vain to find screen work, then became a messenger in Culver City. Skooter Lowry, a Gang member from 1923 to 1928, turned to vaudeville, while toughie Jackie Condon dropped out of pictures, but continued to live in Hollywood.

Joe Cobb, the original Fatty, doubled his weight from 60 to 120 pounds during his eight years with the Gang. As he grew older, he lost some of the poundage, went to school in Texas, then returned to play minor Hollywood roles until 1942, when he took a job as an assembler in a California airplane plant.

Tough kid Mickey Daniels continued to do screen work after leaving the Gang, but never again figured prominently in films. Sunshine Sammy became a tap dancer in New York after his Gang days. Farina, an audience favorite, appeared in a number of Joe E. Brown comedies, then took to the road for personal appearances with his sister, Margaret, and his brother, Stymie, before passing out of sight. Stymie turned up again recently playing the organ at a New York jazz rendezvous.

During their heydey, the youngsters of Our Gang received as many as five hundred letters a week, and no personal appearances were allowed because producer Hal Roach feared they might undermine the group spirit. In the Fifties, the two-reelers were gradually released to television, where they swiftly gained a new audience and startling popularity, becoming the leading afternoon entertainment for children in the New York and other metropolitan areas. While there is no doubt that a fresh generation of youngsters delighted in seeing Spanky McFarland, Alfalfa, Mary Kornman, Fatty Joe Cobb, and Farina, the high ratings made it appear more than likely that their elders were peering over the tops of their newspapers to steal a glance at the familiar Little Rascals whose antics carried them back to another time, perhaps another place, when they, too, had laughed and cried and felt in their hearts the spontaneous carefree delight which is the unique privilege of childhood.

The Dead End kids—Bobby Jordan, Huntz Hall, Billy Halop, Leo Gorcey, Bernard Hunsley, and Gabriel Dell—are not treated in this book, although it is worth noting that Gabriel Dell starred on Broadway in Lorraine Hansberry's last play, *The Sign in Sidney Brustein's Window*.

Only this passing reference will signal the achievement of Elsie Leslie, perhaps the first real child star of America, who created a sensation on the New York stage in 1888 in the title role of a new play, *Little Lord Fauntleroy*, and made later stage appearances as in ingenue before retiring.

These and others have not been included in the present volume, nor have any of the many performers who began their careers as children, though not as stars, and went on to greater fame in maturity. Such a list would include Lila Lee, who began her career as Cuddles in the Gus Edwards Kid Kabaret, Mary Pickford, Buster Keaton, Dorothy and Lillian Gish, and most recently, Natalie Wood. Of all these players, many of whom traveled the vaudeville circuits as children, not one had carried an entire production on their slender shoulders, none had heard the rafters ring with applause for themselves, alone. They had been players in small, often minor roles. Out of the glare of the limelight, they had learned their craft and gone on to solidly based adult careers.

It is to those children who stood in that glare, the child stars of yesterday and today, those remembered and those forgotten, that this book is devoted and dedicated.